C000221826

Stephen Knight

Creator
and Trader

A VISION FOR GROWTH IN THE
UK MORTGAGE MARKET

For my mum, Sheila,
a wonderful lady
who sadly died while this
book was being written.

Stephen Knight
Creator and Trader

A VISION FOR GROWTH IN THE UK MORTGAGE MARKET

Creator and Trader

A Vision for Growth in the UK Mortgage Market

By Stephen Knight

Published by
AAPPL Artists' and Photographers' Press Ltd.
10 Hillside, London SW19 4NH
info@aappl.com
www.aappl.com

Sales and Distribution
UK and export : Turnaround Publisher Services Ltd
sales@turnaround-uk.com

Copyright © AAPPL Artists' and Photographers' Press Ltd 2006
Text © Stephen Knight 2006

The right of Stephen Knight to be identified as the author of this work has been asserted by him in accordance with the Copyright, Designs and Patents Act 1988

Contributions by other authors © each named contributor

Cover photograph © Sampson Lloyd, courtesy AAPPL info@aappl.com

All rights reserved. No part of this publication may be reproduced, stored in a retrieval system, copied, or transmitted in any form or by any means, electronic, mechanical, photocopying, recording or otherwise without the prior written permission of the copyright owner.

A catalogue record for this book is available from the British Library.

ISBN (10) 1904332447 (13) 9781904332442

Design (contents and cover): Stefan Nekuda
stefan.nekuda@chello.at

Printed in Slovakia by Polygraf Print Ltd., Presov
Production Agency: ZoneS   zacco.zones@fastwebnet.it

By the same author:
The Art of Marketing Mortgages

Contents

Acknowledgements

Let's be clear: the growth described in this book could never have been achieved by one person, least of all me. It was achieved by a large number of dedicated, talented individuals working together towards a common aim. I therefore acknowledge with thanks the outstanding contribution of all GMAC-RFC UK employees, past and present.

How often does someone get the opportunity to build a business supported by a global parent with full governance, minimum strategic interference, maximum help and extraordinary patience and tolerance when mistakes are made? I acknowledge with gratitude the roles played in this growth by Chris Nordeen, President of GMAC-RFC's International Business Group, Bruce Paradis, President and CEO of GMAC-RFC worldwide and the entire Executive Board of GMAC-RFC.

In relation to the book itself, I received tremendous help from a number of colleagues who not only provided me with research insights, but who also read draft chapters and gave me honest feedback. Naturally, responsibility for all the words, figures and illustrations that appear in this book rest with me. But I would like to express my gratitude to Anna Bennett; Craig Beresford; Godfrey Blight; Roger Brown; Hans Geberbauer; Mark Gray; Rob Green; Tim Hanton; Stephen Hynes; Jeff Knight; Simon Knight; Eileen McMillan and Barry Searle. What a fantastic team of professionals!

I received external help as well, and would like to express my thanks to Iain Anderson of Cicero, who helped me with chapter 5; Cameron Brown, my publisher; Stefan Nekuda (Niki), who designed the book; Kevin O'Donnell, my editor; Michael Clapper, Paul Fletcher, Tony Hughes, Vic Jannels, Tony Jones, Roger Morris, John Rice, Paul Robinson and David Wylie - all leading packagers who helped me with chapter 7, and Susan Barty and Peter Smith of CMS Cameron McKenna who gave me legal advice in a couple of areas.

I am truly grateful to all of the leading industry figures who contributed to chapter 8. Having their views enriches the book's content significantly. Their names are shown in that chapter.

Wherever I have reproduced a picture or an article from a publication, permission has been sought and obtained, and I am grateful to the publications concerned.

I must also acknowledge the brilliant creative work undertaken over the years by our advertising and marketing agency, Phoenix, not just with the GMAC-RFC advertisements that appear in this book, but also for their creative work behind the strapline "Mortgages for Everyone".

Two chief executives have worked for me during the period covered by this book. Their contributions to our success have been significant. Performing the role of CEO reporting to an Executive Chairman is not easy, but their professionalism and dedication shone through every day. Tragically, my first CEO, Colin Duggleby, was taken from us in the summer of 2003 after a year-long illness. Colin was young, full of vitality, hungry for the company's success and full of integrity. Why life is taken so early from such a genuinely nice person like that never ceases to trouble me.

I am delighted to say that his successor, Bob Appel, is doing a great job and was promoted in the summer of 2005 to run an even bigger operation the company has based in Dallas, Texas. Genuine good guys, both of them, and I thank them for helping me deliver the growth story which is the subject matter of this book.

Before I finish, I am very pleased to acknowledge a very special person indeed. Kerensa Grant is in her thirteenth year as my Personal Assistant. Some murderers get less! In addition to running my office, deciding what and who I am allowed to see, and censoring my output whenever she gets a chance, she not only typed every word of my last book, but also this current book. Since every chapter has had around ten re-drafts, this might give you an idea of how grateful I am to Kerensa.

Finally, I can't conclude the acknowledgements without thanking my wife Lesley, and my sons Tim and Josh for putting up with the long hours involved in writing this book. What patience!

Presentation of product material

Some of the product advertising and marketing material featured in this book has been re-set and scaled down to fit the black and white quarto format. In this process, some of or all of the regulatory material has been deleted so that the main commercial points about the product can be featured with greater prominence.

Glossary of Abbreviations

APR	=	Annual Percentage Rate
ASA	=	Advertising Standards Authority
AVM	=	Automated Valuation Model
B&C	=	British & Commonwealth Holdings plc
BHAG	=	Big Hairy Audacious Goal
BSA	=	Building Societies' Association
CML	=	Council of Mortgage Lenders
CSR	=	Corporate Social Responsibility
DIP	=	Decision in Principle
FMS	=	First Mortgage Securities Limited
FSA	=	Financial Services Authority
GAAP	=	Generally Accepted Accounting Principles
HIP	=	Home Information Pack
HML	=	Homeloan Management Limited
HMSL	=	Halifax Mortgage Services Limited
IMC	=	Independent Mortgage Collection Limited
IMLA	=	Intermediary Mortgage Lenders' Association
KFI	=	Key Facts Illustration
LTV	=	Loan-to-Value
MCCB	=	Mortgage Code Compliance Board
MCOB	=	Mortgage Conduct of Business
MGH	=	Mortgage Group Holdings
MSL	=	Mortgage Systems Limited
PLG	=	Private Label Group
PMPA	=	Professional Mortgage Packagers' Alliance
POSD	=	Point of Sale Decisioning
RAMP	=	Regulatory Alliance of Mortgage Packagers
RMBS	=	Residential Mortgage Backed Securities
S&P	=	Standard & Poor's
SVR	=	Standard Variable Rate

Preface

In October 1989 the German lender, HypoVereinsbank, launched a UK specialist lender, initially called Mortgage Services Limited, and subsequently re-named HYPO Mortgage Services Limited. In 1995, they exited the market by selling this business to Birmingham Midshires, who renamed it Birmingham Midshires Mortgage Services Limited. The business was put up for sale again and, on 28 February 1998, GMAC-RFC purchased from Birmingham Midshires Mortgage Services Limited the principal assets such as the computer system, head office building, people, furniture and so on, to provide a platform for its launch into the UK as a sub prime lender.

The name given to the new business was RFC Mortgage Services Limited and, to assist with early cashflow, it was agreed that RFC MSL would, for a short period, process intermediary-sourced mortgage applications for Birmingham Midshires on a sub-contracted, third party basis, as well as undertaking its own lending. This arrangement ended in 2000.

On 17 November 1998, GMAC-RFC acquired Private Label Group, a company I had founded, comprising Private Label Mortgage Services Limited (the UK's largest packager) and Independent Mortgage Collection Limited (a lead generation company). Until the spring of 2000, Private Label and RFC MSL operated independently but co-operated as sister companies. From 2000 onwards, however, the two businesses were pulled closer together and, until October 2001 - when Private Label ceased trading as a packager - senior executives at Private Label had dual roles, on both the packaging and lending sides of our business.

Between the spring of 2000 and October 2001, I was effectively executive chairman of both Private Label and RFC MSL, which we had by then renamed GMAC-RFC. For the purposes of this book, however, I have kept these jobs separate. In the first five chapters, describing GMAC-RFC's rapid growth after my appointment to the current day, I refer only to my role as executive chairman of GMAC-RFC. In chapter 6, in which I describe the final years of Private Label, I refer only to my role as executive chairman of that company.

This books charts the corporate restructuring which led to the formation of GMAC-RFC in the UK and the company's subsequent rapid expansion. I hope everyone in the mortgage world will find its detail and examples useful and that everyone who reads it, whether in business or not, will find its story of corporate growth stimulating and informative. This book was completed on 31 October 2005.

1 2 3 4 5 6 7 8

VISION AND STRATEGY

In the five years between 2000 and 2004, our company:

- Increased its mortgage business 11 times faster than the market average
- Grew to become the UK's number one non-conforming lender
- Rose to become the UK's number one seller of mortgage portfolios
- Stepped up to the position of Europe's number four issuer of Residential Mortgage-Backed Securities
- Accelerated from being the UK's 60th biggest mortgage lender to become a top 10 lender for the first time
- Developed insufficient humility about our achievements

Sorry about that. Not being humble enough, I mean. But I figure it this way: I have to grab your attention early on. If you think this is another boring old strategy text book, you might throw it at the cat.

In fact, this is a case study of a mortgage lending success story, one that actually worked when the vision was turned into reality. I hope it will inspire anyone working in the mortgage business who thinks it unexciting and staid. It is anything but. I hope, also, it inspires anyone in business who wants to learn some of the secrets of successful business and enjoy rapid growth without seeing the wheels come off the trolley.

Everything major that worked in our "create and trade" strategy is in here, plus a bit more. There were lots of mistakes, of course. I have always been lucky rather than clever. But the bits that worked did so spectacularly well, and I am happy to share them.

The story starts really in the summer of 1998. The company I had started eleven years previously, and which I now owned again (see chapter 6 for the full story), was bumping into a glass ceiling. We believed that we could at least double the £1 billion volume of lending we were generating at the time if we could only persuade our panel of lenders to rebuild their dated administration processes, which were holding us back.

In truth, my company Private Label had run its course as a mortgage packager. We needed to transform ourselves into a lender, selling portfolios of mortgages post completion rather than pre-offer. That way, we would be in control of our own underwriting, service levels and product design, maximising income without the need for a huge capital injection. I described this strategy as being a "creator and trader" of mortgage assets - a model not too dissimilar to a mortgage banker in the US.

Then the phone went. Would I have dinner with Bruce Paradis?

"Who?"
"Bruce Paradis, President and CEO of GMAC-RFC".
"Never heard of him. What's the company name again?"
"GMAC-RFC".
"Spell it".
"I just did".
"Sounds like a bad hand at scrabble".
"It's one of the world's biggest and best known mortgage conduit companies".
"OK, I'm interested, dinner would be great".

On 24 June 1998, we had dinner at the Greenhouse restaurant in Mayfair. We talked about the UK mortgage market generally. Bruce asked me how I would develop the UK business that GMAC-RFC had just launched if it were down to me. This was the perfect opportunity for me to launch into my "creator and trader" theory.

I remember the discussion being terribly therapeutic. The chance to rehearse my "create and trade" idea in front of the CEO of a major US lender that already had its own string of innovations to its name was a great opportunity and learning experience. When these chances come along it seems rude not to grab them!

Bruce seemed to like the strategy. And I liked him. Good job really for, five months later, GMAC-RFC bought Private Label. Eighteen months after that - a delay that was presumably designed to test whether I was house-trained - I was asked to become UK chairman of GMAC-RFC, to implement the "creator and trader" idea.

This part of the book tells you what I did with that mandate. This first chapter describes the top line vision and strategy only. The longer execution chapters that follow tell you how we did it and how we overcame the many obstacles in our way. Figure 1.1 tells you what is to come in this first chapter.

Figure 1.1

The vision

All successful businesses need vision. A clear statement of what you are and what you are trying to achieve. The clarity will be in proportion to the simplicity. I believe that "creator and trader of mortgage assets" achieved that.

We would, as I explained to my Board during an offsite meeting in May 2000, create loans like any other mortgage lender. But we would then trade the loans or books of loans. The result would be that we would maximise our return on capital, potentially establishing a very large lending company relatively quickly, but with a relatively small balance sheet.

Our opportunity would be that we would not be constrained by our own risk and volume appetite: rather, we would be able to undertake any lending that we believed was saleable to the market at large, either by way of securitisation or portfolio sale. Conversely, we would not have the flexibility of a balance sheet lender to take a view on certain products or criteria situations, or to model a product based on its long term viability.

By making this part of the vision crystal clear we were able to immediately engage all important stakeholders, including management, employees and important business partners. They understood why we lent in certain circumstances and did not in others. It was a new concept at the time.

Back in 2000, it required some faith. For example, we would need to become accepted quite quickly by the market as a mainstream lender, i.e. making products available that competed in the high street, since it was clear that we would not be able to fully exploit the distribution opportunities open to us unless we played in the big market.

The competition for mainstream business was fierce. The margins at which we would have to offer new mainstream products would not allow us to viably securitise such assets. We would have to create a brand new market for this approach to succeed, namely the regular trading of whole loan portfolios between lenders. We would have to deliver the correct mix of business to ensure that the assets were saleable in blended tranches.

A few of my colleagues did not grasp the strategy immediately, but most did. I had unflinching support from our parent company, particularly Chris Nordeen (then chairman of GMAC-RFC Europe, now President of our International Business Group), Bruce Paradis and the rest of the executive board. That counts when you are taking big gambles.

The value proposition

The vision is the "what" - a creator and trader of mortgage assets. The value proposition is the "how". How would we deliver against that vision? What were we going to bring to the market that was different? It had better be good, otherwise the vision would never be achieved.

We hit upon "mortgages for everyone in a fast, automated process" as our value proposition. Again, a simple phrase designed for clarity.

Taking the first component first, i.e. mortgages for everyone, we would bring to the market a full product range from mainstream lending (A) through to niche lending (self certification and buy-to-let, for example) (A-) and then to non-conforming lending (B/C) under one brand. No-one else was offering this all-in-one approach then, or since. The traditional approach had been to have different brands in different product sectors.

We believed in competing brands to address different distribution opportunities: something that we subsequently invested in. But not different brands for different products.

We felt that high margin terms, then in place for non-conforming loans, would get closer to mainstream pricing over time. We believed that because of this there was no significant reputational risk in offering "mortgages for everyone" under one brand. Indeed, it would dilute our brand promotion plans to differentiate by product, particularly as we were such a new entrant to the market.

We felt that the growth to which we aspired meant that we had to sign up with the biggest distributors as soon as possible. We predicted that the largest intermediary firms (large brokers, networks, insurance companies) would soon come to dominate volumes as the largest firms do in other markets.

At the time, these firms were really only interested in mainstream loans. Because of this our launch platform with these clients had to be spot on in order to "disturb" their existing lender connections. We would then be able, so we planned, to pull these larger distributors along the risk curve with us and get them interested in products that were mutually more profitable. Our strategy to launch into the only part of the market that really gets you noticed was multi-faceted, beyond just signing up new distributors. While we believed that the margins on niche and non-conforming loans would come down over time nearer to mainstream, we felt that remortgaging in the mainstream market would, over time, remove the existing-to-new borrower subsidy, thereby increasing margins in that sector so as to produce more equilibrium pricing between new and existing borrowers.

Huge discounts and new business incentives have not been ever-present in mainstream. They had been introduced in the early nineties to help beat the impact of the recession. I know this because I was one of the first to introduce them. But as each existing borrower remortgages to a product where the rate and terms reflect an incentive for new business, a step is taken closer to ultimate equilibrium pricing.

This will take many years to achieve: probably the best part of two decades from 1990 - 2010. But if we could be an automated, cost efficient, top 10 player by the time it came about, we would be well positioned for explosive growth in the mainstream part of the market that still accounts for 75% of overall volumes. Business would then be profitable if there was a positive margin from day one in all sectors.

The way I described it at the time is shown in figure 1.2. A form of pricing continuum. Full status, mainstream, low loan to value loans will eventually enjoy a small, positive margin to the Bank Base Rate. There will then be a gradual build along the risk curve until the heavy adverse non-conforming comes in at, say, 2% to 2.50% over Bank Base.

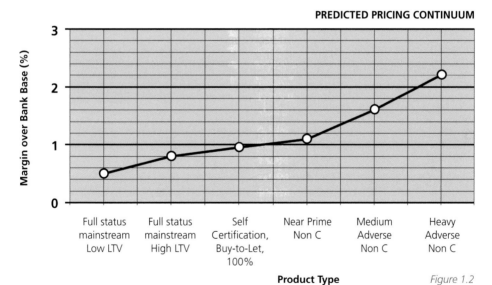

Figure 1.2

Our aim was to be able to generate very high volume - tens of billions of pounds – of all types of this asset (i.e. *mortgages for everyone*) in the right mix so that we could profitably exit through a blend of product type, quality and price.

This prediction of a relatively smooth pricing continuum as you move along the rate curve has not come true yet. Mainstream rates are still heavily incentivised. But not as much as they were. In 2000, when we made this prediction, discounts and cashbacks totalling 6% in the first year were commonplace. Now equivalent giveaways are nearer to 2%. At the same time, the margins on niche and non-conforming loans have come down from the 4% level they were when this prediction was made. The trend is so far looking good although, as ever, the exact timing cannot be accurately forecast.

By clearly stating the value proposition as including "*mortgages for everyone*" we underpinned the fact that we were committed to be in all product sectors. There were some wobbles on this as we were occasionally required to make mainstream loans available at little or no margin. Reinforcing the value proposition reminded colleagues that we had no choice in this regard unless we were to abandon one of the foundation stones upon which our strategy had been based.

The second component of the value proposition was "*… in a fast, automated process*". We did not believe that we would make anything like the impact we needed to by becoming another paper-driven lender offering poor service to its customers.

We intended to automate the process. Our dream was binding credit decisions at point of sale without the need for the old-fashioned, long-winded costly paper chase. Instead of getting behind with paper, we intended to get paper behind us.

As I explain in chapter 4, executing that part of the vision took a little longer than expected. Along the way, we eliminated as much paper as we could, and we eventually delivered the market-leading point of sale decision engine which now gives us a platform for further automation.

Reinforcing the promise of a "*fast, automated process*" allowed us to make clear decisions in relation to products and services that required a labour-intensive approach. We might consider such products or services to be outside of our core business, where I was quite happy to diversify and differentiate, so long as the value proposition for our core business was clearly understood and executed upon.

■ Managing the product mix

We were under no illusion that taking on a strategy of this type would take up a huge amount of management time. It would require daily focus on the amount of business we were taking in to ensure the wheels did not come off the trolley. If we did too much of one sort of lending it could destabilise the portfolios we were hoping to offer for sale to lenders. There was no escape from the fact that the senior management would have to become closely involved day-by-day, and able to make quick decisions that adjusted product intake without presenting an inconsistent or knee-jerk approach to the market.

What we decided to do was to circulate to every member of staff details of the products we had taken in that day, benchmarked against the appropriate targets. In this way we would get staff engaged not just in relation to the volume of business we had achieved, but also the mix between products. It would enable everyone to realise the importance of gathering in business in the appropriate proportions.

An example of an up to date version of that report is reproduced in figure 1.3. It relates to a particular day in 2005. It does not include the business that is accepted by our packagers, branded lenders and remote processors, but it gives a flavour of the importance we attach to this part of the strategy:

EXAMPLE DAILY PRODUCT MIX AND VOLUME MONITORING REPORT

	Number	% of Amount	Amount
A	35	15%	£ 6,300,000
A- Self Cert	105	38%	£ 15,750,000
A- Buy-to-Let	52	16%	£ 6,760,000
B/C	110	31%	£ 12,980,000
B/C Buy-to-Let	1	-	£ 100,000
Total Apps	303	-	**£ 41,890,000**
Daily Target to Year End	-	-	£ 35,000,000
Difference	-	-	£ 6,890,000

First Post Figures V0.6.rep
Produced by Credit & Risk BI Team

☺ *Figure 1.3*

At month end, the product mix programme calculates what volume of business we need on a daily basis flat for the rest of the year to achieve our targeted completions number. The "daily target to year end" is then changed for the next month. A smiley face, or a glum face, shows whether we have achieved the right amount of business on that day against the rest of year target.

Although it sounds a very minor point, to get every member of staff looking out each day for the smiley or glum face had a disproportionately positive impact right across the business. Efforts were re-doubled when the glum face appeared. It helped to reinforce our philosophy that "everyone is a salesperson" when dealing with customers. It made intermediaries and packagers realise that we were hungry for their business and intended to earn it.

Magnitude and direction

Not unreasonably, the business needed a benchmark to show where we were heading. You cannot set off on the sort of growth trajectory we were predicting without giving people an idea of what the ultimate destination looks like. It just does not work without it.

Our view of the future was that over-supply in the UK mortgage market would produce consolidation. We also reckoned that statutory regulation of the UK mortgage market for the first time was at least a strong possibility, and our assessment of the impact of regulation on other markets suggested that regulation was an even bigger driver of consolidation (and commoditisation) than over-supply.

In the insurance company sector, for example, major product lines were now dominated by a small number of large institutions. The diversity of choice that had existed pre-regulation had disappeared. The UK mortgage market was not a direct parallel. Nonetheless, we felt that there would be a small group of maybe a dozen lenders who would collectively dominate mortgage volumes, with regional or niche players making up the rest.

Being regional was not really an option for us. Becoming a niche player was possible, but we just did not feel that it would maximise our growth opportunities. Moreover, niche players have a habit of becoming marginalised as major players push along the risk curve.

We looked at alternative strategies. But, in truth, our heart was not in anything other than becoming one of the group of major league players who would dominate mortgage volumes in the future.

The Board therefore made clear to all stakeholders that our aspiration was to become a top 10 lender, measured by gross lending. We then reviewed with management and staff the then existing list of top 10 lenders by gross lending. This enabled them to see the size of organisation that we needed to become.

We were careful not to put a timeframe on it, other than to say "as soon as possible". I think that all things strategic should be painted in broad brush strokes. Unless being precise to an actual date, or to an actual number, is crucial to the strategy being pursued, it is better to look at ranges that do not restrict you. Magnitude and direction is what counts.

We pointed out that others would be growing and competing with us. We had no idea how successful they would be or, indeed, how well our new strategy would go down. It was not necessary to predict an actual timeframe. I would rather everyone stay focussed on this year's results. If we beat the market this year we would be on our way. Ditto next year, and so on.

Becoming a top 10 lender was an example of what is known in some circles as a BHAG (Big Hairy Audacious Goal). Seemingly impossible, or at least very difficult, they can - if they work well - excite the imagination and lead to above average performance.

The setting of BHAGs was already embedded in the culture of GMAC-RFC. I did not need to introduce it. I thought it was a good concept, so becoming a top 10 lender as soon as we could was our BHAG.

Of course, the ultimate achievement of BHAGs comes about through the successful implementation of a number of smaller goals, each running in parallel. An acronym for small, hairy, audacious goals does not appear to be available.

The competition grid

This is all top line stuff so far. Vision and value. Magnitude and direction. To get our business plan accepted by our US parent required a more detailed analysis. As I re-read the original business plan we produced in 2000, the importance of the competition grid came through.

This is where you plot the things that your competitors do well, and the things that maybe they do not do so well, on a chart. You then overlay the same measurement of your own company. If an apparent strength of yours lands on a square where there is more of a competitive weakness, this is a good starting point for developing a product or service. If either a strength or weakness lands on a competitor's strength area, then you have to be pretty sure that you have the resources to do that thing better.

The most important aspect of the competitor grid is who you put on it. Businesses sometimes make the mistake of comparing themselves with their competitors of the time. But if you are about to embark on a growth strategy, it is important to feature on the grid those with whom you aspire to compete.

Ask yourself the question, who will I compete with if I achieve the growth I want? That can sometimes paint a wholly different picture.

Just as the competition grid needs to comprise those organisations with whom you aspire to compete, so it is equally important to assess how those competitors will themselves develop. An assumption that your organisation will be moving ahead whereas your competitors will stand still is flawed.

Our work in analysing the competition grid suggested to us that, for example, as competition intensified, lenders would be prepared to undertake riskier lending in the search for higher margins. This was not a generally accepted view at the time, when most "big brand" lenders were still rejecting applicants with unusual circumstances or a poor credit history, judging this type of lending to be brand-threatening. But by knowing that this competition would evolve helped us to better discern our future shape. Sometimes, of course, decision-making is not about arriving at the best choice through inspiration or a flash of genius. More often than not, a good decision is arrived at by eliminating the alternatives.

As we looked at the completed competition grid five years ago, there were some clear alternatives to avoid. These were not just because existing, established players had them sown up. It was also because, in at least two areas, we felt that the institutions concerned might be fighting losing battles.

Take, for example, the issue of customer retention. Everybody in our industry is talking about retaining customers because it is cheaper than seeking new ones. But when they discuss the means by which to do this, the techniques are very often potentially flawed and not necessarily in the customers' best long-term interests.

They often involve the customers accepting new terms that may well be an improvement on their existing position, but which are not as keen as those being offered to brand new customers, either by the lender in question, or in the market generally. There are even some lenders paying continuing renewal commission to brokers in an effort to dissuade them from recommending keener-priced alternatives from competitors when a particular new business offer comes onto the market.

My view is that customers are getting increasingly financially sophisticated, and better informed. Any tactic aimed at persuading customers to stick with inferior terms is likely to be flawed. We therefore felt that we had to build a business model that was not dependent upon retaining customers through inertia, and which assumed in its drivers that most customers will increasingly do what is best for them.

The other potentially losing battle we identified related to the multi-product "lifestyle" offerings being made to customers by the big banks and top building societies. The idea behind this approach was that most savings, insurance and borrowing needs can be catered for by one supplier. Inertia would permit a number of cross-sales per customer. But we felt that the value being attributed by many institutions to cross-sales potential was optimistic.

As inertia becomes less prevalent so there is an increasing tendency for the customer to look at each individual product line on its merits. There is also an instinct, often displayed by the public, to avoid having all their product eggs in one basket, sometimes called the "jam jar principle" (in days gone by people saved for the mortgage, electricity and other household bills by putting coins into different jars).

We felt that, over time, unless an institution was prepared to be at the cutting edge of pricing and general terms in *each* of its product lines, the value attributable to cross-sales could be relatively small. We therefore decided to avoid becoming a multi-product supplier, instead focusing all of our energy and resources on being a "monoline" mortgage lender.

Subject to being able to deploy the resources properly, we had access to capital, funding and a fund to use for acquisitions. We also had a senior management group in the US committed to listening to the local culture when deciding whether a core competency was transferable to a new market.

Where there is over-supply, consolidation will take place. But it will often be the last thing to happen. Before that, participants will seek all available survival routes. Mainstream lenders moving into the non-conforming sector was an obvious step in that process. One of our first acts in pursuit of our strategy therefore had to be to see that competition off. We therefore, as an initial act, dropped our non-conforming rates across the board, by up to 2%. This was a difficult decision to get through the Board and the Assets and Liabilities Committee because, at the time, there were no real signs of the big brands getting into the non-conforming (principally sub prime or B/C) sector. All we had to justify our decision was our work on the competition grid. However, we were convinced that it would happen.

Now, of course, some five years later HBOS, Abbey, Britannia, Bristol & West, Portman and a whole host of smaller building societies have firm footholds in the non-conforming sector, often through subsidiary companies. Investment banks such as Merrill Lynch, Lehman Brothers, Deutsche Bank and Bear Stearns have also entered as principals to secure more bond underwriting for themselves.

This competition is a major factor behind margin reduction in all non-conforming elements of the market. We believe that there is further margin compression to come before we will start to see significant consolidation, which must, in turn, call into question the viability of the high prices some investment banks have paid in recent times to acquire mortgage lenders.

The environmental analysis

We felt that the economic and political environment was going to be kind to us. The (relatively) new Labour Government had won with a convincing majority, so we foresaw political stability, at least for a while. Inflation seemed to be well under control and the economy was growing. We predicted growth in gross mortgage lending but we could not have foreseen the shocking events of September 11, 2001, when over 3000 innocent civilians were tragically killed in the US in a series or terrorist attacks and following which interest rates fell dramatically. While the events themselves were deeply saddening the drop in interest rates had a strong stimulating effect on the UK mortgage market and on UK house prices generally. That converted our prediction of a "good market" into a "great market", albeit for reasons that nobody wished for.

We talked in our environmental analysis about the way in which demand for new household formation exceeded the supply of available property, thereby maintaining strong house price growth. We also said that the UK would not be joining the European single currency in the foreseeable future, which was contrary to the view then prevalent amongst many US commentators, who were predicting a "United States of Europe".

The relationship between growth in real incomes and growth in house prices has typically dominated macro environmental thinking in our market. But our view was that regional disparities were increasingly diluting the importance of the "average UK property price". Whilst we attempted to predict a band within which average UK property prices might grow, our most important conclusion from this part of the analysis was to ensure that our distribution coverage allowed no exposure to a particular geographic region.

When making market predictions for the future, we gathered data from a variety of sources and put them all together. The divergence of opinion among these sources was surprising. We did not take an average of these views: rather, we input them as data to our general thinking on the subject and then come up with our own view. This is one reason why I am not in favour of employing an in-house economist, for no one individual can be consistently right on a sustained basis.

I remember well the university professor who predicted a dramatic 30%+ fall in property prices a few years back. It was reported that many people sold their homes as a result of this prediction, believing themselves to be exiting at the peak of the market. What actually happened was that there was double digit growth in house prices that year and the year after. People who acted on that advice ended up being as poor as, well, a university professor.

If there is no great advantage or damage that a small percentage variance to a core number is going to offer or inflict, it is better to project in bands rather than precise numbers. Shapes help you decide strategy, not precise numbers whose only claim to fame will be that they will not be right. As a result of this conservative approach, we were fairly accurate in predicting the type of environment we would see as a backcloth to our growth plans. Not right on everything; but accurate enough not to affect the implementation.

Clearly there would be intense competition among mortgage lenders. We felt that, if there was to be over-supply and a price war, there would be winners and losers within the lending community. No one organisation would necessarily be a permanent winner or loser since that status could change within the course of a year. At any given point in time, however, the losers would be short of assets.

With the help of consultants Mercer, Oliver Wyman we devised a simple calculation that first considered a lender's market share based on the level of its outstanding lending compared with the market as a whole. We then looked at its latest share of gross advances versus the market as a whole. Where the latter understated the former, that was the measure under our calculation by which a particular lender was "under-lent".

It was a "rough and ready" formula, but I was not aware of anybody previously looking at the competitive background in this way. When we totalled the shortfall for each lender we were able to take comfort that we would be able to create a market into which we could sell completed loans - a key to the "trader" part of our strategy, the execution of which is described in Chapter 3.

We were also sure that technology was going to dominate the market in a way that it had not before. If margins were coming down in the face of competition then something had to give. Fortunately, there were costs we could take out, and we intended to do just that, as described in Chapter 4.

Now of course this is not an exhaustive list of all of the conclusions we reached as a result of our environmental analysis. Rather, they are a flavour only of how we went about this part of the strategic process and the shapes we discerned which helped us, in turn, to describe the organisation we wanted to become.

Strengths and weaknesses

All businesses need to look at what they can and cannot do well. There is no point in setting a path that you do not have the resources to deliver against, or where you can be easily outgunned. As a result of our analysis of the competition grid, we had already decided not to engage our major competitors on their ground, and we realised also that we had a brand deficit.

Other potential "weaknesses" included the fact that our competitors had long-established distribution and customer relationships. There was no ready market for selling assets we were unable to keep, and we had no track record in the mainstream market. Moreover, we were burdened by legacy computer systems due to the initial acquisition which had enabled us to enter the UK market in 1998.

But of course, there were strengths. We had no funding or capital constraints. We had strong parent company backing. We were ideally placed to look at the market afresh. There was also a hunger to innovate. If you can tap that then suddenly weaknesses can become opportunities. For example, the fact that we did not have a big balance sheet capacity behind us could be turned to advantage if we could tap the combined strength of the balance sheets of others. Whilst there was no liquidity in the market for traded portfolios, we could create one.

We would need to get the underwriting spot on because our judgment was that the market would only be available to buy *paying* loans. But this is where new technology could perhaps score a treble hit, by (a) making underwriting more predictive and accurate; (b) removing wasteful and old-fashioned human resource and (c) revolutionising service in an industry that had a poor track record in this regard.

The brand deficit might also be turned to advantage by introducing the name of our ultimate parent, General Motors. Previously, the financial side of our business had not typically used the name "General Motors" in its title, and special permission would be necessary. But we felt that recognition of this brand among UK consumers might be valuable.

Last, but not least, were the many years of distribution success we had experienced with Private Label. Longstanding relationships based on trust and mutual understanding had characterised much of Private Label's success. This distribution was now available to GMAC-RFC.

For every weakness, there turned out to be a compensating strength which could be derived from it. Or at least that is how we decided to see it. Any piece of adversity can normally be turned into an advantage.

Branding

Next we had to consider the brand deficit we had versus the established UK lenders with whom we would compete over the next few years. We were at the time of this major strategic review trading under the name RFC Mortgage Services Ltd. Figure 1.4 shows that uninspiring presentation.

RFC Mortgage Services Limited

Figure 1.4

Occasionally, we had to refer to our immediate parent company, which was of course GMAC-RFC. When those occasions occurred we used the then parent company logo as illustrated in Figure 1.5.

Worldwide Capital Partner

Figure 1.5

We judged that a brand overhaul was necessary and we engaged an agency to help us with research and images. What we decided as a result of this research was to (a) drop the RFC Mortgage Services Ltd name (b) introduce to the brand a reference to our ultimate parent, General Motors and (c) get the market thinking of us as a big financial services company.

Our research indicated that customers and intermediaries relate better to a large organisation from whom they derive comfort through size. Moreover, big corporate accounts and other lenders prefer dealing in what they perceive to be their peer group. We were at this time a relatively new entrant to the market and behaving as such. We needed to catapult ourselves quickly into the category of large, trusted lender to get the growth we needed.

We therefore sought and gained permission to use the General Motors name in our logo (the first business in our worldwide financial services company to do so), and we launched our strategy on the back of two brands. We used GMAC Residential Funding for our consumer and intermediary interface and GMAC-RFC for our institutional and public policy interface, both shown in Figure 1.6.

GMAC Residential Funding
A General Motors Company

GMAC RFC
A General Motors company   *Figure 1.6*

General Motors had been in the UK since 1919. It was the world's biggest car maker. People understood it to be large and powerful, so being able to use the name in our logo was important. But we also had a further asset in GMAC, the company that stood between GMAC-RFC and General Motors.

GMAC was already one of the world's largest financial services companies in its own right. So we sought to exploit that connection as well in a major advertising campaign we introduced as part of our launch. Using simple headlines and strong visuals we made the market think of us as GMAC. With headlines such as …

■ Success - it's all in the genes

■ You're usually embarrassed by your parents … we're very proud of ours

■ Who says success isn't hereditary?

… we put across our point in a way that immediately opened doors. It worked. The largest lenders and distributors wanted to talk to us. We were accepted as a large player long before that status was due to us based on our UK results.

Follow-up research showed that the increase in brand recognition was substantial among our target markets: never more so than with lenders to whom we wished to sell assets. We needed those lenders to trust us and to accept our warranties and representations including, where necessary, buy-back clauses. The use of brand in all these areas proved to be another sound decision.

Five years on and the position is different. Our target market recognises the GMAC-RFC name based on our UK achievements. There is no need for us to continually refer to our ultimate parent or have two separate brands GMAC-RFC, and GMAC Residential Funding. They have served their purpose. These days, we are just plain old GMAC-RFC.

To demonstrate that corporate life never stands still, and sometimes turns full circle, General Motors announced just as this book was going to press that it would be exploring the possibility of taking on a strategic partner in the ownership of GMAC. This is so new that it could play out in many different ways, over many different timeframes. One potential outcome could involve a new brand altogether, possibly by the time this book is published. But that is OK. The lessons we learned during the branding exercise mentioned here can be put to successful use again, if necessary.

You're usually embarrassed by your parents...

We're very proud of ours

GMAC Residential Funding

A General Motors company

www.gmacrfc.co.uk

GMAC Financial Services employs 29,000 people in 40 countries and has mortgage assets of $180 billion.

Registered in England and Wales:
Eastern Gate, Brants Bridge, Bracknell, Berkshire RG12 9BZ.
Registered No 3489004

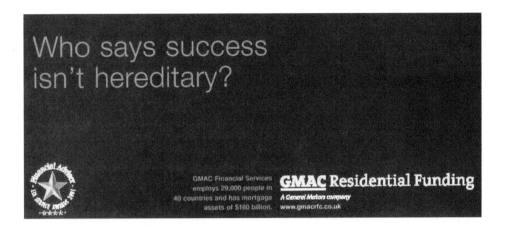

Who says success isn't hereditary?

GMAC Financial Services employs 29,000 people in 40 countries and has mortgage assets of $180 billion.

GMAC Residential Funding
A General Motors company
www.gmacrfc.co.uk

■ Focusing resource on where we made money

Before looking at the results, there is one area where we made what many in the industry thought was an unusual strategic decision, namely to outsource our back office servicing. An explanation of the background to this decision may help.

As the shape of a "creator and trader" of the scale we were proposing became clearer, it was obvious that servicing loans post completion was neither creating nor trading. If we were going to focus so much investment and management attention on a new and quite revolutionary (at the time) front end point of sale decision engine, we could not have the distraction of replacing at the same time the legacy back end system that we had inherited.

We therefore laid plans to outsource our post completion administration, which we specified in 2001 and implemented in 2002. This was just about the time when we sailed past the size of mortgage book which is typically used to indicate that there are sufficient economies of scale to bring the administration in-house. However, this decision was not a result of some secret or inspired knowledge. It was driven by our need to focus resource on where we would be making money, i.e. creating and trading.

I had enjoyed a relationship with Homeloan Management and one of its predecessor companies (MSL) for many years. I trusted them and their people. I knew that we could make it work better for us than keeping the loan administration in-house.

We would need a separate site and a substantial permanent local presence of GMAC-RFC employees. This is because inevitably mistakes would be made by both sides, so a close relationship would be required to resolve them quickly and amicably.

Outsourcing most definitely does not work if lenders leave the administrator to get on with it. It needs to be a partnership. We put one of our best managers, Carol Taylor, on site at HML, with a large team of other GMAC-RFC employees to supervise the work and build a team ethic with the HML employees.

We agreed service standards for all key work and included these in the contract. We introduced a disciplined review framework, including weekly informal, and monthly formal, meetings. We made it work well for us and our business partner, HML.

Of course, we costed the outsourcing route against the option of establishing a new back end system ourselves. Even without the opportunity costs, outsourcing was cheaper, by several million pounds over three years. An extra element in our particular case was our chosen strategy of trading the assets we created. Many of our portfolio purchasers use HML to continue the administration. It therefore seemed beneficial to establish that continuity in a way that could financially reward all parties.

Well over 200 HML employees now work exclusively on our completed mortgage accounts in a bespoke building in Padiham, Lancashire. We have sold many portfolios, issued numerous bonds and coped well with various changes to our administration process, not least statutory regulation. The decision to outsource was right for us.

Results

So, did the strategy work? I gave this away in my opening lines to gain your attention. Figure 1.7 shows the percentage year-on-year growth in gross lending achieved by the market as a whole, with the GMAC-RFC (UK) results alongside:

Year	2000	2001	2002	2003	2004
Market growth	5%	34%	38%	26%	5%
GMAC-RFC growth	90%	173%	83%	46%	31%

Figure 1.7

A business leader should always concentrate first and foremost on performance against the market at large. The best and worst brains among your competitors all come together in the market average. If you are going to assess how well you have done in your time as a CEO then you also need the discipline of a base year. I became Executive Chairman in 2000: therefore, 1999 (the year before I took over) is my base year in all the charts that follow.

Beating the market is what you are looking to do in any growth strategy. In the first five years of deploying our new strategy, we outgrew the UK mortgage market eleven-fold. That is, if you compare gross lending for the market as a whole in 2004 against the base year of 1999, there is market growth of 154%. Using the same comparison, GMAC-RFC (UK) grew its gross lending by 1700%.

But of course, this was achieved from a relatively low base. Some early wins were always going to score big percentage gains. This point is mitigated by the multiple by which we beat the market consistently every year for five years. But, as an alternative measure, we could look at the actual lending levels themselves, as set out in Figure 1.8.

The keen observer will notice a certain symmetry between 2001 and 2004 in that lending has grown by a rounded up, or rounded down (where appropriate), £1.5bn

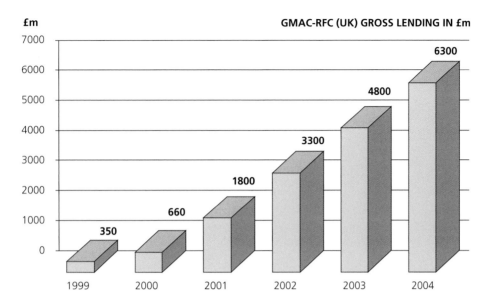

Figure 1.8

per annum. This is a complete coincidence. I had the figures double and treble checked. Those are the numbers. The increase we have achieved in gross lending has seen us rise from what the Council of Mortgage Lenders estimated to be about the 60th largest lender in 1999 to top 10 status at the end of 2004, as Figure 1.9 illustrates:

GROSS MORTGAGE LENDING, IN YEAR

Rank 2004	Rank 2003	Name of Group	£bn	Estimated market share
1	[1]	HBOS	68.4	23.4%
2	[4]	Lloyds TSB	26.3	9.0%
3	[2]	Abbey National	24.9	8.6%
4	[3]	Nationwide BS	23.2	8.0%
5	[6]	Northern Rock	20.1	6.9%
6	[7]	The Royal Bank of Scotland	19.3	6.6%
7	[5]	Barclays	17.5	6.0%
8	[8]	HSBC Bank	13.5	4.6%
9	[9]	Alliance & Leicester	8.7	3.0%
10 =	[12]	GMAC-RFC	6.3	2.2%
10 =	[10]	Bradford & Bingley	6.3	2.2%
12	[11]	Bristol & West	5.3	1.8%
13	[14]	GE Money Home Lending	5.1	1.8%
14	[13]	Britannia BS	5.0	1.7%
15	[15]	Standard Life Bank	4.6	1.6%

Source: CML

Figure 1.9

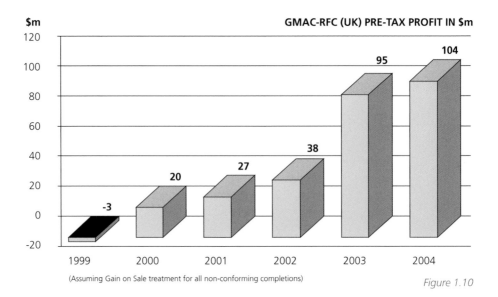

Figure 1.10

(Assuming Gain on Sale treatment for all non-conforming completions)

Any fool can increase lending by more or less giving money away at below market rates. The whole point of deploying business strategies is to create profit. Figure 1.10 confirms the profit numbers according to how I am judged, namely in US dollars using US Generally Accepted Accounting Principles. For ease of comparison between the various years, a consistent Gain on Sale treatment under US GAAP has been assumed for all bond executions even though the execution of some securities in later years required a different accounting treatment to Gain on Sale.

EUROPEAN RMBS SECURITISATION - 2004 ORIGINATOR RANKINGS

	Originator	Total EURm	No of Issues	Share (%)
1	HBOS	20,727	3	17.7
2	Northern Rock	16,263	3	13.9
3	Abbey National	5,963	1	5.1
4	**GMAC-RFC**	**5,200**	**4**	**4.4**
5	Fortis	4,397	2	3.8
6	Paragon	3,932	3	3.4
7	Kensington Mortgages	3,326	3	2.8
8	Bradford & Bingley	2,881	1	2.5
9	3CIF Group	2,871	2	2.5
10	Bancaja	2,590	2	2.2
	Total	**116,911**		

Period: 1 January 2004 to 22 December 2004, Includes: MBS, ABS and CDOs, Source: MCM and RBS   *Figure 1.11*

There is no publicly available information listing portfolio sellers. Our calculation is that we have sold more portfolios over the last five years than all other lenders added together. There is, however, a league table of Europe's largest securitisers of RMBS. As figure 1.11 shows, we grew from nowhere to 4th in this particular table.

In the same table for 2005 for the year to date we are ranked as third largest, a position we expect to retain for the full year unless there are some unexpected issuances in the final quarter of the year.

Wrap-Up

I was aware that, when I presented the proposed strategic plan internally and to our parent company, there were a number of major gambles. For example:

- We needed to be able to establish and get acceptance for a new type of UK lender, namely a "creator and trader"
- We needed acceptance for a "mortgages for everyone" approach under one brand
- We would succeed only if we could manage on a daily basis the exact product mix
- We were proposing to enter the mainstream mortgage market where margins were tumbling, and where we would compete with major lenders
- Our brand would need to be fundamentally changed in order to take on competitors who had a 200 year head start
- We would be attempting to create a portfolio sale market
- We would be introducing to established lender/distributor relationships some brand new concepts, including correspondent lending
- We would be investing in systems which would automate the pre-offer process, initially relating to the credit decision, but ultimately related to the whole process.

One or two "firsts" contained within a strategic plan normally represent the maximum appetite for those whose job it is to risk manage a business. To have this many "firsts" was unusual, to say the least.

But we did it. We introduced them all and we had success with them all. That is why this chapter, and this book, will, I hope, be of interest to all mortgage market practitioners. Much better to have a case study that worked than a text book which might not.

As you reflect on this strategy, and the chapters that follow, you will realise that I am giving away much of our "secret sauce". But I look at it like this: only tomorrow's innovations will really hurt our competitors. They already know about yesterday's.

In Chapters 2-5 I now explain in detail how we turned our vision of a successful mortgage lending business into reality in record time. It is a story of executing a clear and concise strategy with determination. For the time being, at least, spare the cat.

1 **2** 3 4 5 6 7 8

CREATING THE ASSETS

We had to outperform the market. It was as simple as that. And not by a small margin either. To secure top 10 lender status from virtually a standing start within a reasonable timeframe would require us to achieve new business volumes that exceeded the general rate of market growth many times over.

Stepping up to channel conflict

It was clear in the summer of 2000 that we would not reach our goals by relying on one product - our non-conforming "menu" - and one distribution channel - packagers. Our strategy required "mortgages for everyone" sold through every distribution channel available to us. This meant addressing demand from intermediaries who preferred to deal directly with lenders, and by providing an additional specialist team focused on the largest of those relationships. We would identify those who would benefit most from being treated as corporate account customers.

This, of course, is the classic channel conflict. We had hitherto specialised in dealing with packagers only. We realised that packagers were going to remain an extremely important distribution channel. We also acknowledged that they would be disappointed if we made our product range available to the intermediary market at large, since some of these intermediaries may have previously dealt with us through packagers.

But we knew that we had no choice. The packager channel, however important it was to us, could not on its own deliver either the breadth or the volume of lending that we needed to achieve our goal.

The right person in charge

To successfully implement this change of distribution approach, while keeping the existing packagers as happy as possible, required strong management. In our particular case, this part of the business was in good hands. I had worked with Godfrey Blight since 1985, first at Citibank and then at Private Label. I had no hesitation in appointing Godfrey as Sales Director of GMAC-RFC, charged with establishing, and then meeting, our ambitious sales targets, opening up new distribution channels and minimising channel conflict.

Focusing on packagers

Reporting to Godfrey, and initially heading our packager division, was John Rice, who is now Managing Director of RAMP. We have always served our packager channel with a dedicated sales resource. Although this meant on occasion that we might have several salesmen visiting customers in one area of the country all on the same day, we believed that we gained more with specialism than we lost with duplication.

We were open about our intentions, demonstrating with our actions that the packager channel remained important. As well as announcing that we would be widening our product range, and opening up new distribution channels, therefore, we took a number of initiatives to reinforce our commitment to packagers. These included:

- An immediate rate reduction that pushed our non-conforming product range to the top of the best buy tables

- The introduction of "Platinum Partner" status for those packagers contributing substantial volume (delivering a number of benefits including enhanced procuration fees)

- An extension of the remote processing/correspondent lending package that had been started by my predecessor

Although all three initiatives combined to make us hard-to-ignore for packagers, it was the last point that was market-changing. Correspondent lending had been very successful for us in the US. It still is. Recent statutory regulation has required us to amend our correspondent lending package in the UK, but, back in 2000, we were free to offer the full benefits and we certainly opened eyes and doors.

Correspondent lending had been introduced into the UK business by my predecessor, Chris Nordeen, who was at that time chairman of GMAC-RFC Europe and acting CEO of RFC MSL. I pay tribute to Chris for this. What we did was roll out his initiative on a larger scale.

Correspondent lending allowed the packager to appear as the lender. Offers of advance were issued in the name of the packager, using our technology and on-site underwriting staff. The offer noted that the loan would be "sold" post offer, but pre completion, to GMAC-RFC. For a packager to be able to present itself as the lender meant that it was in a position to attract demand from those intermediaries who only wanted to deal directly with a lender. We would therefore give to our top packagers the means by which to compete with the new Intermediaries Direct channel we were also starting.

This was our commitment to the packager channel. We would do everything that we could to enable it to "attract" business. What we would not do was to try and "contract" that business by forcing it down a channel with which it was uncomfortable.

In business you have to add value, and compete on your product and service proposition. It is healthy to increase your competitiveness, but unhealthy to try and reduce your competitors' competitiveness.

No other lender was offering correspondent lending at that time. The ability to control the processing up to completion stage, and to build their own brand, rather than that of the lender, were extremely popular features to packagers.

A packager is reputationally exposed to its least efficient lender. It was commonplace at the time for packagers to have to make frantic telephone calls to lenders to try and find a particular application in a pile of outstanding cases that had been chased hard by an intermediary who was a regular customer of the packager. Correspondent lending changed all that.

The packager was now in charge of its own outstanding cases. It could make its own priorities. It could deliver the service to which it had always aspired. The application file never left the packager's office. It was always in complete control.

A knock-on benefit to us was that, as we expanded the number of correspondent lenders, so we further diversified and increased our own processing capability. Intermediaries who wanted GMAC-RFC products had a wider choice. If they wanted to deal with us directly then they could. But if they felt that they could get better service using one of our correspondent lenders, then we were happy to allow them to do that as well.

As we priced to lead the market, and introduced our different categories of packager, so our non-conforming business increased. Within two years, we had 80 packagers in their different guises delivering regular business to us. Although the majority of the business came from those with whom we had correspondent lender and remote processor arrangements, we were also being used by all the other major packagers as well. In fact, within two years, we had passed Kensington as the number one non-conforming lender, measured by sub prime completions first mortgage volume.

Correspondent lending had a great three year run, transforming what lenders were prepared to offer to the packager community in terms of service and delegated control. Most of the major non-conforming lenders now offer some form of decentralised processing deal to their largest packagers, and we are proud to have instigated this change in process.

The prospects of statutory regulation, however, meant that correspondent lending could not continue in that guise. Regulation envisaged that any organisation which presented itself as the lender, even one that "sold" all of its business post offer, would need to be regulated as a lender in its own right. This was disproportionately complex and expensive, so compromises had to be found.

The reason behind the introduction of correspondent lending was often misunderstood, and deliberately so by those lenders unable or unwilling to provide a similar service. What we knew, however, was that the branding and processing elements were the main factors, and these could be retained by substituting "branded lending" for "correspondent lending".

Under our branded lending deal, packagers could still produce offers in their own name, but "in association with GMAC-RFC". Instead of stating that the loans would be "sold" to GMAC-RFC post completion, the offer made clear that GMAC-RFC was the lender. The remote processing arrangements remained intact.

Most correspondent lenders therefore transferred to become branded lenders. Some gave up the pursuit of branding, but retained the remote processing capability. By M-Day (when statutory mortgage regulation began in the UK) on 31 October 2004, we had three categories of packager delivering business to us, namely:

■ Branded lenders (all of whom had remote processing)

■ Remote processors (no branding)

■ General packagers (no branding or remote processing)

We had also increased the product range that we made available to packagers by including self certification and buy-to-let products, thus enabling them to offer a broader service to their customers. Indeed, an early decision had been to release the "STAR" no-income-stated product (previously exclusive to Private Label) to the full packager network - a very popular move at the time.

The result of all of the product and service initiatives we undertook with packagers was that our new business from this source increased ten fold between 1999 and 2004.

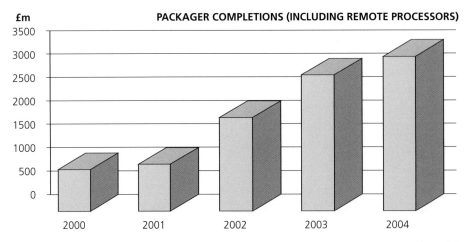

Figure 2.1

We have, we believe, demonstrated beyond any shadow of doubt our commitment to the packager channel, which is continuing. We have shown at the same time that we will not step away from channel conflict or change our plans because one channel does not like what we are doing.

What we have consistently done, however, is to ensure to the best of our ability that each channel receives the products, service and responsive sales management that will enable them to compete with any other channel, thereby attracting business in a way that increases standards and customer choice.

Intermediaries direct

There are some intermediaries who prefer to deal direct with lenders. Normally they are large companies, but they do not have to be. They may belong to a network or be individually registered. They may sometimes use a mortgage club and sometimes not. It is, however, a sizeable demand and no lender of the size we wanted to become could ignore this demand.

To address this sector we established a new distribution channel, which we called Intermediaries Direct. To set up this new national sales force for GMAC-RFC, we appointed Rob Green, one of the top sales managers from Private Label.

Rob's starting point with this new channel was the Private Label database of 14,000 intermediaries, about 3,000 of whom had sent in an application in the preceding six months. He started with six regions and about 10 full time sales people (all transferred from Private Label) and set out to grow the intermediary direct channel in parallel to our other channels.

Today, the national intermediary direct salesforce has 30 regions and a regional management structure below Rob. But this salesforce still uses in practice the tried and tested sales techniques that had made Private Label so successful. These are the 15 core rules:

1. Recruit salesmen with a good personality, who communicate clearly, who have a will to succeed and who will be remembered by intermediaries after they have left their office

2. Positive feedback is not a closed sale: always ask for the business and focus subsequently only on the physical application you get as a result of a sales visit

3. Do not send a salesman out on the road without proper preparation and training, which must include understanding fully the point of sale technology

4. Have a disciplined approach to the "sales cycle" from appointment-making through preparation, objective-setting, the initial greeting, the closing and the follow-up

5. Ensure that all salesmen are up to date with the workings of, and "sell against" points related to, competitor products

6. Always follow up the sales call with a telephone call, email or letter

7. Get your salesmen to learn in each sales call what business is being given to competitors and on what products, and maintain an efficient way of getting that information to a central database to be analysed by the product development team in marketing so that trends can be discerned, adjustments made to your own product range or competitor terms challenged

8. Manage individual salesmen using the statistics that relate business calls to business generated, strike rates and repeat usage, benchmarking these against expected norms

9. Continually focus your sales team on the 80/20 list which always applies (this near universal rule says 80% of your business will come from 20% of your contacts)

10. Selling can be a lonely job: make your salesmen feel important, give them support, a nice car, and continually catch them doing something right

11. Sales managers should be continually in the field, keeping in touch with the customers: poor decisions will be made by desk-bound sales bosses

12. Make sure your salesmen have scripts and sales angles that the intermediaries can use to promote particular products to their best effect

13. Strike up a relationship with your competitors in the field, be friendly and help them where you can: aggressive rivalry is wasteful, inelegant and unpopular with intermediaries

14. Salesmen should care a lot about their intermediary customers' problems: if an issue does arise, they should go out of their way to resolve it, as their customers will remember that and respond well to it

15. An organisation that can have fun, and not take itself too seriously all the time, will present a confident and attractive image that will be remembered

Simple rules, most of which will be followed by the majority of successful salesforces. The most important factor is the production and use of statistics that relate business generated to sales calls made, benchmarked against the expected company norm.

Handled in the right way, this is the sales tool which will tell you in hard facts whether intermediaries have responded to the sales messages you have given them. It will prevent salesmen from chasing lost causes, and will present the opportunity to maximise business from those intermediaries who are responding well.

Rob and his sales managers produce regular reports showing field staff how they spent their time, how much business resulted and how successful their strike rate was against the company benchmark. As rule 2 says: "positive feedback is not a closed sale".

This approach was born out of the early days of Private Label, many years previously, when salesmen used to come back to the office full of "positive feedback". I used to give them the bank paying in book and ask them to pay some of that feedback into our account to help pay the wages! It is a culture thing: successful salesforces judge themselves on what business they get, and ruthlessly apply their time to those customers who "walk the talk".

Successful application of this approach enabled our salesforce to become "farmers" rather than "hunters". This meant that they were growing and nurturing increasingly longstanding relationships rather than continually hunting new contacts with whom they had never dealt previously.

One way in which sales activity has radically changed since those Private Label days is in the use of technology. With online Point of Sale decision making now a key part of our package, the sales team has to sell the benefits of the technology as much, if not more so, than the products. They have to know intimately how it works, what its foibles are and how best to present it. Non technically-minded field staff may find themselves exposed in today's online and computerised world.

To address new or irregular users, we established a telesales team. This unit has also been successful, generating hundreds of millions of pounds worth of new business each year. They also sometimes grow new contacts to a sufficient size so that they can be passed on to the national salesforce.

We could not be sure how the intermediary direct channel would take off. We knew there were an increasing number of intermediaries who wanted to deal direct, but we did not know how many. Good people, with a disciplined sales approach, were our main assets in building this channel from scratch, to a level where it would contribute the majority of our new business in 2005, including corporate accounts.

Corporate Accounts

We judged that regulation would mean fewer but larger intermediary firms. Customers would require, like never before, the advice of an intermediary, faced as they were with increased choice delivered by an increasingly sophisticated and competitive market. So the good intermediaries would get bigger and more powerful, requiring a corporate account approach if we were to maximise business from them.

We chose another top Private Label sales manager, Roger Brown, to lead this channel. Roger's first job was to identify what a corporate account looked like, then describe how it would interact with the new intermediary direct salesforce, and establish a target list for new corporate account customers.

I felt that it was so crucial to have a salesforce dedicated to the corporate accounts channel, that I asked to personally receive a monthly note from Roger describing the latest results against previous month, with an added commentary. This continued for about 18 months until Roger persuaded me that the outstanding growth he was achieving did not really merit my individual attention, even though he assured me he was enjoying it!

As we looked at how the future of corporate accounts might develop, we not only saw mortgage clubs and networks becoming pivotal, but also large brokers and estate agents becoming quasi-institutional in their own right. Estate agents were of particular interest to us because we were at that time poorly represented among our distribution partners by the UK's leading estate agents.

Typically, estate agents had been more focused on fast-moving mainstream mortgages, leaving complex niche and non-conforming loans to their broker partners. One of the many advantages in us launching mainstream products was that we were able to attract the attention of estate agents to whom we then introduced our wider product range.

It took us a few months to get everything together, particularly the separate recording of new business from corporate accounts. We launched our new channel in October 2000 with just half a dozen names including John Charcol, Mortgage Intelligence and Legal & General. Notable new appointment successes in our first year were Sesame, Bradford & Bingley and Friends Mortgage World.

Then came new major estate agency "catches" in Countrywide and Mortgages Direct (Spicer Haart), followed by Norwich Union, InterAlliance, Personal Touch, PMS and Bankhall. More recently were added Millfield, St James's Place, Connells, Sequence and Openwork. Our corporate accounts channel grew from six firms in 2000 to over 30 today.

Added to the intermediary direct business we were receiving outside of corporate accounts, these two new channels combined achieved £3bn of completions in 2004, from a standing start in 2000. In 2005 this figure will be over £4bn.

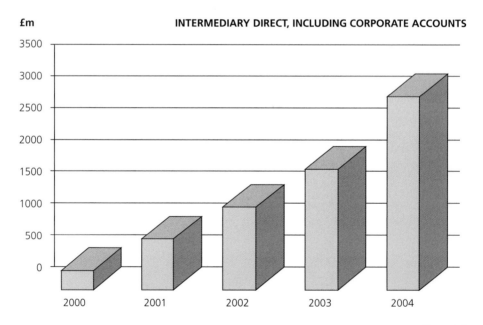

Figure 2.2

Although our competitors had followed us into the remote processing markets so far as non-conforming packagers were concerned, few, if any had targeted these facilities at estate agents or, for that matter, large brokers. Yet the ability to control the administration from start to finish, and to be remunerated as a packager, was as much of interest to estate agents and large brokers as it was to the packager community.

We had caught these distributors' attention with our headline-grabbing mainstream, self certification and buy-to-let mortgage products. Once we had their attention we talked to them about non-conforming products. We are responsible for a number of big well known mainstream players now distributing non-conforming mortgages when they had rejected such business previously.

Each corporate account had to be treated individually. They had management at the centre who needed to regularly review progress. We had to persuade that management to allow us representation in their newsletters, and at the regional sales meetings. There were roadshow launches, targeted mailings, exclusive products and any number of different marketing initiatives all negotiated and relationship-managed through the centre.

The idea from a lender's perspective was to get "under the skin" of your key corporate account contacts, making sure that they realised how important they are to you, and seeking ways to build profile and recognition for your company with their business-getters. They know that of course, and they are often hard taskmasters on behalf of their end customers in negotiating the best products and product terms. But if the relationship is made to work well, with professional specialist sales resource focused on it, there are fantastic rewards to be had.

Exclusive products are increasingly a feature of the relationship with corporate accounts. Sometimes there will be a bespoke exclusive product aimed at a particular market need that the corporate account has identified. Mostly, however, it will be transparently more attractive terms available to the corporate account than are available in the market direct.

If you have one distribution channel generating £4bn of business, for example, there is every justification for recognising that fact while, in turn, giving their business a boost by creating more competitive leverage for them in their markets.

We have found that the right sales management combination is to have a small team of professional corporate account managers, each focusing on a few firms only, giving them close, individual attention and really getting inside the relationship, supported by good interaction with the regional sales teams and bespoke, responsive marketing support. We have been lucky enough to have won quite a few awards on this journey, but the one we received from Legal & General, our biggest corporate account, for their "best relationship manager" - GMAC-RFC's Paul Huxter - helped to confirm we were on the right track.

While a good corporate accounts manager can successfully manage a relationship centrally, there needs to be regional coverage to meet up with the business-getters. This is where you need top co-operation and co-ordination between your central corporate accounts managers and your regional salesforce. The connection has to be seamless.

Our system works particularly well because the individuals running corporate accounts and the national salesforce respectively have worked with each other, and for Godfrey, for 10 years plus. Stability of sales management, if you can achieve it, is worth a certain percentage of sales growth each year on its own.

Another important point in that set-up is that all business generated is credited to the regional salesman and also to the manager of that particular corporate account. There might be a double count in that, but the motivational benefits outweigh the cost of effectively paying twice.

More recently, as communication techniques and habits have changed, there has had to be an even more sophisticated level of penetration of the corporate accounts relationship including website links and intranet coverage. Our corporate accounts channel now has its own dedicated person within the marketing department for support with new marketing initiatives.

Further technology enhancements are planned that will form even greater links in the future. Launching a separate corporate accounts channel was a major move for us in attacking those new business volumes, and we see only further growth in this channel.

Investing in distribution

The competition grid I mentioned in chapter 1 allowed us to spot one strength of ours that lined up with a relative weakness of our competitors, namely our willingness to make strategic investments - minority stakes if necessary - in distribution companies. GMAC-RFC has been an acquisitive company and I was encouraged by Chris Nordeen to establish from day one a fund that would fast-track the governance of such acquisitions.

The fund established as its primary goals a wish to either influence distribution or to help us make future distribution decisions by moving us up the learning curve. We were encouraged not to lose money, although that is not always easy when you are investing in somebody else's business.

We decided to use the fund to address areas of the market not catered for by the three channels mentioned above. It was difficult to go out and source these opportunities: rather, we would have to wait for them to come to us, then recognise them when they did. I guess that, during the period from 2000 to 2004, we were presented with as many as 50 different investment opportunities. We chose only three:

■ High Street Home Loans (HSHL)

Investment opportunity number one presented itself when HSHL, one of our branded lender remote processors, approached us on the basis that one of the founding partners wished to exit the business. The remaining partner, Gary Forrest, and his team were committed to developing the HSHL brand with a unique product range serving the smaller packager.

We knew that, as our packager channel was evolving, we could increasingly only satisfactorily serve the bigger players, so this seemed a perfect fit. Chris Nordeen had already made a small strategic investment in HSHL. So the proposed new investment would involve increasing our existing minority shareholding to 100%.

We agreed to do this and took full ownership in February 2003. An exclusive product range was launched, designed to appeal to the smaller packager. Progress has been steady and pleasing, with HSHL further differentiating its service more recently by continuing to offer a manual underwriting service while we have become automated. We have thus become fans of the "competing brand" approach in circumstances where there are unique distribution channels with no obvious overlap.

■ National Guarantee (NG)

The second investment came about when we were approached by one of our top branded lender remote processors, NG, who wished to complete their transition from B2B (Business-to-Business) to B2C (Business-to-Consumer). This required a further investment, to which we agreed by way of a minority 40% stake.

NG's target market is non-conforming products and it places its business with other lenders as well as with GMAC-RFC. But by the close co-operation this investment has generated, we have been able to learn much about the challenges of the B2C non-conforming model in the current competitive market conditions. Eventually, as we grow still larger, we will have to consider the B2C channel ourselves, so our experience of working with the NG investment has greatly assisted our thought processes.

■ Mortgage Ventures Limited (MVL)

The third investment was also in B2C, but this time in a company - MVL - that specialised in the mainstream sector. MVL owned two broking firms - one established (Chase de Vere), and one to be launched (Purely) - and the 37% minority shareholding we purchased is teaching us about the B2C model in the mainstream market. As with NG, we are not involved in any aspect of running the business.

Taken as a whole, our investments are either actively addressing a market that we are unable to serve ourselves in a viable fashion, for example, small packagers, or - in the case of NG and MVL - we are learning about the dynamics that exist in B2C within two different market sectors. All investments are therefore playing a role in both creating assets to form part of our growth, and teaching us about our ability to create more assets in the future.

B2C generally

What we have learned about B2C is that the viability dynamics are on a knife edge, delivering profit or loss, dependent upon small percentage differences in key performance ratios. The two most important components are cost per enquiry and enquiry-to-application. If the former is higher than average, the latter has to be spectacularly good. If the former is average then if you are a couple of percentage points out on the latter you will turn profit into loss. Paying for the business only when a loan completes, which is what happens in B2B, seems positively civilised by comparison.

Four of our five current executive directors on the GMAC-RFC statutory board were involved in an experiment in lead generation in the late 1990s (see Chapter 6). Even then, the trend had started under which fewer and fewer consumers respond to off-the-page offers. Those that did were disproportionately window-shoppers with no specific transaction to pursue.

Scroll forward to the world of statutory regulation where, to advertise any mortgage product, requires three rates to be shown (the initial rate, the reversionary rate, and the APR), and it is easy to see why most B2C players have downgraded their advertising budgets. We have witnessed the use of purchased leads, leaflet drops in national newspapers at a million a time, data mining (pre regulation) and a whole host of other techniques, but have not seen any of these turn into sustained success. Even the old-fashioned branch network approach of our major top 10 competitors is starting to be overtaken by technology, as lenders close branches or re-focus them as multi-sales outlets.

Purchasing qualified internet leads is the only current approach we would observe that looks remotely viable. If the lead provider can establish with the consumer that there is a transaction to pursue, and can provide leads according to the ability of the purchaser to service them (i.e. turning the supply on and off at short notice) then this can work since, instead of the large capital outlay that would be required in a TV, national press or leaflet campaign, payment can instead be made lead-by-lead.

You still need the means by which to convert the leads. We know of no B2C operation that has worked viably over a sustained period of time without the need for a high customer fee to pay for this. A disproportionate number of telephone and field-based staff are required to turn enquiries into actual applications.

There is no shortage of innovation in the area of lead generation by the internet lead providers. You can now purchase web spot advertising so as to appear high up on a search engine list when people key in the word "mortgage". There is even a provider that picks up leads where there has been a mis-spelling of the word "mortgage" in order to intercept them and feed them out.

ING Direct has been highly successful in establishing itself in double quick time as one of the world's largest retail investment companies with the simple proposition of a market-clearing benchmark savings rate, delivered cost effectively over the internet, working with a linked current account. Its marketing budget must be huge, and that is a certain outlay in return for uncertain results. But it shows it can be done. We think that we will have to add a B2C distribution channel sooner rather than later.

Lenders as distributors

The UK mortgage industry has been slow to catch on to this particular concept. There seems to be a reluctance on the part of UK lenders to work closely with competitors on particular product lines. This is changing, mainly due to the growth in the non-conforming sector, but too slowly in my view for the opportunities that are available.

More and more lenders are seeing the sense of trying to keep non-conforming applicants rather than rejecting them and passing the business to their competitors. If lenders in those circumstances are not ready, able or willing to undertake non-conforming lending themselves, then a partnership with a competitor is the obvious solution. The customers can be served and retained, with the lending risk passed on to another institution.

The most commonly used method for addressing this issue is for one institution to pass leads to another. But passing rejects to another organisation does not work. We have tried this and various other methods, including an arrangement we had with Chelsea Building Society where they effectively acted as a remote processor for our non-conforming loans. That was more satisfactory than the simple passing of leads, but not much more. It is all to do with the time lag needed between rejection and selection.

Most human beings either cannot or will not understand a rejection and a selection at the same time. A time break is needed to come to terms with the rejection before the mind is clear enough to make the selection.

The idea behind these referral schemes is that the customers will cope with being rejected for the product and lender they initially wanted, and be ready to immediately select a different product from a different lender. They will not: at least not in any significant volume.

I liken this situation to arriving home one night to be told by your partner that the relationship is over. As part of this dramatic announcement your partner then introduces a friend for you to consider as an alternative. However fabulous the friend might be, you will want to understand and process the rejection first, before being ready to select a different way forward! (Well, most of us would!).

I have not seen one of these schemes ever work properly, and make real money, even when the rejecting lender is within the same group of companies as the proposed alternative lender. The time break needed between rejection and selection is ignored at huge opportunity cost, the length of which will rely very much on the individual customer.

The only formula we have known to work is the one we have implemented with Amber Home Loans, a non-conforming lender that is a wholly owned subsidiary of Skipton Building Society, where the customer is never 'rejected'. This arrangement has already contributed to our overall volumes, and it is one that we would like to replicate further across the industry.

Amber was already a successful non-conforming lender in its own right. But demand for its non-conforming product range was greater than its balance sheet appetite. We therefore offered a way to increase that capacity.

Under our contract, both sides agree the credit parameters and Amber processes the application just like any other, completing it onto their balance sheet. They can therefore accept business where they cannot lend, but we can. The case is accepted and the mortgage completes just like any other Amber loan.

Amber then has a put option on us every calendar quarter for those mortgages that are within the agreed target range and which fit the target criteria. These loans are "sold" to us. We honour the agreed customer terms, and Amber frees its balance sheet again for more lending. The cycle is refreshed, but Amber continues to "own" the customer and, importantly, is seen to positively accept applicants that, before, it might have needed to turn away.

The sales process is not interrupted. Customers are not "rejected" and referred to what they may regard as an unwelcome alternative to the lender they had originally selected. This sort of partnership is more common in the US, and leaves some risk with the "selling" lender.

But this can be compensated for by the volume of business which can be done under the slicker process, and not just in the target lending areas. A lender that can offer a fuller product range by virtue of a partnership like this will attract more of the business it can do itself, as intermediaries experience habit-forming familiarity.

The income which the selling lender can generate from the purchasing lender, alongside retained customer fee and insurance commissions, goes straight to the bottom line and can dramatically improve the return on assets (as there are few, if any, assets retained) and return on capital (as no capital is needed to back the sold assets). Another great application is to "rehabilitate" the paying customers back onto the selling lender's prime product range with a customised fee-free remortgage deal after a typical two or three year redemption penalty has expired.

Whether it is balance sheet capacity, risk, appetite, speed to market, or lack of specialist underwriting, this type of arrangement can address those needs in a way that "passing of a reject" cannot.

Products

However clever and insightful your distribution management, nothing actually happens without good products. We have attempted to deliver over the years any number of non price/non product reasons why intermediaries and packagers should deal with us, such as the branded lending/remote processing package; automated point of sale decisioning; incentives; good account management; excellent service and so on.

Good execution in these areas will always give you more sales than you would otherwise have achieved, based on a good range of products. But in our experience, these areas are enhancers rather than motivators. They will not get you business unless your core product range is right.

■ Market Intelligence

I have already mentioned one of the important cogs in the product development machine, namely the constant data feedback we get from every sales call, as the fieldstaff ask what products their intermediary customers are selling outside of our own range and why. Supporting that input must be constant marketing research, every hour of the day.

Our product team, based in the marketing department, tops up the information it receives from the sales fieldstaff by going into our competitors' websites, teleresearching a cross section of our intermediaries as to which products and lenders are attracting them at any given point in time, and even receiving details of competitor product launches and how particular products and services are being positioned.

We also have a number of loyal intermediaries and packagers who feed material and information into us. Intelligence-gathering can never stop. It must be renewed and refreshed daily.

Every lender does this. I know that, on occasion, our product launch material is on the desk of a competitor marketing director before it is sometimes in the conscious product portfolio of our fieldstaff. It is healthy because the customer benefits. Once a trend is discerned (never react to a single piece of feedback) a competitor's product that is doing damage can be targeted either with a comparative sales aid or a price re-adjustment within our own range.

In the mainstream, self certification and buy-to-let markets it is easier to compare price and terms. With non-conforming it is more complicated, because every lender prices slightly differently according to the amount of adverse lending they will accept. We have therefore developed software that looks at over 60 different customer profiles and then finds the best rate for that profile from our product range, and from the products offered by our chosen basket of competitors.

It requires us to constantly input the changing terms being offered by competitors. But the payback comes when, at the touch of a button, you can see how you compare with all of your competitors, just some of your competitors or one competitor in particular.

Using a "traffic light" method, the system flags green where we have a cheaper rate in that particular customer profile, red where we do not, and amber where we are the same. Our aim is to be the cheapest in the non-conforming sector up to 75% LTV in at least 50% of instances, and this software makes it easy to adjust pricing to achieve that aim.

■ Mainstream

We knew as we embarked on this journey that it was the competitiveness of the mainstream products that would get us noticed by the large intermediaries, particularly the estate agents and corporate accounts we had targeted. The national press were only interested in reporting mainstream products that get onto the best buy tables, so we bit the bullet and launched as a mainstream lender even when these products occasionally lost us money.

We did not know how, or even if, the market would accept mainstream products from us. GMAC-RFC had experimented with a couple of exclusive launches via Private Label, but addressing the wider market was a different thing altogether. Our first ever open market mainstream product was a two year penalty-free fix designed to go straight to the top of the best buy tables. That got people talking about GMAC-RFC straight away. We promoted the "mortgages for everyone" strapline and started pumping away at the message that we were in all sectors of the market.

It worked. The whole package of stressing our corporate heritage, alongside our "mortgages for everyone" message, and our eye-catching products brought us large volumes of mainstream business. More importantly, it started to get us noticed and talked about by the major distributors. If we ever exceeded our target product mix for mainstream business we would make the replacement products slightly less competitive. Then, just as the market thought that we had gone quiet for a while, we would shake it up by launching something new that went to the top of the tree. As I covered in chapter one, management of the product mix is a daily event right across the business, demonstrating that a strategy for growth on the scale that we had implemented is seriously management-intensive.

As the press started to pick up on our product competitiveness, so also did the wider market. We started getting appointed to the panels of the largest distributors. People began eagerly anticipating news of our latest product launches.

We managed to create an atmosphere that GMAC-RFC was "the lender to watch", which also filtered through to the employment market, where we started to get good people approaching us for jobs. We were recruiting sales staff heavily as the applications rolled in, both on the corporate accounts side and within the national salesforce. There was also a positive knock-on recruitment impact right across our business. But the growth was not just founded on mainstream lending: it was based on "mortgages for everyone".

■ Self Certification

When we had to replace our no-income-stated "STAR" product, we introduced a wide range of fixed, discounted and tracker self certification products, some leading the field and available to 90% LTV. Because of this we seized a market opportunity when one of our largest competitors tightened its self certification criteria and raised rates to limit demand for a while.

We reduced ours, won a massive increase in business and established a great foundation for further expansion. You have to be ready to move quickly.

■ Buy-to-let

To complete the "niche" range we also launched a buy-to-let suite of products. The buy-to-let market was enjoying rapid growth. From an insignificant amount of lending ten years ago, buy-to-let had grown to represent about 6% of the overall market, so all major lenders needed to be in this market to keep up with competitors.

Like any evolving market, the products available in the buy-to-let sector were priced cautiously initially at a higher price than mainstream. As the supply:demand ratio changed in favour of the end customer, so the product terms became much more attractive. The pricing of buy-to-let loans is now much nearer to mainstream, and the market has enjoyed significant innovation, in which we have played a part.

Recognising the great performance quality of buy-to-let lending, we introduced an 89% LTV product, increasing the amount we would lend over and above the industry norm of 85%. This initiative helped buy-to-let borrowers chasing higher property prices, although we restricted the product to a 3 year fixed rate loan where stability of monthly payment was guaranteed.

We also introduced a brand new buy-to-let product offering options of 100% and 110% rental cover. With rents reducing as a result of increased supply of privately rented accommodation, buy-to-let borrowers were finding it difficult to complete purchases using the standard industry formula of the rent needing to cover 125% of the mortgage payment.

What was eye-catching about this particular offering was that the interest rate and general terms were the same irrespective of the rental cover calculation used. All that transparently changed with this product was the arrangement fee charged.

These options were increasingly welcome, and contributed to us becoming a leading lender in buy-to-let, just as we had become in self certification and non-conforming.

■ Non-conforming

The main engine room of our non-conforming growth was still our "menu approach", which ensured that customers only paid for the credit issues they had: something that other lenders' "boxed" ranges did not do. But we soon came to realise that this approach did not always suit the intermediary direct channel. Increasingly, intermediaries dealing direct relied on mortgage sourcing and had neither the time nor the inclination to construct an interest rate using the menu approach.

This is not surprising when you understand that the menu effectively allows three thousand variations. As a result, we were not building sufficient non-conforming traction in the intermediary direct market. The unique menu, with which most mortgage sourcing systems could not cope, was holding us back in that channel. We therefore decided to introduce a second non-conforming product range - our own version of a boxed range designed for the intermediary direct market, while retaining the menu for the packager sector.

This approach has certainly contributed to our volume success, although having two product ranges in the same brand can cause its own difficulties. It is something we are reviewing as this book goes to press. The benefits are clear, though. They are that the boxed range easily sources on the mortgage-sourcing systems, while the menu range plays to the strengths of the packagers in terms of their ability to give advice and guidance to brokers on more complex products.

■ Lifetime Mortgages

One product we have not introduced is the lifetime mortgage. I have fairly fixed views about this, which came out in an unplanned manner at the CML Annual Conference in December 2003. I was on stage immediately after Anne Gunther, the CEO of Standard Life Bank. I was due to give a speech describing GMAC-RFC's strategy and why it was different to everybody else's.

Anne delivered her presentation and announced that Standard Life Bank would be entering the lifetime sector. Much to the horror of our marketing team present, I therefore decided it would be a good time to voice, slightly tongue-in-cheek, my views on this product which is primarily aimed at helping older members of our community "unlock" the value in their homes by remortgaging. When it was my turn on stage I diverted from my script and said something along the lines of:

"I can assure Anne that she will have no competition from us in the wrinkly sector. The thought of dealing ten years after completion with an incontinent borrower who is unable to remember where he lives, fills me with horror".

The comment got a great laugh, which was the intention. A journalist picked it up, however, and wrote a piece with the headline "Knight's wrinkly jibe shocks brokers". I doubt very much that it did, and no broker is quoted as having been shocked.

The sentence in this article that caused a high degree of subsequent mickey-taking from colleagues and friends in the industry for some weeks afterwards, however, was when the journalist wrote "Knight, himself 49 ...". In other words, at least from the perspective of a young journalist, "you are almost a wrinkly yourself, mate". Fair comment. To be fair, I'm still a little way off a lifetime mortgage although most of us will get to that time of life eventually.

My whole concern about the lifetime sector is that you are lending to people at the brink of their vulnerability. You may conclude a deal with a sensible, well educated and erudite couple in their late 60s or early 70s where they fully understand exactly what the deal is. Then some problem occurs ten years down the line when, to put it a little more sensitively than I did at the CML Conference, they may not be quite so compos mentis.

As their dependants try to unravel the deal, claiming that their parents cannot remember the specifics, there is a high risk of reputational damage. Who is going to believe a big institution when there is a picture of a frail, elderly couple who are saying that they never really understood what they were getting into?

I know that applicants and their dependants are all supposed to sign documents witnessed by solicitors to state that they understood the terms and conditions of the mortgage. But there is nothing to stop people saying subsequently that they did not actually understand all this material. No lender wants to enforce a loan against a vulnerable borrower.

While that is an ever-present commercial risk of dealing with the public, it is a clear and present risk when lending to people on the cusp of vulnerability. This point, together with the fact that lifetime mortgages, with all their extra paper and "high touch", cannot fit our vision statement of "delivering mortgages for everyone through a fast, automated process", means that we will not be joining this sector for the foreseeable future.

Maybe I am wrong with this judgment. Maybe others will make handsome profits from this sector while the demand:supply ratio allows higher-than-mainstream margins to be achieved. But it is one product that I do not fancy at all reputationally.

■ Summary

This is a brief run through of a product range that delivered eleven times the rate of market growth. The biggest single factor other than the timing of particular product launches, and the constantly evolving product designs, was the availability of a full product range from mainstream through niche to non-conforming, i.e. "mortgages for everyone", all under one brand. It allowed intermediaries to develop habit-forming familiarity with us. Moreover, it got us noticed, because nobody else did it.

Presenting the products

Good products can still get lost in bad presentation. By constantly researching with our customers how they would like to receive our products, we have been able to stay refreshed in their minds. Initially we made individual products available as individual guides. This did not invalidate one set of material when a separate product was withdrawn.

But as we increased our range so our customers told us that they wanted all of the products at a glance. We therefore started to produce A4 guide booklets showing all the products along with sales angles and key criteria.

Our remote processors still favour the A4 booklets. But our intermediary direct customers created a different demand. They relied heavily on mortgage-sourcing systems, emails and websites. They need only a DL size guide which is essentially produced on A4 and folded into thirds. At this size it can fit into pockets or all types of hand-held folder. An example of such a guide appears alongside, and on the next two pages.

There is nothing particularly revolutionary in the design, although I hope we have always maintained the core discipline of such items in making them easy to use, visually attractive and unambiguous. The purpose of mentioning this item is to make the point that lenders should not put out information in the form that they think their intermediary customers would like.

You must research, and then update that research, in order to move with evolving tastes. If you can link all of your marketing material together in one campaign, as we did in the summer of 2005 with our cricket advertising visuals, then you will get even more bang for your marketing buck.

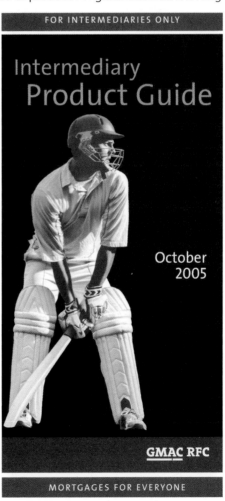

FOR INTERMEDIARIES ONLY

Intermediary
Product Guide

October
2005

GMAC RFC

MORTGAGES FOR EVERYONE

Product Summary

(£) **Mainstream Incentives** Remortgage: Free legals & no application fee (alternatively £300 Cashback available on 2 year discount) **Purchase:** £300 Cashback available on 2 year discount only.

(£) **Self-Cert Incentives** Remortgage: Free legals & no application fee or £350 Cashback **Purchase:** £350 Cashback

We will issue cashback via the solicitor on completion. Standard remortgage legal costs will be conducted at the expense of GMAC-RFC. Work over and above a standard remortgage will be charged to the borrower. For full details of what this service covers, please visit www.gmacrfc.co.uk/freelegals.

Mainstream

Criteria	2 Year Fixed (01 Jan '08)	2 Year Discount (01 Jan '08)
PAY RATE	4.75% to 90% 4.95% to 95%	4.95% to 90% (1.54% Discount) 5.20% to 95% (1.29% Discount)
ERC		3% to 01 Jan '08
ARRANGEMENT FEE		£545
INCOME MULTIPLES		Up to 4.5 + 1 or 3.75 x joint to 75% 4 + 1 or 3.3 x joint over 75%
FEATURES (25%)		Fast Track available
LOAN SIZE/LTV		£250,000 = 95% £350,000 = 90% £500,000 = 85% £750,000 = 75%
AGE		Min 18, Max 75 at end of term
LET TO BUY		Yes
FIRST TIME BUYERS		Yes
REVERSION RATE		SVR (6.49%)
INTRODUCER PAYMENT		0.35%

(25%) 25% redemption free overpayment allowed within any 12 month period

Buy to Let

Criteria	Full Term Tracker	2 Year Discount (01 Jan '08)	2 Year Fixed (01 Jan '08)	3 Year Fixed (01 Jan '09 Purchase only)	5 Year Fixed (01 Jan '11)
PAY RATE	5.24% to 75% (BBR + 0.74%) 5.49% to 85% (BBR + 0.99%)	5.24% to 75% (1.25% Discount) 5.49% to 85% (1.00% Discount)	5.09% to 75% 5.19% to 85%	5.19% to 89%	5.24% to 75% 5.44% to 85%
ERC	4%, 3%, 2% in first three years	3% in the discount rate period only	3% in the fixed rate period only		5%, 5%, 4%, 3%, 2% to 01 Jan 2011
ARRANGEMENT FEE	A) £545 B) £1295 C) £1495	£545	£545	£795	£545
INCOME MULTIPLES	A) 125% of BBR + 1.00% B) 110% of BBR + 1.00% C) 100% of BBR + 1.00%	A) 125% of BBR + 1.00% B) 110% of BBR + 1.00% C) 100% of BBR + 1.00%	125% of BBR + 1.00%		125% of BBR + 1.00%
FEATURES	No up-front paperwork and references required. Maximum 25 properties in total with a cumulative value not exceeding £3 Million				
LOAN SIZE/LTV	£300,000 = 85% £400,000 = 75% £500,000 = 65%				
AGE	Min 25, Max 75 at end of term				
LET TO BUY	No				
FIRST TIME BUYERS	No				
REVERSION RATE	n/a			SVR (6.49%)	
INTRODUCER PAYMENT	0.50%				

Self-Cert

Criteria	2 Year Discount (01 Jan '08)	2 Year Fixed (01 Jan '08)
PAY RATE	4.95% to 75% (1.54% Discount) 5.25% to 90% (1.24% Discount)	4.95% to 75% 5.25% to 90%
ERC	4% to 01 Jan '07 3% to 01 Jan '08	4% to 01 Jan '07 3% to 01 Jan '08
ARRANGEMENT FEE	£545	
INCOME MULTIPLES	Up to 4.5 + 1 or 3.75 x joint to 75% 4 + 1 or 3.3 x joint over 75%	
FEATURES (25%)	Self-Cert available for Employed and Self Employed. Right to Buy available up to 75%	
LOAN SIZE/LTV	£350,000 = 90% £350,000 = 85% £500,000 = 75%	
AGE	Min 21, Max 75 at end of term	
LET TO BUY	Yes	
FIRST TIME BUYERS	Yes (Max LTV 85%)	
REVERSION RATE	SVR (6.49%)	
INTRODUCER PAYMENT	0.50%	

Get an instant, binding decision at gmacrfc.co.uk

All the information shown is summary information only. For use by intermediaries and professional financial advisers only. It is not intended as an advertisement and must not be given to or distributed to members of the general public.

IPC October V1

The fold out inside pages of the new pocket-sized product guide

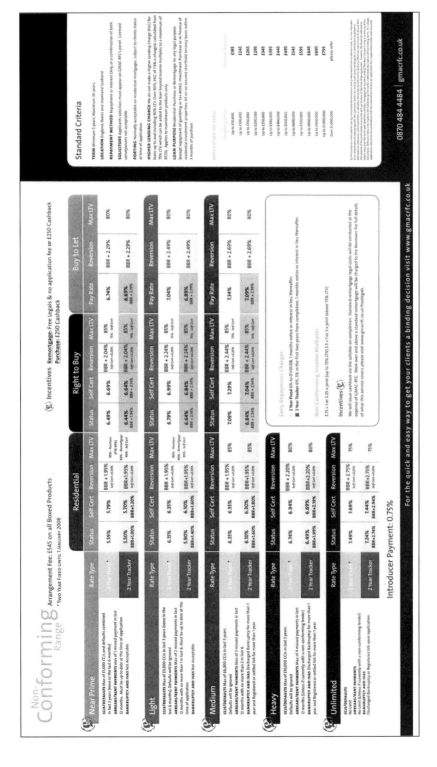

Mortgage-sourcing systems

As recently as 1995, I recall a survey which indicated that only a minority of intermediaries used mortgage-sourcing systems. How much has changed in this past decade! A recent similar survey showed that an overwhelming majority of intermediaries use these systems, and understandably so. Product choice has now grown to such an extent that it is difficult to put together a manual comparison of suitable products for consumer selection or consideration. Sourcing systems are well placed to provide that service.

Figure 2.3 shows the number of products available on Moneyfacts, a leading mortgage-sourcing company, on one day in 2005. It illustrates the competitive environment in the UK market:

Moneyfacts™

www.moneyfacts.co.uk

Moneyfacts' representation of the UK mortgage market on their online systems on 21 September 2005

- 5,485 Mortgage products
- 1,400 Buy-to-let products
- 31 Equity Release products

Other Factors

- Approx 1,296 Self Certification borrower type
- Approx 2,836 First Time Buyer borrower type
- Approx 2,787 Remortgage borrower type

Reproduced with the kind permission of Moneyfacts

Figure 2.3

The sourcing systems have not been slow to expand their range of output and technological sophistication, now permitting intermediaries to compare products by a large number of categories, such as two year fix, three year fix, trackers, discounts, penalty-free etc., while also overlaying initial rate, APR, total cost of payments over selected periods and many other criteria. The greater the usage potential, the more lenders need to dedicate resources to ensure that the input to the sourcing systems is as accurate as possible.

We have found over the years, particularly where the sourcing systems have manually input the data we have sent them, that there can be a normal degree of human error. We have also found that when, for example, we have changed the arrangement fee on all our fixed rates, and inputted only those changes to the sourcing systems, the arrangement fee on our variable rates has mysteriously changed as well. So important these days is the role of mortgage-sourcing companies that we dedicate full time resources in our marketing department to monitor their output every day, and to validate products on the system. This has become even more important to us as mortgage-sourcing systems have started to introduce Key Facts Illustrations, where they are required by statutory regulation to be accurate to as little as £1.

I know that most other lenders take a similar approach. Some do not and try to dissuade intermediaries from using the sourcing systems, instead, referring them to that particular lender's own website. But this just comes back in my view to trying to "contract" business rather than "attract" it. If your intermediary customers prefer using mortgage-sourcing systems then go with it, rather than try to dissuade them.

These days, we have close links with all the mortgage-sourcing systems and, as this book goes to press, are close to introducing a click-through link which would enable intermediaries, when in MBL and Trigold (two of the largest), to click through to our website in order to get a point of sale decision. They can then return to the mortgage-sourcing system without ever having to exit it.

This is a joint investment designed to make the life of intermediaries easier. Another example is the initiative we and several other non-conforming lenders took with Trigold, to try and assist with the more complex comparison of non-conforming products.

Over the five years in which we have been creating assets in such volume, our relationship with every mortgage-sourcing system has not been as rosy as it is today. Where the sourcing systems have also acted as mortgage distributors in their own right, we have found it unattractive when a competitor's product has popped up onto the screen of a user without prompt, and sometimes in circumstances where the product concerned is not the best in its sector.

Equally frustrating have been the occasions when our monitoring has uncovered a particular product of ours not appearing at all. Sometimes this would be human error, but on more occasions than we think is healthy, there was a disproportionate incidence of such error when our product was a best buy, undercutting a similar product that the sourcing system, in its distributor role, happened to be promoting.

I cannot prove a direct link, and never have had proof of anything underhand. Maybe therefore it was the case that these errors did occur disproportionately when there was a product clash, and the whole thing was an unfortunate coincidence. Post regulation, we are not aware of any similar problems so it looks like, coincidentally, the bug has been fixed.

I believe that, these days, all the sourcing systems offer a great service to intermediaries and, if I were the regulator, I would relieve them of the need to produce KFIs to an accuracy level of £1 in return for them guaranteeing the accuracy. It would then be quite easy for the sourcing systems and the lenders to come to an agreement that apportioned liability according to where an error occurred, with the result that the suppliers took the heat, and relieved some of the pressure on intermediaries.

There is little real damage that, say, a £10 difference in the monthly payment, or a £100 difference in the total cost of payments, can do to borrowers, so why not get proportionate in our regulation? Working with the mortgage-sourcing systems, co-operating where possible with new initiatives, and supplying data input and monitoring resource, has been an important component of our successful volume growth. I have observed with interest how the evolving comparison tables produced by the mortgage-sourcing systems have created their own supply and demand in terms of lenders designing products in such a way that, under a certain comparison, they are a best buy. If you dam the river at one point, water always escapes somewhere else. Business always flows in whatever direction it wants to take.

Electronic delivery

Postal mailings still have a role to play in the marketing mix, but are going to be much less important than electronic communication in future. We find that short, sharp messages sent by email are much more welcomed by time-starved intermediaries than a pack sent in the post. E-communication also means that we can deliver the latest product news to our intermediary customers real time, and by the second.

Our point of sale decisioning system has helped us target those emails, because it has shown us the peak times that intermediaries like to be online. If your customers are actually sitting at their PCs when an email arrives it is four times as likely to be read. We know this because, when the email sets up a link to our website, our marketing agency tells us that the hits we subsequently get are four times the industry average.

Emails allow us to interact with intermediaries, bring our brand to life, and visually illustrate product and sales points that would not come alive in the post. Cricket was our advertising theme in 2005, so - to further promote use of the website and e-delivery generally - we launched an online cricket game in conjunction with the publication "Mortgage Solutions". This had the added benefit of raising profile for us and for our cricketing adverts.

The game was accessible by visitors to either our website or the website of "Mortgage Solutions". Intermediaries played the game with the prize of winning a pair of tickets to one of the cricket test matches.

The prize was sought after. Mortgage Solutions promoted the game heavily, as did we. We got more intermediaries to our website and then created what is known as "viral marketing" (the "tell a friend" effect).

We do not know the extent that this game enhanced recognition of our cricketing advertisements and other similarly branded promotional material, but we are sure that it must have had a positive effect, because the coverage for our online game was the equivalent of a large advertising spend.

Lenders seeking a strategy for growth need to understand how best to communicate with their intermediary customers in a crowded market. It is important to get the balance right between website, email, text, phone, face-to-face, interactive and promotional mailings. Consistent messages and imagery are key, which is where technology plays a vital role. Some research we undertook in 2005 showed just how much intermediaries' use of technology had ballooned. Some 84% of brokers used five or more different online systems. This compares to just 26% in 2003 and 45% in 2004. The top 5 online systems identified in this research of over 1000 intermediaries were:

1.   Halifax

2.   GMAC-RFC

3.   BM Solutions

4.   Abbey

5.   Cheltenham & Gloucester

As a result of this shift, most lenders are expanding the capability of their websites. Desktop messengers to alert brokers to the launch or withdrawal of a product, broker profiling, online video channels (an intermediary would rather view someone explaining a product than read about it), updates, dial in conferencing and so much more.

We have either introduced, or are working hard to introduce, all of these items, and we were pleased to receive the coveted 'eee commerce' award from "Money Marketing", demonstrating that we were up there with the best for e-technology. It is where all lenders need to be.

Role of advertising

There is no doubt that, for a mortgage lender, the role of advertising has changed. It used to be that you could measure the success of a campaign by the number of enquiries a particular advertisement generated. But those days have long gone. Pick up any of the trade press magazines and the advertisements look like so much wallpaper. In the national press, regulation has as good as killed individual product advertising, with perhaps the occasional exception.

I have already mentioned the ugliness of three interest rates in a national press product ad. It is one reason why we advertise in the trade press only, even though the number of intermediary enquiries we generate would not, on the face of it, justify the expenditure.

What we are doing with our trade press advertising campaign is planting messages and images in the minds of the intermediary readers. As they flick through what is now more than 20 such publications a month, they will see our ads without necessarily registering them in their minds. When we then mail, email, telesale or call on those intermediaries, we find they are familiar with us and our products much more when we are advertising than when we are not.

They can then often find themselves more predisposed towards the sales and marketing message we subsequently give them because of this familiarity. This is not a formula that I can prove. What I can say, however, is that we have never had a period of increased sales that has failed to be accompanied by an increase in advertising expenditure over the same period. The more memorable you can make your advertisements, the better this process is likely to work.

Advertising not only gives the opportunity to promote subconscious familiarity. It also allows you to communicate an image. An advertising campaign that has

Number 18 in a series of 32

Over 3000 options from 4.68%

GMAC Residential Funding is your first choice for most of your non-conforming clients.

Not only does our non-conforming menu offer pricing for individuals with over 3000 product options covering the widest range of mortgage solutions for your clients; on top of that we're also offering a 1.25% discount to August 2003.

SOMETHING TO SMILE ABOUT

We like to give you something to smile about. What else would you expect from the UK's leading non-conforming lender?

For further information on our new products call 01344 477 477, or visit our web site

www.gmacrfc.co.uk

David Copland
Pink Home Loans

GMAC Residential Funding
A General Motors company

Mortgages for everyone

Number 18 in a series of 32

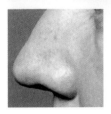

Buy To Let - Tracker
From 4.72% (**APR 4.9%**)

Mark Harris
Savills Private
Finance Ltd

For Mark Harris it's as plain as the nose on his face. GMAC Residential Funding's new Buy to Let Tracker mortgage offers some of the lowest tracker rates on the market. At LIBOR +0.69% (to 75% LTV) or LIBOR +0.89% (to 85% LTV) for the life of the loan, our new Buy to Let Tracker mortgage means easier budgeting for your clients.

Just as no two noses are ever quite the same, so it is with our new and improved range of products that cater to a variety of your clients' needs. Together with our 0.50% introducer fee, this gives you another good reason for choosing GMAC Residential Funding.

For further information on our new products call 01344 477 477, or take a nose around our website:

www.gmacrfc.co.uk

GMAC Residential Funding
A General Motors company

Mortgages for everyone.

humour will promote the image of a confident organisation. A visual that is strong and powerful is more likely to scream out from the page. If that is then the same image that you use on your product guides and other marketing material your retrieval rates will be higher.

A good lesson we have learned over the years is that the fewer the words the better. This is a shame. I like words. There are quite a few of them in this book. But they no longer work in an advertising context. We used to advertise products using a full page of text. We could really give a complicated product a good going over, squeezing out every last drop of sales potential. But such an approach no longer works when there are so many trade publications, and so many advertisements competing with so many other messages. You have a few seconds to reach the subconscious of the reader, and you will not do it with words alone.

Another so important factor is to refresh your campaign regularly. However much you are in love with one particular set of visual images, they soon produce diminishing returns. That is another shame because of all the design work that goes into a new campaign. But it is how it is, and those lenders who still trot out the same advertising style year after year are either wasting their time or they are in such a market-dominant position that it does not matter.

In this section I look at four of our campaigns, starting in 2002 with "Body Parts". The idea behind this campaign was to take a full face photo of a well known intermediary and then zoom in on a body part (don't worry, all family-friendly stuff here). This was sufficiently striking in its own right, but enhanced by the fact that an intermediary reader of such an advertisement might be attracted to why a peer was featuring in such a campaign.

A competitor copied this approach some years later, by featuring intermediaries and making them look like angels. Even we would not go that far!

Number 8 in a series of 32

KEEP ON TRACK WITH OUR BUY TO LET
Tracker rates from 4.76%

Ray Boulger
Charcol

With some of the lowest tracker rates on the market, Ray Boulger thinks GMAC Residential Funding's Buy to Let Tracker is a real eye-catcher! Unlike so many competitors who offer attractive tracker rates for a short period only, our new mortgage is linked to 3-month LIBOR for the life of the loan. Available for purchase or remortgage to 85% LTV, rates start from just **4.76%** (to 75% LTV) and can only be changed by the market, not by us.

Our Buy to Let Tracker means easier budgeting for your clients. Add in a generous allowance for rental assessment, favourable redemption terms - not to mention our 0.50% introducer fee - and this gives you yet another good reason for choosing GMAC Residential Funding for all your clients' mortgage needs.

For further information on our new products call 01344 477 477, or visit our web site

www.gmacrfc.co.uk

GMAC Residential Funding
A General Motors company

Mortgages for everyone

In the three examples I have chosen to illustrate this campaign, you will see that we featured the smiling mouth of David Copland (Pink Home Loans), the nose of Mark Harris (Savills) and the left eye of the mortgage market's "professor" Ray Boulger (John Charcol).

The first and last advertisements in that sequence promoted individual buy-to-let products. The middle ad featured our non-conforming menu. But I am sure you get the idea. We followed up on that campaign with unusual attention-grabbing visuals that would either amuse, or catch the eye, because they were not the standard, boring financial institutional approach. There was a very tall lady marrying a very small man to promote our two year mainstream fix which was "High on benefits, low on rates". A "cool" double bass player promoted our new buy-to-let product, and a lady golfer sinking a long putt promoted a 'winning' aspect of our buy-to-let range.

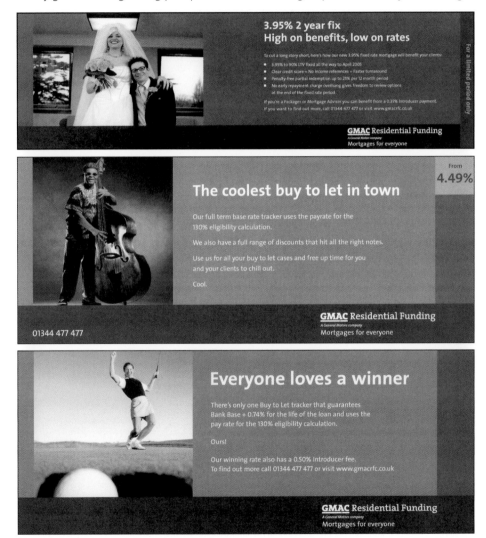

In 2004 we chose powerful black and white sporting photography using spot colour to highlight a "support" message. It was very important with this campaign to match the copy with the exact visual, which started to get a bit restrictive. But the controlled athlete, and the powerful boxer receiving inspired words from his trainer, are good examples of this particular campaign.

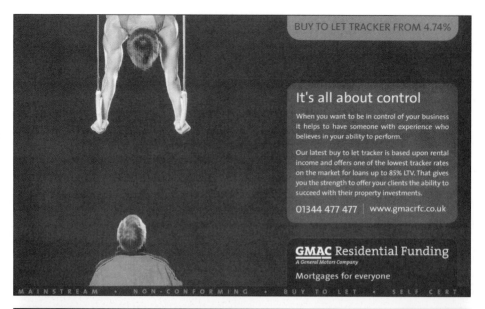

BUY TO LET TRACKER FROM 4.74%

It's all about control

When you want to be in control of your business it helps to have someone with experience who believes in your ability to perform.

Our latest buy to let tracker is based upon rental income and offers one of the lowest tracker rates on the market for loans up to 85% LTV. That gives you the strength to offer your clients the ability to succeed with their property investments.

01344 477 477 | www.gmacrfc.co.uk

GMAC Residential Funding
A General Motors Company

Mortgages for everyone

MAINSTREAM • NON-CONFORMING • BUY TO LET • SELF CERT

For authorised intermediaries only

NON-CONFORMING
2 YEAR FIX FROM 6.59%

Giving you the edge

A few inspiring words can make all the difference, especially when backed by years of experience.

Put your trust in a non-conforming champion. Our extensive range of mortgage rates deliver a fairer deal for your clients and help you punch your true weight.

0870 484 4484 | www.gmacrfc.co.uk

GMAC Residential Funding
A General Motors Company

Mortgages for everyone

MAINSTREAM • NON-CONFORMING • BUY TO LET • SELF CERT

My favourite is the one that we chose for the summer of 2005, to coincide with the England v Australia Ashes Test cricket series. Our marketing team believed that England had a real chance to make this an exciting Test Match series and not just the usual Australian walkover. In fact, England won, and the public and media euphoria that accompanied this victory made our cricketing images even more powerful. Controlled luck!

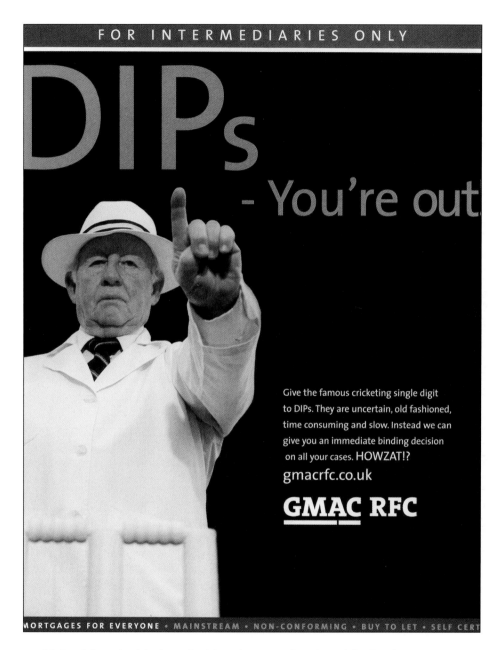

Maintaining the black and white photography, the cricketing images gave us more copy potential than any previous campaign. As the illustrations show, we were able to feature an umpire giving DIPs (Decisions in Principle) the famous cricketing single digit (where the umpire raises one finger to show that the batsman is out); a batsman "knocking the non-conforming competition out of sight"; a bowler promising online decisioning in a "seriously fast delivery" and "Howzat for a self cert mortgage?".

FOR INTERMEDIARIES ONLY

5.95% knocks the non-conforming competition out of sight

Our non-conforming range starts from 5.95% for purchases and remortgages. So go on-line and see how easy it is to get a binding decision today.

gmacrfc.co.uk

GMAC RFC

MORTGAGES FOR EVERYONE · MAINSTREAM · NON-CONFORMING · BUY TO LET · SELF CERT

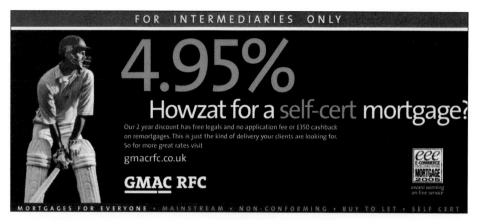

Interested observers will note how the copy has shortened as the campaign has evolved over the years. Advertising therefore continues to be an important component of the marketing mix. We would not contemplate sales growth without it.

Advertising Standards Authority

Here is a brief diversion. It is a story related to advertising which illustrates that things are not always as straightforward as they may seem.

Our product development team spotted a trade press advertisement on 7 October 2002 promoting a competitor's sub prime fixed rate as *"…the best two year fixed rate terms in the sector right now"*. We had similar products available at *lower* fixed rates over a *longer* term in two of the three categories being promoted. We did not think that Lender X's products could therefore be described as "best" in the sector.

Figure 2.4 puts the relevant terms of the two products alongside each other. There were slight differences in arrears levels, application fees etc., but nothing material. The main comparators were, as shown, namely rate, term and level of County Court Judgments accepted. I refer to the competitor as Lender X, since our strange experience was with the Advertising Standards Authority, to whom we complained, and their procedures, not with the lender:

Lender X´s fixed rates					
Full status	5.75%	To	October 04	With	£5000 CCJs
Self cert	5.99%	To	October 04	With	£7500 CCJs
Unlimited	6.29%	To	October 04	With	No max CCJs
GMAC-RCF´s fixed rates					
Full status	5.69%	To	January 05	With	£3000 CCJs
Self cert	5.89%	To	January 05	With	£3000 CCJs
Heavy adverse	6.49%	To	January 05	With	£7500 CCJs

Figure 2.4

Lender X would not change its advertisement and, as the ASA will not comment as to whether a particular advertisement contravenes the relevant code (they require a specific complaint), our product team made it official. With hindsight, we should have just let it go.

The ASA invited both sides to make representations, but neither side was allowed to see the other's input. So how would the ASA know whether one side was making it up?

Anyway, the ASA's Executive notified both parties that it would make a recommendation to its Council to the effect that Lender X should withdraw the advertisement. Our complaint had been *upheld*.

But Lender X contested this recommendation, so the ASA appointed what it described as an expert, to assist them with the complexities of the case. The next thing we heard was that the ASA, after receiving the expert's report, had overturned its original decision, and our complaint was *denied*.

The ASA does not reveal the identity of its experts until after its final recommendations have been decided. We made it clear to the ASA that we would have objected to the appointment of this particular expert had his identity been revealed beforehand. He was one of our suppliers. His company also supplied the group that owned Lender X, who were a bigger customer. We felt that he should not have been appointed because of this.

Some months later, the expert wrote to me saying that his company had now introduced corporate governance rules that would prevent him from acting as an expert witness in the future where clients were involved. Too late!

It was not just the conflict of interest that concerned us. I knew the expert personally. So far as I knew, he had not been actively involved in the UK mortgage market for many years. The UK non-conforming market had moved on from its early days. It no longer specialised in serious adverse credit. Most borrowers had light adverse credit backgrounds. In his report, the expert did indeed refer to the fact that Lender X accepted more adverse credit loans than we did, and we got the impression that this had been an important factor in the expert's deliberations.

Our principal complaint to the ASA was this (their response, under advice from the expert, is shown in italic).

1. The acceptance of marginally extra adverse credit by Lender X was irrelevant to most borrowers. CACI, the independent research company, had published statistics, based on a 50% sample of non-conforming completions during the research period, showing that 79.56% of these borrowers had CCJs to a value of £3000 or less. Therefore, four out of every five borrowers would have qualified for all of Lender X's product and all of GMAC-RFC's. The lower GMAC-RFC fixed rate over the longer term should have prevailed in any product comparison as to which was "best".

   ASA response: *The data was unrepresentative* (even though it was a 50% sample!).

2. Via its Committee of Advertising Practice General Media Panel, the ASA had earlier issued a Help Note confirming that the use of the word "best" in an advertisement should relate to every product being sold unless it is clearly stated that the claim relates to specific products only.

ASA response: *This does not apply to complex financial products* (even though there was no such caveat when the Help Note was issued).

3. As our fixed rates lasted three months longer than Lender X's, this extra period - when Lender X's borrowers would be paying their Standard Variable Rate, but our borrowers would be paying a lower fixed rate - should be factored in showing the GMAC-RFC products to be "best" by a long way in terms of total cost to pay during the period covered by the redemption charge.

ASA response: *Four weeks after the advertisement appeared, Lender X introduced a replacement set of products with a January 2005 end date. We have therefore assumed that they were the products advertised* (even though they were not).

The first two responses were incomprehensible enough. But to base a decision like this on products which the advertiser *did not* advertise, and which they only introduced four weeks later was, in my view, truly bizarre.

It is the ASA's policy to write to the editor of the publication that carried the original advertisement to highlight their decision. But I think that this backfired a little because the publication concerned could obviously not make head nor tail of what the ASA were saying, and published an article entitled: *"ASA sub prime confusion"*.

I suppose all this is largely academic today because the FSA is in charge of financial promotions. But if you are scratching your heads about how this decision was made, welcome to the head-scratching club.

The role of PR

Diversion over. Back to creating assets.

In one sense, the role of PR has not changed over the years. Journalists need good stories and good contacts they can trust. Lenders need to use PR to positively position their company in the marketplace, to provide thought leadership in their chosen sectors and maximise the newsworthiness of their products and services.

A press article is much more likely to be read in detail than an advertisement, so the PR machine can never stop, just as the journalists' quest for news never stops. To address this, a lender of significant size needs in-house PR specialists as well as a specialist external agency. Research-based surveys are a good way to get news coverage. It is an area of interest for the reader and can help inform the market. Awards are another big PR area. The PR team needs to be constantly relationship-building with journalists and editors to head off stories as well as placing stories. There is no other activity within marketing where you need to react so quickly. Accessibility to journalists, ability to comment and speed of response, are the key differentiators between those who get reported regularly and those who do not.

Press comment should not just be related to your company. The press team need to be ready and empowered to make balanced and thoughtful comment on all related areas including the economy, the housing market, regulation and so on.

An aspect of the role that has changed, however, and not for the good, is the extent to which lenders are now on the back foot responding to stories which a media environment that was less competitive would find too trivial to report. Ted Farnsbarns from Chorley (a fictitious name, of course) gets one application held up and that gets reported as "Broker slams lender's service".

We have had a bit of that and it is tiresome. You investigate the case and find that the broker has only sent you three applications in the last two years, all of which turned out to be massively complex.

Now the media do a great job when they expose malpractice or bad service. But what is often missing is the test of proportionality. Most of the busy, top professional mortgage brokers do not brief the trade press when one case goes wrong. They pick up the phone to the senior management of the lenders. So by definition, the brokers who feed these stories to the media are very often the small ones.

Even if the complaint is unjustified, the moment is lost for the accused, and a follow-up letter or article just draws attention to the previous piece. It is something that today's PR staff have to live with, but it is not particularly productive or enlightening. In the end, it is also itself-defeating since the emotive headlines do not have the same impact that they used to. Fortunately, the positives of a crowded, hungry trade press outweigh this one negative. The mortgage market is well served by a wide range of weekly, bi-weekly and monthly magazines, and your PR professionals, in-house and external, have as much to do to gain attention for your message as the advertisers must do to scream out off the page.

News reporting has changed in that, supplementing the printed magazines, are the publications' websites and e-news offerings. An ability within the PR team to write "bite-sized" news items for use with this media is becoming an important skill.

We receive regular reports from Lansons, our PR agency, showing who has mentioned us and how many times. We benchmark this against competitors and calculate an equivalent advertising spend, so that we can compare the effectiveness of PR against an equivalent advertising budget. PR is a sophisticated business these days. It is impossible to separate our PR investment from our volume growth success. We are briefing and speaking to the press every day, coming up with new angles for news, and responding to their enquiries. "Hiding" has never been an option.

Internal communications

In many large organisations, internal communications is a HR responsibility. I have never followed the logic in that. Your staff deserve to be addressed, sold to, and made to feel good, by your best communicators. This important job belongs to the marketing department. I do not believe that an organisation seeking growth can maximise its opportunities unless it has a clear internal communications strategy. What is important to the organisation must be what is important to the staff. If your people are to have enthusiasm and energy when dealing with customers, suppliers, regulators, the media, competitors and each other then they will need constant supplies of both from their employers.

We, for example:

■ Regularly circulate news stories and share press releases

■ Make a big fuss about awards and milestones

■ Inform all staff about our products, services and key sales messages prior to launch

■ Promote our advertising, PR and direct mail campaigns, explaining what we are doing and why

■ Keep staff up to date on industry news

■ Actively promote charity events and initiatives

■ Encourage quotes and feedbacks

Front cover of InformALL, our in-house staff communications magazine

In the Top 10

In June 2005, the Council of Mortgage Lenders (CML) confirmed that we were joint Top 10 lender for 2004, advancing £6.3 billion in mortgage loans – a staggering increase of 31% on the previous year, in a market that only grew by 5%.

In the last 5 years, we have enjoyed meteoric growth, overtaking 50 lenders, most of whom had a 200 year head start. In fact, to achieve the status of 10th largest lender, GMAC-RFC has outgrown the market rate of growth eleven fold. Let us all work together to ensure we stay in the top 10.

We asked some associates what it meant for them to be working for a Top 10 lender:

"Our success in such a short space of time is a true reflection of the nature of the company. Since joining I have been impressed by the company's innovative and market leading approaches, the energy and commitment of the associates and the desire to continually improve. All this gives us a great foundation for moving up the list!"

Danny Pittam,
Graduate Management Trainee

"It feels like we've left the pack and joined the front runners."

David Foster, L&D

"I am exceptionally excited about the opportunities the company continues to create from its growth."

Franki Mathews, Facilities

"I went into my building society last week, it was pretty good to see the GMAC-RFC logo displayed prominently in their 'mortgage marketplace' as a featured lender, ahead of their own product, and also ahead of my former employer, a high street lender for whom I worked for 100 years (or was it only 15 ?!)."

John Rawstron, Padiham

	Gross mortgage lending 2004		
Rank [2003]	Name of group	£bn	Estimated market share
1 [1]	HBOS	68.4	23.4%
2 [4]	Lloyds TSB	26.3	9.0%
3 [2]	Abbey National	24.9	8.6%
4 [3]	Nationwide BS	23.2	8.0%
5 [6]	Northern Rock	20.1	6.9%
6 [7]	The Royal Bank of Scotland	19.3	6.6%
7 [5]	Barclays	17.5	6.0%
8 [8]	HSBC Bank	13.5	4.6%
9 [9]	Alliance & Leicester	8.7	3.0%
10 [12]	**GMAC-RFC**	**6.3**	**2.2%**
10 [10]	Bradford & Bingley	6.3	2.2%

Other famous 10ths

10th most popular London musical – Chitty Chitty Bang Bang

10th favourite children's tv show of all time – He-Man & The Masters Of The Universe (1982)

10th most popular kids' character – Homer Simpson (The Simpsons)

10th largest football ground – Sheff Wednesday – 39,800 (person capacity)

10th tallest building in the world – Central Plaza, Hong Kong (78 stories, 1227 ft)

10th tallest tower in the world – Liberation Tower, Kuwait City, Kuwait, 1,221 ft

10th largest country (in area) – Sudan 966,000 mi² (2.4 million km²)

10th month of the year – October

10th most expensive city to live in– Oslo, Norway

10th least expensive city to live in – San José, Costa Rica

10th most popular film of all time in the UK – The Seventh Veil (1945) - Estimated Admissions 17.9m

10th best place to live in the UK – West Oxfordshire

Joint top 10th selling record of all time – I'm A Believer (The Monkees) and (Everything I Do) I Do It For You (Bryan Adams)

A page from InformALL dealing with the announcement by the CML that we had made their top 10 list

This list is not exhaustive. We have monthly departmental "cascade" meetings, using a common brief, but using an informal "roundtable discussion" style, a quarterly worldwide communication magazine and our own bi-monthly mag, called InformALL, featured here, where we have the right blend of light-hearted and serious content to ensure that it is read.

Our main priorities for 2005
Focus on: Embedding Treating Consumers Fairly (TCF) into business-as-usual

We spoke to Chris Sowinski, the TCF business champion, to find out more about it.

What does TCF mean for GMAC-RFC?

Firstly, we need a clear picture of our way of doing business before assessing the TCF implications. For example, we have renamed our TCF programme as "Treating Consumers Fairly" to avoid potential confusion, and recognise that we traditionally mean intermediaries when talking about "customers". In essence, TCF means making sure that consumers understand what they are buying and the risks that they are taking on.

But surely we treat consumers fairly already?

To a point, yes of course, and our corporate Vision and Values make this very clear. One of the challenges businesses will face is demonstrating fair treatment. This means that we have to be pro-active and continually look for areas of potential consumer detriment. If we identify problem areas, it is a senior management responsibility to put things right. In areas where we already have good TCF practices, we should keep records of success and review periodically.

> "If we identify problem areas, it is a senior management responsibility to put things right. In areas where we already have good TCF practices, we should keep records of success and review periodically."

So, are there any rules or guidance from the FSA that we can follow?

No, although there is an increasing amount of material available both from the FSA and other industry sources. Unlike mortgage regulation, the FSA has decided not to issue TCF rules and guidance. The important thing for us is to understand the principles of TCF and then apply them in the context of our business. This means that subject to adhering to the principles, we can make and own any TCF changes ourselves.

What are our competitors and brokers doing about TCF?

One intermediary lender has issued a TCF brochure to its intermediaries, and others like us, are building their TCF plans, having related them to the context of their particular business and way of operating. Brokers have been fairly quiet up to now, but are increasingly realising that TCF, is an important element in their success. We aim to help inform brokers of our approach to TCF. It is important for us to recognise TCF as an opportunity instead of an obstacle.

Where can associates find out more about our TCF work?

Our ongoing TCF communication plans are at an early stage, but in due course we plan to have a page on the UK intranet. In the meantime, there are various sources of information (see right). I am also happy to come to team meetings to run awareness sessions.

> Brokers have been fairly quiet up to now, but are increasingly realising that TCF, is an important element in their success. We aim to help inform brokers of our approach to TCF. It is important for us to recognise TCF as an opportunity instead of an obstacle.

Progress so far...
>> **TCF Board Committee established**
>> **Identified TCF changes to Arrears Policy**
>> **TCF Gap Analysis complete**

Coming up...
>> **Senior Manager training**
>> **TCF Board Policy**
>> **Cascades to all associates**
>> **Departmental action planning**

More information:
>> TCF Committee Members:
Chris Sowinski, Liz Barley, David Botting, Alan Dawson, Tony Fisher, Paul Fulford, Sam Hussain, Marc Plato, Tony Rogers, Carol Taylor and John Wright.

>> FSA website: **www.fsa.gov.uk**

>> Chris Sowinski: **01344 783005**

A page from InformALL promoting TCF

I cannot overestimate the importance of "selling" internally, using the best techniques employed to sell externally. To build a successful brand, you have to do it from the inside out. This is too often missed by other lenders. But never by those who enjoy substantial and sustained growth.

Fun!

My first job was working in an orange juice factory, but I got canned because I couldn't concentrate.

Then I worked in the woods as a lumberjack, but I just could not hack it, so they gave me the axe. After that I tried working in Kwik Fit but found I was getting tired all the time, it was really exhausting.

My best job was being a musician, but eventually I found I wasn't noteworthy. I studied a long time to become a doctor, but I didn't have any patience. My next was a job in a shoe factory; I tried but I just didn't fit in and got the boot.

I became a professional fisherman, but discovered that I couldn't live on my net income. I managed to get a good job working for a pool maintenance company, but the work was just too draining. So then I got a job in a workout center, but they said I wasn't fit for the job.

After many years of trying to find steady work, I finally got a job as a historian until I realised there was no future in it. Then I worked at Starbucks, but I had to quit because it was always the same old grind.

I found that I couldn't focus when I worked in the opticians. Finally I started working as a florist where I have really blossomed.

Have you found your perfect job?

Handy tips

If you've had too much sun and ended up with sunburn, soothe the sting by rubbing some full strength white vinegar into it. You could also add a cup of baking soda to a warm bath and soak for a while.

Those same two items will help relieve the itch of an insect bite. Cover the area with a paste of baking soda and water, or dab some white vinegar on the bite.

Tennis balls lost their bounce? Put them in a hot dryer for fifteen minutes, the heat will rejuvenate them.

If you like to practice your putting, but hate the bucket of balls, store those golf balls in an egg carton, it is the perfect size and will fit neatly on a shelf out of the way.

If you burn your tongue on something hot to eat (hot coffee or soup) put a teaspoon of sugar on your tongue and hold your tongue against the roof of your mouth and let the sugar melt. This will keep your tongue from getting sore from the burn.

Place candles in the freezer for at least 3 hours prior to burning and they will burn much longer.

Shady Tips

>> A mousetrap, placed on top of your alarm clock will prevent you from going back to sleep.

>> Clumsy? Avoid cutting yourself while slicing vegetables by getting someone else to hold them while you chop away.

>> Keep the seat next to you on the train vacant by smiling and nodding at people as they walk up the aisle.

>> Don't waste money buying expensive binoculars. Simply stand closer to what you want to look at.

>> Thicken up runny low-fat yoghurt by stirring in a spoonful of lard.

>> A next door neighbour's car aerial, carefully folded, makes an ideal coat hanger in an emergency.

>> Before attempting to remove stubborn stains from a garment, always circle the stain in permanent pen so that when you remove the garment from the washing machine you can easily locate the area.

The mind boggles

1. What starts on four legs, then on two, then on three?

2. So you can spell coke, joke, poke but how do you spell the white of an egg?

3. Using the mathematical signs plus, minus, divide and multiply and as many brackets as you need to make the question mark equal to 9. 3 3 3 3 3 = ?

4. The number of minutes that have elapsed since it was 11.16am is half of the number of minutes before it will be 12.19pm. What is the time now?

5. Everybody has me but nobody eats me. Everyday I get bigger but not fatter. Those with plenty want me less and those with few want me more. I'm seen but never heard. Who am I?

(Answers below)

Answers

1. A human! A baby crawls, a kid walks, and when you get old, you have a cane!
2. 'Albumen' - which is the white of an egg. Did you think it was 'yolk'?
3. 3 / -(3 - 3) + (3 x 3) = 9
4. 11.37am
5. Hair

Why oh Why

Why is it that people say they 'slept like a baby' when babies wake up about every couple of hours?

Why does a round pizza come in a square box?

Why do people pay to go up tall buildings and then put money in binoculars to look at things on the ground?

If money doesn't grow on trees then why do banks have branches?

Why do toasters have a setting so high that could burn the toast to a horrible crisp?

Why do fools fall in love?

A page from InformALL that's just pure fun!

Wrap up

Where we ended up was quite different to where we started. From a one product/one distribution channel starting point we launched "mortgages for everyone" across three main distribution channels plus some investments and, more recently, initiatives with other lenders.

We built on a previous core competency in product design by making our research and competitor analysis even more sophisticated. We never stopped advertising and promoting to the market at large, while making specific initiatives more targeted than ever.

We expanded our sales and marketing teams with even more talented individuals, as we tried to make GMAC-RFC the "lender to watch". We made everyone realise that, while one department is not more important than another in a hierarchical sense, sales and marketing are the most important functions in the chronological sense. If insufficient business is coming through the door, then there are no assets to complete; manage post completion; trade away; risk manage; add up; comply and all the other great departments that are needed to make the whole thing tick.

We understood, and continue to understand, that chronology. It all grinds to a halt if you do not get business through the door. We were lucky enough to have created billions of pounds of it. We made top 10 lender status. But could we trade these assets?

GMAC-RFC becomes UK's 10th largest lender

GMAC-RFC has bucked the trend of slow lending levels and managed to achieve top 10 status.

According to the Council of Mortgage Lenders, GMAC-RFC was ranked as the 60th largest lender in the summer of 2000. It is now ranked as the 10th largest.

The company provides mortgages for everyone from mainstream through niche to non-conforming firms.

Last year, it advanced £6.3bn in mortgage loans, an increase of 31 per cent on the previous year in a market that only grew by 5 per cent.

To achieve the status of 10th largest lender, GMAC-RFC has outgrown the market rate of growth 11-fold.

Stephen Knight, executive chairman of GMAC-RFC, said: "We are no longer an organisation that is directly comparable to the specialist, niche lenders with whom we compete in certain markets."

Mr Knight added: "Our growth has been achieved by offering mortgages for everyone in all sectors of the market under one brand, with the competitiveness, breadth and innovation in the product range matched by market-leading service initiatives, such as our instant, online binding decision, while most other lenders offer decisions in principle.

"We are on track to record double digit growth in a market that is likely to contract by 20 per cent."

Financial Adviser. 11 August 2005

1 2 **3** 4 5 6 7 8

TRADING THE ASSETS

The contrast between the "creating" and "trading" sides of our business could not have been starker. With the former, we knew that the market was there: it was just a question of whether we could increase our share in the way that we needed to. On the trading side of the business, large parts of the market we needed were missing. We had to create them from scratch.

So far as the mainstream (A) and self certification/buy-to-let (A-) products were concerned, we realised that the rates we would have to offer to gain share would not make securitisation a profitable exit route, at least not initially. So, in relation to this class of asset, we would definitely have to create something brand new: a liquid portfolio sales market.

Of course, the securitisation market was not new. But, having initially emerged from the centralised lending model of the 1980s, it had largely disappeared in the downturn of the 1990s and it was very immature for non-conforming UK RMBS. There was therefore plenty of development and educational work needed for that exit route to also be regarded as truly liquid.

Markets evolve. A few years later we were able to profitably securitise A and A-assets. We also sold a non-conforming tranche by way of a portfolio sale. But, back in 2000, it was all very raw.

There was no doubt that this was an enormous gamble. We were cranking up the creation side of our business beyond all previous recognition. If we had not been able to similarly expand our trading capability then we would have exceeded our balance sheet limits and, almost certainly, have had to exit the assets created at a loss. Our plans, which were at that stage concepts, simply had to work, and we did not have time on our side either. By the end of 2000, the new initiatives we had taken on the product creation side were building loans at a fast pace.

Creating the demand for portfolio sales

Now, to be fair we did not invent the idea of lenders selling portfolios and whole loans to each other. That had been going on for years. But there was no liquidity in this market and no regular players.

There were one-off trades that, in almost all instances, reflected the selling lenders' exit from the market, either by withdrawal or merger. Our goal was to create a market where purchasing portfolios was built into the business plans of enough lending institutions to make a market, with GMAC-RFC identified as the company that always had assets to sell.

In our strategic review, we had developed a calculation of the amount by which certain lenders were "under-lent" (see Chapter 1). That gave us a broad basis for identifying the total potential demand for portfolio sales, if only we could crystallise that demand in the minds of the lenders involved.

We therefore came up with six reasons why they should buy portfolios from us. It was the classic sales technique of creating the demand, before then selling into it. We sought to persuade a largely reluctant market (there were some exceptions) of the following points:

1. **Speed.** Sometimes, a lender needs to build assets quickly. Perhaps to reach a target, or to make the year end figures look better. But there is no guarantee that launching a new product range will deliver this. It takes time for loans to build: moreover, you have to factor in reaction from competitors. But when a portfolio is purchased, all of those problems are solved. The purchasing lender selects the required volume of assets and they are all there in the form of paying loans, ready to go. If you are under-lent today, you can be fully lent tomorrow

2. **Positive margin.** Market competitiveness meant that new business was being written at cheaper and cheaper rates. Some marginal products were either unprofitable, or breakeven at best. Buying a portfolio from us, however, always secured a positive margin over cost of funds. That's because we always offer portfolios of blended A and A- assets, delivering a positive weighted average margin to the cost of funds

3. **Distribution.** Securing sufficient distribution was a problem for a number of lenders. The largest distributors were seeking to leverage their size by appointing smaller lender panels. Generally, all lenders were increasingly having to go toe-to-toe with the industry's most aggressive marketers. Buying a portfolio from us, however, gave lenders the chance to tap into our distribution arrangements and sales approach. Regular purchases would turn us into a very effective new distribution arm for the purchasing lender

4. **Replacing redeeming borrowers.** The front book/back book price differentiation was increasing year-by-year the number of mortgages being lost by each lender through redemption. Buying portfolios from us was a way of replacing that attrition at a stroke

5. **Diversified risk profile.** Most lenders have established risk profiles for their loan books, which they would diversify by buying a portfolio from us. This also brought the benefit of being able to "road test" a particular product line in a reasonably anonymous way, perhaps to inform an internal debate as to whether that product should be launched by the purchasing lender in its own right at a later date

6. **Profitable.** The volumes that we were generating, and the cost efficiency of our model, allowed us to accept a premium on the portfolios that made it profitable for both seller and buyer

The fact that we had dealt with and paid the intermediaries, and offered representations and warranties that would not be available from packagers or intermediaries, were all additional positive factors. If you are going to create a market that did not previously exist, you are going to have to convince people that they need something they did not need before, or did not know they needed. One thing we realised from day one was that we would have to insist on no "cherry-picking". If buyers were allowed to deselect whole classes of assets from the portfolios they were prepared to purchase then this could have left us with a distinctly lop-sided balance sheet.

At the margin, lenders did deselect certain loans following due diligence, and it is always relatively easy to accommodate that because one man's meat is another man's poison. It was the wholesale deselection of classes of asset, for example, insisting on no mainstream loans or no buy-to-let, that we had to, and did, resist.

Getting started

The first person to head our asset sales programme - Julia Morris - reported directly to me. Julia was an experienced executive at GMAC-RFC, having worked in the two predecessor companies that had been part of our purchase and initial launch into the UK. Despite having to travel to some parts of the country to which she would prefer not to return, Julia did an excellent job in laying the groundwork for our future success.

Julia's career ambitions lay outside of asset sales so, once we had established the foundation, Julia transferred to our Continental European business and we recruited Steve Khan, who had worked for me some years previously at Private Label, and who had since gone off to do a marketing job at Platform Home Loans. Steve also did a great job in building our asset sales proposition before he was headhunted to do a similar job at Lehman Brothers.

Fortunately, Craig Beresford was by then on the team and Craig has built the asset-selling side of our business up to another level where, without doubt, we are recognised as number one in this particular specialist business. However, it took a while to get there. While the securitisation team was visiting major cities in Europe and the US, the portfolio sales team were enjoying visits to Scarborough, Barrow in Furness, and all places north.

On one occasion, having made their way to Newcastle, they were told that the person they had booked in to see had forgotten about the meeting. A new meeting was fixed up for the following day, so the ever resourceful team drove to Scarborough speculatively to see someone else on the spur of the moment and actually did a deal. Good job because, when they returned to Newcastle the following day, they could not agree a price and would otherwise have returned home empty-handed.

In the early days, we tried to sell a £50m portfolio of loans to the significant Staffordshire Building Society, only to find at the end of our pitch that we were talking to the tiny Staffordshire *Railway* Building Society who only wanted 50 loans. We asked a heavily-limping treasurer of one of our buyers if he was a golfer, and got the reply "not since I lost my leg". In a no-star hotel in Yorkshire one of our team was propositioned by a female OAP at the start of the evening, only for the feisty lady to re-appear in the lift at the end of the evening (our man graciously declined her offer of a nightcap in her room). No successful business is built without good "road stories", and these are some of the printable ones.

When we present portfolios for sale we produce what we call a stratification document. You cannot sell "thin air". Buyers want to hold something in their hands, something real, something that we actually have ready for sale. Figure 3.1 is an extract from the sort of stratification that we started to supply to potential purchasers as the initial negotiating point of a portfolio sale. We have assumed that the buyer in this illustration has expressed interest in a portfolio of loans valued at around the £350m mark in total.

We are showing a typical mixture of fixed and variable product taken from our mainstream, self certification and buy-to-let product ranges. This is broadly the sort of blended product mix we like to achieve, and our portfolio sales team spend a considerable amount of time slicing and dicing the book to come up with the most attractive portfolio we can make available to the buyer within our blending rules.

A typical GMAC-RFC Mortgage portfolio will be established and created to comprise a blend of our current balance sheet across all of our lending platforms and might look like figure 3.1.

It is of course for the buyer to project its own profitability based on its current cost of funds. We undertake our own modelling based on the margin over prevailing swap costs for the fixed rate portion of the portfolio, and the margin over Bank Base for the variable rate portion of the portfolio. As we can never know a buyer's blended cost of funds, it is generally accepted practice to relate the variable element to prevailing Bank Base.

EXAMPLE OF AN ILLUSTRATIVE £350m BLENDED DEAL

Bank base rate is 4.50%
Overall portfolio Weighted Average (WA) margin over bank base is therefore 1.04%
Swap rates are 4.50%
Fixed rate margin over swaps is therefore 1.12%

Rate Type	Number	Total Balance	no. as %	Value as %	WA Int Rate
Discount	837	£127,234,385.91	34.04%	35.97%	**5.42**
Fixed	1254	£175,444,659.13	51.00%	49.60%	**5.62**
Tracker	368	£51,050,060.84	14.97%	14.43%	**5.58**
	2459	**£353,729,105.88**	**100.00%**	**100.00%**	**5.54**

Product Type	Number	Total Balance	no. as %	Value as %	WA Int Rate
Mainstream	457	£69,005,522.40	18.58%	19.51%	**5.15**
Self Certification	1492	£227,454,685.51	60.68%	64.30%	**5.62**
Buy-to-let	510	£57,268,897.97	20.74%	16.19%	**5.68**
	2459	**£353,729,105.88**	**100.00%**	**100.00%**	**5.54**

Figure 3.1

The sales start building

In 2000 progress was initially slow. Our first trade was a £39m portfolio of "STAR" product loans that Private Label had originated for GMAC-RFC as part of a pilot exercise that I cover in more detail in chapter 6. We followed this up with an even smaller £14m trade in November of that year.

The assets we were creating really only started to build ready for sale in 2001. It was not until we exited them that we were able to say with any confidence that an active portfolio sales market had been created.

In that year, we really hit the road and started to develop strong demand. The four portfolio sales we achieved in 2001, with a total value of £330m, did not reflect the groundwork we had laid for future years. That would be retrieved later, as we started to receive advance orders, allowing us to originate assets with an end investor in mind.

In 2002 asset sales rocketed to £1.5bn, featuring five new buyers, most of whom had been attracted by our prior year sales activity. The trades were spread throughout the year and included one massive deal - £649m to Mortgage Express - which paved the way for a longer term arrangement with that buyer.

In May 2002 we had also introduced Britannia Building Society. Britannia and Bradford & Bingley plc (through their subsidiaries Britannia Treasury Services and Mortgage Express respectively), apart from being old connections of our group via Private Label, were also a departure from the small to medium sized lender to whom we had traditionally sold up until then.

We needed this contrast because the assets were building so quickly on the creation side of the equation that we needed bigger outlets. We certainly exploited these in 2003 with a total of £1,263m going to Bradford & Bingley, and £304m going to Britannia, out of total sales amounting to £2.3 billion in that year.

By 2004 we were selling a portfolio every four weeks, reaching a full year figure of £2.6bn. Figure 3.2 shows the build up of portfolio sales year-by-year.

PORTFOLIO SALES YEAR-BY-YEAR

Year	No. of loans sold	Volume sold £m	% increase on prior year
2000	469	£ 43.2	N/a
2001	3116	£ 329.2	662.1%
2002	13333	£1481.5	350.0%
2003	19310	£2311.6	56.0%
2004	20622	£2602.9	12.6%
2005 to Q3	19719	£2660.5	2.2%
Totals	**76569**	**£9428.9**	

Figure 3.2

The appetite curve

All this demand did not just come our way. We had to go out and get it. In many instances we had to create and anticipate it. The risks we were prepared to take, in terms of launching products ahead of "the appetite curve", under-scored our success. We describe "the appetite curve" as the speed with which our portfolio buyers will accept new things. If we believe that, after so many months, sufficient buyers will be prepared to buy loans with characteristics that they will not accept today, that is "the appetite curve".

If we launch a new idea today, our risk is that we are wrong in the timing. Our reward lies in being able to continually launch market-leading products. Figure 3.3 shows "the appetite curve" for three different illustrative developments:

1. Dropping the rates on new lending such that the weighted average margin on the portfolio we will be offering for sale is less than the agreed norm for the premium required

2. Introducing new buy-to-let criteria allowing 110% and 100% rental cover options

3. Launching a capped rate product

THE APPETITE CURVE

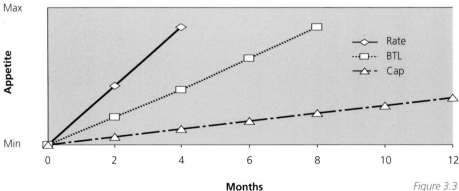

Figure 3.3

What figure 3.3 illustrates is that, in time of fierce competition, our purchasing lenders know that we have to reduce rates to win business. They would rather have cheaper assets than reduced assets. They can get quickly up "the appetite curve" in terms of paying the same premium for lower-yielding assets, knowing that we will correct that as soon as we can.

The buy-to-let change is more radical. Buyers need to be persuaded that this is good lending. Enough of them need to change their lending rules to accommodate the new criteria. This takes a bit more time.

The risk is always there that an insufficient number will change. But, in my illustration, enough lenders get to maximum appetite, albeit a little slower than a more straightforward concept such as the interest rate play.

In contrast, a capped rate mortgage is very tricky. It is no good GMAC-RFC buying a cap and trying to pass that on to the purchasing lender, because the hedge counterparty may not accept the new lender on the same terms, or at all.

If the purchasing lender has to purchase the cap then it may run up against its own balance sheet constraints regarding the use of such derivatives and/or may not be able to get acceptable terms, meaning that the capped rate products would have to be removed from the portfolio being purchased.

Our estimate is that an insufficient number of purchasing lenders would get to maximum appetite within a reasonable timeframe, if at all, on a capped rate product. We therefore never launch such products.

The first two examples are actions we actually have taken over this past year. We discussed them of course with our purchasers. But it is unrealistic to expect your business partners to accurately predict what they will buy until they can see the completed loans, the LTVs and how much of the portfolio they represent .

The risk is ours, but it is a calculated risk. We balance the speed with which the assets will build with the estimated speed at which we think we could get a sufficient number of purchasing lenders up to maximum appetite. If we get it wrong we are stuck with the assets.

But taking risks like this is the only way to stay ahead on the creation side. If we based our products and criteria only on what our asset buyers say they will take today, we would lose our speed-to-market and reputation as an innovator. This would, in turn, reduce our effectiveness as a volume portfolio trader. We have to back our ability to influence change and present acceptable blended risk to our buyers in accordance to how we see the market developing - not where it is today.

We have in total, since we set about creating this market, completed 55 trades with a total value of £9.42 billion selling a total of 77,000 loans, as summarised in figure 3.4.

The vast majority of the trades shown in figure 3.4 are from repeat buyers. This is important for us. We are no different to any other business in this respect. Repeat customers are always the most cost efficient for a business and the best endorsement to have.

It means that they are happy with the quality of the assets we have previously originated for them and have found their portfolio-buying programme to be viable and profitable.

HISTORICAL PORTFOLIO SALES DEAL CALENDAR

Month		No. of Trades	No. of Loans	Value in £m
Jul	00	1	227	29.0
Nov	00	1	242	14.2
Feb	01	1	438	49.5
May	01	1	991	95.7
Nov	01	2	1687	184.0
Feb	02	2	1382	147.6
Mar	02	2	1773	191.5
May	02	1	1363	152.8
Jun	02	1	481	54.5
Sep	02	1	5969	649.5
Oct	02	1	496	59.8
Nov	02	2	1869	225.8
Jan	03	1	628	74.3
Mar	03	1	3884	467.1
May	03	1	2170	255.9
Jun	03	1	1195	156.6
Jul	03	1	1225	150.7
Sep	03	2	2218	248.3
Oct	03	2	2279	245.8
Nov	03	3	5711	712.9
Feb	04	2	4693	546.5
Mar	04	1	1977	273.2
Apr	04	1	1084	140.3
May	04	1	940	113.1
Jun	04	2	2727	339.2
Jul	04	1	989	120.1
Aug	04	1	934	122.2
Sep	04	1	2201	300.8
Oct	04	1	534	69.9
Nov	04	2	3741	481.6
Dec	04	1	802	96.0
Feb	05	2	2652	347.8
Mar	05	1	996	124.9
Apr	05	2	2855	393.9
May	05	2	2619	351.9
Jul	05	1	826	104.9
Aug	05	3	4225	571.7
Sep	05	2	5546	765.4
		55	**76569**	**9428.9**

Figure 3.4

Third party servicing

It turned out that most lenders did not have the systems capability to accept a steady stream of incoming mortgage portfolios. Even some lenders that owned third party servicing companies did not have this capability. There is no doubt, therefore, that the availability of independent third party servicers, notably HML, has been pivotal to the development of this sector.

By the time we came to transfer our own post-completion servicing to HML, eight out of every ten of our portfolio buyers had set up servicing arrangements with them. When our own post-completion administration transferred to HML, the transfer of data became even slicker.

At the touch of a button, in the course of a working day, hundreds of millions of pounds worth of mortgage loans were transferred from one HML client to another without any significant administration issues. The purchaser not only enjoyed a seamless transfer, but also had separate reporting and administration for these assets.

Borrowers received their "goodbye" and "hello" letters from seller and purchaser in a well-timed communication process, with no disruption to the administration of their mortgage accounts, and rarely raising a query.

Getting the contract terms right

As we initially entered this market, we assured our potential portfolio buyers of one of our core values, namely "succeeding with integrity". We would buy back or appropriately compensate lenders in respect of loans which turned out not to meet pre-agreed expectations.

We have rarely been asked to take action under this clause, which is testimony to our quality assurance staff as well as to the due diligence role undertaken by the purchasers. But when we have been asked to take appropriate steps, we have always done so gladly. It is thus that we have been able to establish a reputation among portfolio buyers for being an organisation that means what it says in terms of being committed to long term partnerships.

Our sale and purchase contract has now matured into a largely re-usable document. Both we and our regular purchasers are able to minimise the amount of legal work on future trades by using a contract with which all sides have become familiar. We believe that the balance of warranties and representations contained within that contract are fair to both sides, and that it actually provides the purchaser with a higher measure of protection than would be the case had they created the loans themselves.

The contract provides for the purchaser to honour the mortgage terms we have agreed with the borrower. This is one of the reasons why portfolio sales activity is good for the customer. It is by definition in this overcrowded, over-supplied, highly competitive mortgage market of ours that we would have only been able to generate the business in the first place by offering competitive customer terms. These are then binding on the purchaser. This is one reason why portfolio sales activity in the

UK has grown to such a significant proportion without controversy, because core terms have been honoured.

Some parts of the contract do require specific performance pledges, such as when the loan moves onto the lender's standard variable rate. The customer allows that to be discretionary on us when the loan first completes, so that discretion passes to the purchasing lender. But it would be a reputational risk for us if the purchasing lender set an uncompetitive standard variable rate.

We therefore insist on a cap, relating to the highest margin that a discretionary variable rate could be set against a public benchmark such as Bank Base or three month LIBOR. This occurs in all instances where the purchasing lender is not a well known institution with its own established, standard variable rate. If that clause is unacceptable to a particular purchaser then we have been known to pull out of portfolio sale transactions, such is our determination to maintain our reputation and protect the borrowers.

Continuing arrears reporting is also a necessary contract term. It has been important to us to receive regular statistics on loans we have sold. We established this requirement long before Treating Customers Fairly, the latest UK regulatory strategy and philosophy, became talked about as if it was a new concept to lenders.

While the contract is the most important document within the entire portfolio sale transaction it is only one part of an activity that can take a full three months from start to finish. Some readers of this chapter may be experienced traders in mortgage portfolios. But for those who are contemplating this activity, figure 3.5 illustrates the typical stages, and actions required, in a new trade:

Two to three months before deal completion
- Buyer identified (this can reactive or proactive)
- Key pool parameters agreed with buyer - size and timing of deal and due diligence
- Example pool delivered for pricing
- Initial pricing agreed

6 weeks before completion
- Contract issued to buyer

4 weeks before completion
- Sale pool built and delivered to buyer
- Final pricing agreed on sale pool
- Due diligence carried out on sale pool

3 weeks before completion
- Any due diligence removals done

1-2 weeks before completion
- Contract agreed
- Contract signed and exchanged
- Press release agreed
- Exit letters approved and agreed

Day before completion
- Pre-completion statement issued day before completion for calculation of payment on completion date
- Pre-completion statement agreed with buyer

Completion day
- Completion statement issued
- Completion statement agreed with buyer
- Funds transferred
- Legal completion of contract
- Exit letters sent out to borrowers and solicitors
- Press release sent out

1 week post completion
- Reconciliation completed within 5 days of completion
- Beers all round!

Figure 3.5

Success diversifies previously simple markets

The above statement is true in most markets, most of the time. What started out for us as the sale of a couple of hundred loans to a single buyer, has now spawned sub markets, new competitors, new types of buyer and some pretty esoteric structures.

Into the first category fits Amber Home Loans, a subsidiary of Skipton Building Society, which has quite openly adopted our mantle of "creator and trader". Amber regularly buys portfolios from us (and sells loans to us as well - see chapter 2). What Amber does with some of the assets it buys from us is to mix them with loans it buys from other lenders to meet demand from smaller lenders for lower value portfolios.

It was always inevitable as our business grew that we would start to introduce minimum thresholds below which it was not viable for us to sell portfolios, given the actual and opportunity costs. The relationships which we have built up with large, buying institutions means that selling in very small blocks of up to, say, £75m is no longer cost effective.

That is the case with many portfolio sellers, with the result that the premium that can be achieved on the sale of smaller portfolios is greater than on larger trades, to reflect the demand/supply position. If you have the time, the patience and the administration to break down the portfolios you have into smaller units, you are not only meeting a sound demand, but also making a proportionately larger profit. Good luck to Amber for seeing this opportunity!

An interesting reflection on how the market, and sub market, have developed was contained in a structured finance commentary issued by Standard & Poor's (S&P), the rating agency, on 6 June 2005. Commenting on the evolution of the portfolio sale market in the UK, S&P listed by way of illustration 45 whole loan trades that had taken place between 2000 and the date of the report.

S&P acknowledged that these were "sample transactions" because there was no publicly held information available as to the size of the portfolio sale market. However, we were identified as the seller in 27 of these 45 trades (60% of them) demonstrating our market dominance.

But what caught my eye was the fact that Amber was identified as the seller in nine further trades (20%). My understanding is that at least half of the assets sold by Amber in the nine trades specifically mentioned in that list had been created by us and sold to Amber in the first place! So our market share was more like 70%.

The other sub market which has started to take off is investment banks acquiring mortgage portfolios that they then securitise. Increased supply in the availability of mortgage portfolios is keeping premiums down, while a frothy international capital market is increasing the profits achieved by securitisation. This particular sub market may not always be with us in volume, but, for the present, it is certainly viable for all concerned, particularly those who have launched new businesses based on the constant availability of portfolio purchase demand.

We have not chosen to exploit this demand in volume because (a) our regular buyers give us more demand each year than we have available supply and (b) the warranties and representations that are perfectly acceptable and viable in the portfolio sale market are different from those typically given in the securitisation market, and we see no reason to change.

The creation of the portfolio sale market has allowed new lenders to launch. Freedom Finance has launched innovative self certification and non-conforming product ranges as a regulated lender in its own right, but is selling virtually all of the loans it originates to other lenders by way of portfolio sales. The business has been created because the portfolio sales market exists: another example of consumer benefit through extended choice.

As the market has become more sophisticated, so some lenders have established specialist subsidiaries to buy and sell portfolios of mortgage loans. Sometimes, when the parent is a building society, one of the objects of these new subsidiaries is to create profits which helps to provide greater membership benefits on the mutual side of the business. Figure 3.6 shows a table of some of the lenders who are active in portfolio trading through wholly owned subsidiaries.

Amber Home Loans (Skipton Building Society)
Britannia Treasury Services (Britannia Building Society/Platform Home Loans)
Derbyshire Home Loans (Derbyshire Building Society)

EMEX Funding (Cheshire Building Society)
Mortgage Express (Bradford & Bingley)
North Yorkshire Mortgages Limited (Scarborough Building Society)
Rooftop Mortgages (Bear Stearns)
West Bromwich Mortgage Company (West Bromwich Building Society)

Figure 3.6

Changing structures

As demand for portfolio purchases increased, we evolved different structures to meet it. For example, in 2003 we signed with Mortgage Express (ME), the UK's first forward sale agreement. ME has renewed every year since, so hopefully it works for them. The important elements of this contract are in the public domain due to parent company Bradford & Bingley's normal stock exchange reporting.

The demand from ME was for a regular supply of mortgage loans. It did not want to continually "take its chances" with each new portfolio, paying a premium that was subject to a competitive bid from others, and not necessarily getting the level or spread of assets they required due to commitments we had made elsewhere. We therefore proposed a forward sale agreement which would include a schedule describing the characteristics of the sort of assets we wanted to sell, and which they wanted to buy.

Limits were imposed such as maximum weighted average life of fixed rates, the minimum blended margin over Bank Base, percentage limits on certain categories of loan and so on. The list is long enough for ME to be satisfied that it is getting the assets it requires, but short enough for us to be able to viably create those assets to order. The list also avoids negatively affecting the breadth of the product range we offer on the creation side of the business and does not restrict our ability to deliver the blend of assets required by other purchasers.

A rolling due diligence programme, by which ME staff are checking the assets as we build them, means that any quality problems with particular loans are sorted out well before the quarterly fund transfer dates. An agreed fixed premium reflects our preference for this sort of guaranteed demand, and minimum/maximum options on the quarterly tranches enable both sides to plan by staying within pre-agreed limits. As evidenced by its longevity, this is a highly satisfactory new type of agreement to emerge from a maturing portfolio sales market.

We have developed a hybrid structure to secure demand from the emerging interest of European investors looking for alternatives to purchasing RMBS. European banks or financial institutions which are not regulated entities in the UK and not resident in the UK usually find there are barriers to taking direct ownership of UK mortgages. But the whole point of portfolio sales is to transfer risk from seller to buyer in its entirety. So we had to come up with a solution.

Our talented capital markets team, particularly Craig Beresford, Mark Gray and Joe Smallman from our broker-dealer unit, GMAC-RFC Securities, developed a hybrid between portfolio sales and a normal securitisation, under which we sell the mortgages into a special purpose vehicle which then issues credit-linked notes to a single investor, as opposed to the market at large.

The structure is, essentially, a "private placement" where we retain legal ownership of the mortgages and continue the servicing via HML. But the economic benefit of the mortgages passes to the investor, thereby negating regulatory and withholding tax issues, but still removing the assets from our balance sheet. We have successfully completed one trade to a European buyer using this structure, and we expect to repeat it in the future, both with that investor and others.

Through lending, on the other hand, is not a structure we are likely to repeat, even though it was one of our first attempts at trying to create differentiated demand. What we had in mind when developing Through Lending was to top up our ability to make competitive mainstream loans available right at the cutting edge of pricing.

Our *"mortgages for everyone"* philosophy means that we have to compete in the mainstream market at whatever price has been set by our competitors, and we do. However, the management of the product mix means that we could occasionally do with more lending supply in that particular sector, which Through Lending was designed to deliver.

Through lending was a mixture of the old Private Label model, and the new portfolio sales structure. We would first agree a detailed product design with the purchasing lender, rather as Private Label used to do. We would then launch that product into the market, offering and completing the loans in the GMAC-RFC name.

On the day of completion, however, we would transfer the loans to the purchasing lender, as noted in the mortgage offer. We would receive a pre-agreed premium for creating these assets, the lender would access our distribution channels and our intermediary customers would enjoy increased supply from us of competitive mainstream product.

One of the first problems we encountered with this idea was that we were only able to attract the interest of the small to medium-sized building societies. So instead of rolling the resultant products out to all of our distribution, we had to instead use the concept only for specially targeted exclusives for particular distributors. Valuable enough, but never generating sufficient volume to be truly worthwhile.

The administration was also very complex. It is much easier to transfer a large portfolio of loans than to do it loan-by-loan. Moreover, it was not always possible to persuade the purchasing lenders to offset the costs they were saving by participating in this arrangement against the premium they would be paying, meaning that the product design model by which we created the end customer terms was not as generous as it should have been.

Through Lending should have offered purchasing lenders something different. One of the downsides of purchasing a portfolio is that you have to largely accept what is on offer, or not make a purchase. With Through Lending, the buyer gets to participate in the actual product design and, thereby, receives only the loans it expects.

However, after a couple of years of experimenting with this structure using three different lenders, we decided to quietly file it under "good idea, but strangely didn't work". Of course, if a mainstream lender came along with £500m of funding, we do have the appropriate cleaning equipment with which to remove the dust from this particular concept!

From strength to strength

In its structured finance commentary of June 2005 mentioned above, S&P estimated that the portfolio sale market had reached £10 billion. In fact, they said it might be even more than that. We think that it is probably slightly less. Whichever way you look at it, however, the evolution of portfolio sales as a viable and liquid funding mechanism has significantly improved the way in which the UK mortgage market operates.

By introducing a new type of funding, which removes risk entirely from the selling lender's balance sheet, it has not only facilitated a much more efficient use of capital in the market, but has also allowed new lenders to launch, bringing diversity of choice to consumers.

Large numbers of mortgage lenders have been able to use portfolio-buying as a way to add distribution, diversify risk, replace redeeming borrowers and create profit. Some organisations have been able to create new, sub markets as a result of our involvement.

The quality of lending has also improved. We have our underwriting effectively audited by a dozen or more outside institutions every year. We have to get it right to trade the level of assets we sell every year.

As the portfolio sale market grows, it is likely that the larger financial institutions, particularly investment banks and European investors, will start to dominate the purchasing demand in the way that the more traditional lenders do today. The structures under which assets are transferred will, as a result, become increasingly more complex.

As I reflect on all this some five years later, my overriding emotion is one of relief that it worked. If we had not been able to kick-start a portfolio sale market then our strategy would have been in tatters. Risk and reward: proportionate bedfellows in my experience.

We expect to be responsible for about a third of all portfolio trades by value in 2005: perhaps a little bit more if we take into account the re-selling of assets we originally created. Our percentage market share may drop year-on-year, but the actual amount we trade will increase.

It is interesting that the market appetite for RMBS has currently increased to such a level that we have deliberately chosen to include A and A- asset in mixed collateral bonds rather than sell them as portfolio sales. We calculate that we have achieved superior market execution down this route, even taking into account the fact that we retain residual risk in a securitisation in a way that we do not with a portfolio sale.

This is not a trend that is about to dominate, because we are a committed partner and know that the repeat portfolio sale business we enjoy reflects our loyalty to the sector in continuing to bring forward portfolios that are of interest to our buying customers. But it is a trend that will affect premium rates for as long as those market conditions remain.

The relative merits of portfolio sale versus securitisation were also identified by S&P in their structured finance commentary, as shown in figure 3.7. It provides a useful link to the other part of our trading activity, namely securitisation.

A COMPARISON OF TWO FUNDING OPTIONS AVAILABLE TO MORTGAGE LENDERS - A WHOLE LOAN SALE OR A SECURISATION

Whole loan sale	Securisation
Profit up front	Profit over time
Cross-selling opportunities	Potential to create instruments by selling this profit over time
Assets clearly removed from balance sheet for accounting purposes	New accounting rules will require most securitised assets to be recognised on-balance-sheet
Additional diversifier of funding	Widely-used and understood funding source
Additional form of liquidity/different profit model	Continues to be a very strong form of liquidity/benchmark
Economic option for smaller-sized pools	Offers economies-of-scale/ability to issue large quantity of debt
Ability to buy exact volume of specific loans	Flexible environment/ability to structure risk through tranching

Reproduced with the kind permission of Standard & Poor's

Figure 3.7

Securitisation

The UK non-conforming RMBS market, as we now know it, was still in its infancy back in 2000. The ratings agencies were still wary of modelling the credit risk, and the audience of investors was limited to a few UK institutions. At that stage, even the majority of investment banks did not want to get involved.

Yes, there had been some successfully issued securities. Indeed, we had already issued three bonds prior to my appointment. These had also caused a bit of a culture shock internally. Our staff at that stage still comprised largely the people we had bought in with the initial acquisition. They were used to the approach of a balance sheet lender.

Securitisation was a relatively new funding tool for most employees. The need to drop day jobs and explain our sales approach or underwriting criteria to visiting investors, or to supply a level of data integrity never required before, required a high degree of cultural change which does not happen overnight.

One of the biggest challenges we faced, however, was the lack of performance data related to non-conforming loans. It is always the same: the market can't take off without performance data, but there is no performance data until the market takes off. Our first four transactions therefore employed the traditional senior/subordinated structure, but we wanted to improve execution.

We solved this problem in the short term by looking beyond the issue of the performance data itself. What the investors were ultimately worried about was losing money. They wanted the performance data so that they could assess this likelihood. With help from Bear Stearns, we put together a structure that brought in a new party.

AMBAC Assurance is a monoline assurance company that provides guarantees on financial transactions. AMBAC did understand, and respected, our lending practices and had studied the performance of the loans in our first four portfolios. They therefore agreed to provide a wrap which meant that, if there was ever default on the bond payments, AMBAC would step in.

This structure required us to pay a fee to AMBAC for the insurance. But the existence of an AAA rated insurance wrap brought with it significant differentiation, and extra security for the investor. In fact, we used the structure on eleven consecutive deals, such was its popularity.

It was not without its challenges. Because some investors had a worldwide exposure to AMBAC, it meant that on occasion they could not participate in particular bonds to the extent that they would have liked, or at all. But overall, the innovation of the AMBAC wrap, introduced for the first time in November 2000, was undoubtedly a milestone in kick-starting our securitisation programme onto the next level.

As we progressed through 2001, the assets were piling up as our "creation" strategies were working. Then, when one particular portfolio sale deal broke down because the purchaser pulled out at the last minute, a concern was expressed about our exposure to a sudden reduction in demand from portfolio purchasers generally, given the level of A and A- business we were generating. The concern centred around the fact that portfolio selling was still very much in its infancy in the UK, and was only a single solution so far as the exit for our A and A- business was concerned.

A reduction in short term demand from portfolio purchasers never in fact materialised. As we pushed more asset into the market, so it grew and diversified. Nonetheless, we agreed to nail this particular concern by making our second bond in 2001 a mixed collateral deal, thereby proving that we had a second exit route available to us.

We held back some of the A and A- asset that would normally have been offered for portfolio sale and matched these with non-conforming loans. We felt we would get better execution if we could have a straight 50% in each asset category, which meant delaying the trade until the portfolio of loans in question reached the target level of £800m. This of itself caused concern from our parent as we were virtually betting the entire year's net income on a deal which not only dwarfed in size any other bond we had previously issued, but which also represented a departure from the so recently established precedent of using non-conforming collateral only for securitisations.

So far as we were concerned, the deal was progressing normally. A date for pricing had been fixed - 11 September 2001 - with completion due the following week. Initial indications were that we would achieve satisfactory pricing. Then the tragic and extraordinary events of 9/11 occurred, the very day pricing was to take place. Naturally, all bets were off. The markets closed down for the following two weeks, and opened only tentatively thereafter. The uncertainty - not just in the financial markets - which followed 9/11 produced some commentary to the effect that markets would never again return to normal.

But we felt that our markets were more resilient than that. Nothing had changed in relation to the fundamentals of the business. We were therefore confident that we could still get the deal away, albeit maybe on less attractive terms than originally envisaged.

This proved to be the case. With great help from AMBAC who, at a difficult time for a New York firm, worked closely with investors to allay credit concerns, we priced the deal soon after the markets re-opened, at levels not that dissimilar to the pre 9/11 indications. We closed on 2 October 2001 and everybody breathed a sigh of relief at this most emotional and turbulent of times.

As others started to issue more securities in the non-conforming and mainstream sectors, so the overall market became more liquid. There were many investment banks and their clients presenting to investors and explaining how the UK market worked. This was great news for us. If you are selling breakfast cereal then it is great to have your competitors telling everyone that never missing breakfast is important for good health. The market increases for everybody.

More and more investors saw how healthy the RMBS market was, so we were less exposed to the dictation of terms by a small group that had previously dominated the demand side. As the non-conforming side of our lending business started to grow at an even faster pace, to reflect our pricing and distribution initiatives, we were able to issue securities more frequently and on increasingly favourable terms.

The year 2002 was our biggest to date in terms of issuance volume (over £1 billion). But the following year we beat this with just one bond. This turned out to be a major milestone. There was some apprehension internally and externally as we announced that we proposed to bring to this still fledgling UK RMBS market its first £1 billion non-conforming bond - particularly when we also said that we had decided to make this particular deal our first ever multi-currency execution.

We had been concerned for a while at the limiting nature of issuing in sterling, and trying to create investor demand from UK institutions only. Having some dollar and euro-denominated paper would mean some hectic roadshows for our capital markets team and the lead banks, but we reckoned that the time was right and that the deal could be done.

Not all of our advisers agreed. On more than one occasion we were implored to down-size the bond. There was a good deal of nervousness about sentiment towards the UK housing market. But our team disagreed with this advice. As Stephen Hynes, our Capital Markets Director, said "I understood how well intentioned the advice was. It's just that I didn't agree with it. I felt that this was a risk worth taking".

So, in March 2003 roadshows were set up in Europe and in the US. One particular itinerary period from this roadshow sticks in the mind of Stephen Hynes as it involved London → New York → Boston → Washington → Charlotte → San Francisco → Los Angeles → Seattle → London all in seven days. Phew!

Generally speaking, the demand in the US was stronger than in Europe, mainly because the US investors understood the collateral that much better, and had less pessimism about the UK housing market. Nonetheless, it seemed odd selling bonds backed by UK non-conforming collateral in the US market, where we had to strike a favourable comparison between our product and the securities offered by US-based firms.

The undeniable fact was (and is) that lower losses are sustained in the UK than in the US on residential mortgage lending, particularly non-conforming. There's also no doubt that familiarity with GMAC-RFC as one of the world's largest securitisers helped our US adventure.

The European leg of the roadshow was undertaken by Mark Gray, then our Head of Securitisation, and included London, Dublin, Paris, Frankfurt, Brussels, Spain, The Netherlands, Norway, Sweden, Finland and Austria.

The roadshow was so fast-moving, with travel arrangements often booked at the last minute, that our party arrived in Helsinki only to find that all hotels had been booked due to there being a medical convention in town. The only accommodation left for the presentation team was a trade union hostel located in a wood about 30 miles out of town. The team stayed out of bed as long as possible by playing pool and watching the sun go down at half past midnight.

The reward for this dedication beyond the normal call of duty was not just a pile of Air Miles with which to subsequently take the family on holiday. The main prize was that the deal was done. In a difficult market, and against the predictions made by some market participants, we managed to execute a successful trade.

In this way, we had delivered yet another first on the trading side of our activity to match the new records we were achieving with our asset creation. The first £1 billion UK non-conforming bond had been brought to market by GMAC-RFC UK.

Although demand continued to be strong in the US, with the US dollar-denominated parts of the bonds selling within the spreads achieved by US non-conforming issuers, we were determined to overcome the concerns expressed in the European market about UK mortgage market collateral. This really paid dividends in 2004 when we were able to attract investors from Belgium, France, Spain, the Netherlands, Luxembourg, Austria, Italy, Portugal, Switzerland, Scandinavia and Germany, just at a time when the US demand had started to wane a little. But we had another record to crack.

At £1.5 billion - $2.8 billion - our June 2004 security was GMAC-RFC's largest ever single trade. Although our parent company regularly securitises $1 billion plus per week, it had never at that stage executed one individual deal of this size. There were the usual concerns about risking so much net income on one trade, accompanied by worries about the level of available demand. But our hard work in preparing and educating the market paid off so far as this issue was concerned.

It was not only fully subscribed, it was actually over-subscribed, breaking new records for the market as well as within GMAC-RFC internally. This second mixed collateral bond cemented our position as the UK's leading issuer behind "the big three" of HBOS, Abbey and Northern Rock, who were the only companies to beat us on volume, mainly because they were bringing to market a steady stream of securities supported by back book collateral. As we progressed through 2004 and into 2005 we discerned a further step-change in demand. Far from being the nervous market we had identified in 2000, requiring an AAA insurance company wrap to bring new investors to the table, there was demand for more riskier tranches accompanied of course by wider spreads.

When we looked at our proposed deal for September 2004, we therefore concluded that a better execution could be achieved by returning to the senior subordinated format. We had generated eleven deals totalling in excess of £7 billion with AMBAC so that particular guarantee arrangement was ended on the best possible terms.

The next five deals were executed without the wrap, at ever tighter spreads. It turned out that that first £1 billion bond back in 2003 had been a particularly important milestone for another reason, because spreads tightened in our favour for two years thereafter.

We now find that there is not only strong demand deep into the structures we are bringing to market, but also keen interest in the residuals we hold in respect of previous deals. Previously, one of the important considerations in the GMAC-RFC approach to securitisation, was the fact that we kept a significant amount of "skin in the game" (risk participation) on each deal through our residual holdings.

We felt that with this development the market had moved even further than we had anticipated it would when we started to get bids for these positions. We have partially sold a few, thereby freeing up capital. We see this trend continuing, opening up new avenues of funding and profitable product lines, all of which assist the end borrower in terms of diversity of choice.

As at September 2005, total securities issued under GMAC-RFC UK's programme amounted to just under £12 billion across 20 trades. Figure 3.8 sets them all out in more detail:

TOTAL SECURITISATIONS FROM FIRST TO LATEST

Series	Issue Date	Volume £m	Credit Support	Lead Manager
RMAC 1999-NS1	26-Mar-1999	97.2	Senior / Subordinate	Deutsche Bank
RMAC 1999-NS2	21-Sep-1999	130.0	Senior / Subordinate	Barclays Capital
RMAC 2000-NS1	15-Mar-2000	225.0	Senior / Subordinate	Deutsche Bank
RMAC 2000-NS2	22-Jun-2000	195.0	Senior / Subordinate	Barclays Capital
RMAC 2000-NS3	09-Nov-2000	180.0	Ambac Wrap	Deutsche Bank
RMAC 2001-NS1	28-Mar-2001	225.0	Ambac Wrap	Bear Stearns
RMAC 2001-NSP2	02-Oct-2001	825.0	Ambac Wrap	Barclays Capital
RMAC 2002-NS1	27-Feb-2002	600.0	Ambac Wrap	Deutsche Bank
RMAC 2002-NS2	15-Jul-2002	525.0	Ambac Wrap	Bear Stearns
RMAC 2003-NS1	12-Mar-2003	1,000.0	Ambac Wrap	Barclays Capital/ Deutsche Bank
RMAC 2003-NS2	25-Jun-2003	500.0	Ambac Wrap	Bear Stearns
RMAC 2003-NS3	29-Sep-2003	550.0	Ambac Wrap	Deutsche Bank
RMAC 2003-NS4	03-Dec-2003	500.0	Ambac Wrap	Barclays Capital

TOTAL SECURITISATIONS FROM FIRST TO LATEST (continuation)

Series	Issue Date	Volume £m	Credit Support	Lead Manager
RMAC 2004-NS1	03-Mar-2004	750.0	Ambac Wrap	Bear Stearns/ Deutsche Bank
RMAC 2004-NSP2	29-Jun-2004	1,500.0	Ambac Wrap	Barclays Capital/ The Royal Bank Of Scotland
RMAC 2004-NS3	29-Sep-2004	500.0	Senior / Subordinate	Barclays Capital/ Credit Suisse First Boston
RMAC 2004-NSP4	15-Dec-2004	800.0	Senior / Subordinate	Deutsche Bank/ Merrill Lynch
RMAC 2005-NS1	02-Mar-2005	757.5	Senior / Subordinate	Deutsche Bank/ HSBC
RMAC 2005-NSP2	09-Jun-2005	1,100.0	Senior / Subordinate	Credit Suisse First Boston/ The Royal Bank Of Scotland
RMAC 2005-NS3	28-Sep-2005	700.0	Senior / Subordinate	Barclays Capital/ Merrill Lynch
		11,659.7		

Prepared as at 30 September 2005

Figure 3.8

Wrap up

With portfolio sales, we created a new market. The result has been a growing, diversified market that is delivering benefit to all. What we did on the securitisation side of our business was slightly different, stimulating demand and helping an existing market to develop and mature, and achieving some major milestones and new records along the way.

No longer is the market for UK non-conforming RMBS dominated by a small group of interested investors. The structures, and the risk involved, are now more widely understood. We regularly issue in three currencies and attract roughly 60 investors from up to four continents for each deal.

Despite having the backing of a great parent, we took our own risks and reaped the rewards. We created it - £ billions of the stuff - and we traded all of it, validating the strategy.

1 2 3 **4** 5 6 7 8

AUTOMATING THE PRE-OFFER PROCESS

The paper pile

The mortgage industry is sometimes great at spending millions to avoid losing thousands. And never have millions been more squandered than on the traditional paper chase which typifies the processing of an average mortgage application. When I took over as executive chairman of GMAC-RFC in the spring of 2000 I found that we were, in various different combinations, depending on the circumstances, either gathering in ourselves, or asking our packagers to gather in, the following pieces of paper:

- Employment reference
- Previous employment reference
- Payslips
- P60s
- Bank statements
- Bank references
- Existing lender's reference
- Previous lender's reference
- Landlords' reference
- Mortgage statements
- Previous mortgage statements
- Valuation report

These were the requirements that we were applying to our packagers, and therefore the same as those proposed for the new intermediary direct channel we were establishing. Of course, we did not get all that paper on every case, but we got most of it on most cases and it cost an absolute fortune to administer.

We were at that time a small lender. Number 60, as estimated by the CML. We had advanced just £350m the previous year. Yet we and our packagers employed, quite literally, hundreds of people to pile this paper up. For, as practitioners with any kind of history in this market know, it is not a straightforward question of applying for a reference and getting a response.

Less than half the references came through without chasing. We would often chase several times. While we were doing all this, the customers would also chase us. Or their intermediaries. Or their estate agents. Or their solicitors. Or sometimes all of them on the same day.

When all these documents did come in, we had to interpret them. And, of course, the telephone calls were not straightforward either. They would lead to call backs, arguments, the production of more paper … and so the cycle went on.

We did not, at the time of my appointment, have an intermediary direct channel - that was launched shortly afterwards. But we had agreed to undertake the processing of mortgage applications up to offer stage on behalf of the lender from whom we had purchased the building, staff, computer and general infrastructure which we had used to launch as a non-conforming lender 18 months previously. So we had direct experience of all this frenetic, paper-based activity as well as insisting that our packagers endured the same wild goose chase.

For that is all it was. Chasing our own tails for information we already had access to or which added nothing to the risk assessment, causing mortgage applications to be delayed for weeks on end which, in turn, promoted quite unnecessary suffering. But we were no different to the rest of the industry in this. What I describe is pretty much the industry standard approach at the time for application processing.

Some lenders even practise it today. It is quite extraordinary because all the information we needed to assess a borrower's propensity to pay was already available to us without all this paper. The information that was not available did not really matter in the scheme of things. As I said in my first book, published in 1997:

"Pre-offer processing is still too paper-based. With higher level credit searching and mature credit scoring systems now in place, there is no need for all these paper references. Mortgages should be offered within seven days or sooner, and paid out immediately thereafter, relying on title insurance. I expect that development to be with us very shortly. As the internet becomes more widely used, interaction between users and providers should permit mortgage application forms to be completed on screen and in an interactive way".

So I passionately believed in this long before I actually had an opportunity to do something about it. The year 2000 was my first chance, because I was actually running a mortgage lender. But my disrespect of paper reference-gathering was not just influenced by the millions of pounds we had squandered on this process at Private Label, acting for various lenders. It went back farther than that to my days as a management trainee at the Halifax.

An early induction into paper-scepticism

As I moved around various departments I had spells in further advances, in new applications and in arrears. As I absorbed my experiences from this training I formed the view then, in the mid to late 1970s, that the traditional way of mortgage underwriting was hopeless at predicting levels of arrears, or differentiating between good or bad customers, and was too one dimensional in its approach.

When dealing with further advances, I recall cases where borrowers who had started off borrowing three times income were, by the time of their application for additional borrowing, actually paying the equivalent of four times. This was mainly due to rising rates, but sometimes due to employment changes.

However, their attitude to credit was good and they were making their mortgage payments on time. But as they were already over the lending limit for income multiples they could not borrow any more - even a couple of thousand pounds more.

We expected them to be able to afford it when we put rates up. But we then told them they could not afford it when they came to re-borrow.

Even if the application was well within LTV levels, and even if the borrowers had an outstanding track record with us, I was instructed to turn them down. But I was allowed to lend to somebody else who, on paper, was borrowing just three times income but who, in my opinion, had lifestyle issues which made me think they would find difficultly in paying.

When I then did my stint in arrears, my view in this area hardened further. I found people who had borrowed twice their income, but who were in serious difficulties. I remember one chap - a high flying executive in an oil firm - who would rather face the repossession we had threatened than sell some of his ponies "because his daughter loved them so much".

Even as a young man in my early twenties, I started to doubt very much whether manual underwriting would ever be much good at being predictive. We had all these people and all these rules trying to check things that were never going to be the cause of the arrears anyway. As I worked on the files relating to borrowers in arrears, I rarely found an example of subsequent problems that could have been foreseen at manual underwriting stage.

Unemployment, relationship breakdown, sharply rising interest rates, economic conditions and a whole host of unpredictable occurrences seemed to be the reasons why people got into arrears. Yet none of that could be predicted by amassing a huge paper file of the type everyone told me was the way to underwrite mortgage applications.

I thought then that the best a good underwriter could achieve was the first payment down statistics (how many borrowers do not make the first monthly payments). If they are low then the underwriting has been good. If subsequent unemployment or lifestyle issues cause the loan to go into arrears later, then this is not something that manual underwriting would have picked up in any event.

I had only just embarked on my career in mortgages, but I had serious questions and concerns about all these practices and procedures that were enshrined so authoritatively in the big lender manuals that looked down on us from the shelves in such a brooding and imposing way. The more I read them, the more nonsense I thought some sections were.

I therefore questioned my line managers about this, but my queries were received with a mixture of indifference and a "rules is rules" approach, albeit dressed up in politeness. The politeness and patience, no doubt, to reflect my youthful naivety, and the "rules is rules" attitude to try and drill into me at a relatively young age that rules are there to be followed, not to be questioned.

Fast forward to Private Label and, once again, I am arguing until I am blue in the face with the lender panel to reduce or eliminate their paper-gathering, but with modest success. Twenty years after my experiences at the Halifax, people were still holding on to the traditional methods. Now, in 2000, was the time I could actually do something about it.

Blame the parents

In my experience, the most influential underwriting factor when assessing a mortgage application is the borrowers' parents. Yep, the parents. What they taught their kids about commitments.

Are they to be taken on lightly, and discarded if they no longer suit? Or are they to be entered into cautiously, and always honoured?

Unfortunately, it is not practical to include a parents' interview in the mortgage application process. Pity! In the absence of this the next best thing is to assess the manifestation of that advice, namely the borrower's attitude to credit.

Attitude to credit

This can be done at the touch of a button. With the information-sharing that has been available to lenders for some time, it is possible to see how borrowers have performed on other credit transactions. Like their credit cards, for example. Or personal loans. Maybe other forms of credit. This will tell you about the borrowers' attitude to credit. Are they consistent? Or are they erratic? Do they always borrow the maximum? How many commitments have been taken on?

These are all considerations that a mortgage lender really needs to know. Now that the majority of lenders share information about mortgage performance, it is even possible in most cases to look at that in an automated way. Assessing how somebody has performed on their existing credit is the most influential part of the mortgage underwriting process. The continuing development of credit scorecards and automated systems makes this possible in a few seconds.

Over-reliance on attitude to previous credit is potentially difficult for some first time buyers. Not the majority because, today, the average first time buyer is over 30 and can normally demonstrate a track record on non-mortgage financial commitments. For those youngsters starting out with little or no credit history, however, I accept that a little more investigation is necessary. That has to be priced into the service, and many lenders are happy to do this in order to secure the first time purchaser. They hope that a customer for life can be secured, with potential for other cross sales. Lenders like us who have now automated the underwriting process still attract a fair share of first time buyers because most do have a financial track record. But I accept that those without a financial track record probably go elsewhere.

Scoring a winner

Lenders have for some time had sufficient information about the performance of their existing books in order to derive meaningful statistical extrapolations. A credit scorecard may be less predictive if it is compiled generically, or if it uses data from other lenders. That does not mean it is invalid: it just means that it may be less valid than it would be if based on a lender's own loan book performance data.

Scoring purists would argue that the new generic scorecards can be more predictive than proprietary cards. Either way, credit scoring was delivering to lenders the ability to profile applicants with a high degree of predictability as to whether they had the ability and propensity to pay, with attitude to credit a key input to that score.

My thinking, as I eagerly took on this issue shortly after my appointment as GMAC-RFC executive chairman, was that we could automate our process so as to discern attitude to credit, and feed this into an overall credit profile, thereby giving a meaningful predictive decision within seconds of keying the appropriate information. We would then be able build a mortgage book of such consistency and predictability that we did not need all that superfluous paper-based information.

It did not matter whether someone was borrowing four times their income or two times their income. This was always an out-dated, one dimensional tool in my view. Individual circumstances and lifestyle choices mean that the rigid application of income multiples will not predict affordability or subsequent loan performance. What mattered was whether the borrowers had demonstrated a positive attitude to credit and whether they were statistically likely to be good payers in future.

Even if we verified their income down to the last penny, and lent them only three times at outset, a few interest rate rises and a job change could make that the equivalent of four times income anyway, as I had directly experienced. So what were we actually trying to achieve?

Some of the employers' references we were getting from small companies were not always entirely believable. Our requests for lenders' references were simply an excuse for those existing lenders to try and stop the borrowers moving their mortgage to us. Before we got the reference the borrowers had often been persuaded by a tempting new offer, not previously available, made by the existing lender.

I knew we would need some manual tasks. We would need to telephone employers, for example, to ensure that people worked where they said they worked (or ring their accountants in the case of self employed). We would also need to introduce robust Quality Assurance checks to constantly inform and update our automated processes. But all the paper references could be thrown out of the process without any reduction in the quality of underwriting, in my view.

Error, influence and leverage

One reason this would come about is because we would omit error, influence and leverage. These are three terms which we do not hear many people talking about when it comes to the manual underwriting of mortgage applications. Yet they are highly dilutive of consistency and predictability.

Error is fairly straightforward to describe. It is the process by which human beings underwrite applications every day in different parts of the country and in different circumstances on behalf of their employers. They may involve the mis-calculation of LTV limits or misinterpretation of paper references. With an automated underwriting process, this does not apply.

We then come to influence. If an underwriter does not like an application, and turns it down, there then begins the process of influence. Either the applicant, or the intermediaries, or some other professional in the chain, seek to influence the underwriter that the application is better than at first thought.

I do not know what percentage of initial decisions are overturned in the lending industry. But I bet the number of applications involved run into tens of thousands. But you cannot influence a computer.

Then there is leverage. "I've given you nine good cases recently. This case may not be a great one, but if you don't do it, you won't get the next nine". How often is that said by brokers? Often it is used as the basis to squeeze through a case that really did not look that good. You try leveraging a computer.

For the very reason of the inflexibility mentioned above, I knew that the automation of the underwriting process would turn some intermediaries off. The system would have to offer something that was pretty spectacular in return. But it could.

A binding credit decision made at point of sale, within seconds of keying the required information, could revolutionise the whole delivery of a mortgage application. It could provide a platform for a subsequent dream of mine, which is the point of sale, binding offer. More of that later in this chapter.

As I write this book in 2005, there are still those who pay homage to manual underwriting. The credit rating agencies, for example, still increase the costs of securitisation for loans where income is not verified by paper references. Other industry commentators and policymakers still suggest from time to time that an automated process is not as good as a paper pile. Gathering-in irrelevant paper, and subjecting yourself to error, influence and leverage, is somehow better, according to these arguments. Extraordinary!

Does the precise income multiple really matter?

An interesting related income multiple point arose as we designed our 25 year customised fixed rate, covered from a policy perspective in chapter 5. We were looking to make this product as attractive as possible to ensure that the consumer appetite for long term fixes was fully tested. It occurred to us that long term rate stability could justify a higher income multiple. So we looked first at the average salary in the UK for the previous ten years, which was £22,253 (source: Office of National Statistics). We then applied an average income multiple of 3.3 to this salary and calculated the monthly payment arising from the resultant loan at the average existing borrower rate for the same period, which was 7.21% (source: MoneyFacts). This calculation showed that average borrowers in the circumstances described paid out 23.8% of their gross monthly salary on mortgage payments.

We then took the minimum salary that we were proposing for the new 25 year customised fixed, namely £30,000, and applied to that figure the same rate of average income growth over the next ten years as had applied over the preceding ten years. Using an income multiple of five (the highest available on the new product), we discovered that, at a 5.95% fixed rate, such borrowers would pay out on average 24.7% of their gross monthly salary.

In other words, if they borrowed five times income under our new product at a fixed rate of 5.95% they would pay as a percentage of their monthly salary the same that a borrower on average income would have paid out over the last ten years on a 3.3 x income loan. We therefore launched this product with a maximum 5 x multiple (the exact multiple varied according to the fixed rate content).

It is easy to see how this calculation can be applied to the mortgage market more generally. Sections of the market are worried about mis-declaration of income, such that somebody might be effectively applying for a higher multiple of income than the rules allow. But our calculation shows that, even if that is the case, it may not be as important as previously thought. The payment equivalent of 5 x income is what borrowers at the average variable rate have been paying out over the last ten years anyway.

Self cert on the TV

Later, the issue of loan-to-income came under the spotlight when the BBC programme Panorama highlighted the use of self certification in the mortgage market. The programme argued that abuse of this product was widespread and causing house prices to rise disproportionately.

The programme featured mainly one lender that was not always undertaking Quality Assurance checks. Mystery shoppers had been able, with hidden cameras, to show that a few individuals on this lender's branch staff, and some intermediaries, were seeking to persuade applicants to massage income in order to obtain a higher loan than the one to which they were entitled using the traditional income multiple approach.

It was unusual for a lender to undertake no checks at all. Most lenders would have picked up a problem by way of an affordability model, the manual sense check or the credit profile.

The house price connection was even more extraordinary given that the growth in house prices was so clearly related to a series of consecutive rate reductions, growing real incomes and a shortage of household supply versus the demand for new household formation. Because it was TV, however, it led to all sorts of comment by the written press and to a thematic review by the FSA.

The regulator found, as the industry knew it would, that the use of self certification mortgages was not widespread as a percentage of total lending. It was a niche product with restricted LTV and loaded rates. Only those needing to use it actually did.

Moreover, arrears levels on self certification mortgages were not too different to mainstream, clearly disproving the idea that people were taking on unaffordable debt. Even if people were mis-stating their income (and there was precious little statistically sound data to prove this), they were not doing so in a way that materially affected affordability. The programme's premise, that verifying income in a paper-based way, and rigidly applying income multiples, was the only "safe" way to underwrite was simply out of date.

Even now, over a year later, the debate about self certification rumbles on, sometimes with some truly daft comments attached. Changes in employment patterns mean that more people are on fixed term contracts at work. Many have a more significant proportion of their earnings related to performance then ever before.

Some have income from several sources, additional to their main job. All these borrowers are prime candidates for a self certification product, and those who would seek to prevent such employed applicants from being able to take out a mortgage are being irresponsible and deeply unfair.

More and more people are self employed now. Lenders are perfectly able to assess the credit quality of such applicants and to predict affordability and propensity to pay. The idea that the delays and extra expense involved in verifying income in the old-fashioned way is going to help anyone is terrifying in its naivety.

The programme also sought to blur the lines between "fast-track" and "self certified". This introduced a broader canvas on which the programme could paint its picture. Unlike the single lender which had disproportionately attracted the programme's attention, most major lenders "fast-tracked" certain types of mainstream loan. They did this because making customers wait around for non value-adding paper references was an economic cost to all parties.

The information available from credit bureaux, combined with fraud databases and statistical models, provided a safer, more reliable and more efficient process for verifying income. Fast-track evolved to reflect this. It was a perfectly sensible development applied to mainstream lending, and is a process for better underwriting not a self certification look-alike.

Self certification is different. For a start it is a separate product selected by the customer, normally because of volatile or hard-to-prove income, in contrast to fast-track, which is an underwriting process selected by the lender for its mainstream lending. Self certification loans typically carry a higher rate and a lower initial LTV requirement. They share a characteristic with fast-track in that there is no income verification by way of paper reference, but there are these key differences.

There is no evidence I have seen to support widespread mis-use or consumer detriment arising from the existence of self certification or fast-track products. There will be consumer detriment, however, if these products become the subject of prescriptive rules based on theories and fantasies far removed from the serious business of predictive underwriting.

The road to automation

But back to the year 2000. I had to convince the board, and then the rest of the business, that full automation was the way forward. There were many discussions and even more sceptical colleagues.

It was more straightforward to convince the credit team of the benefits of automation. They could immediately see the advantages in terms of increased quality. The main issues arose with operations and sales. There was a subconscious desire to hold onto the traditional way of doing things.

Operations staff in particular sometimes wanted the new system to do old jobs. The sales team was worried about how intermediaries would react to such a "black and white" underwriting approach, without influence or leverage.

The board was persuaded, and it empowered our credit team to re-engineer our underwriting process. So the team set about specifying an automated process, and looking for a supplier. Team members considered a number of routes forward. Building our own bespoke system from scratch, using different suppliers for various different components, was a strong contender.

However, GMAC-RFC had already introduced in the US a decision-making engine called Assetwise, for which our colleagues were seeking a European showcase. The system worked differently in the US in that applicants' details were keyed in and the computer found the best terms for that particular applicant amongst the GMAC-RFC range. As it is such a commoditised mortgage market in the US, intermediaries and their clients were interested in understanding the rate they would pay at a particular moment in time.

In the UK, we felt that demand would be different. Intermediaries largely know, and have sold to the customer, the product they will be offering before applicants' credit details are entered. So we needed to convert the system to UK needs and re-write to our specification, which turned out to be a longer lead-in time than we had initially planned. The system we ended up with, however, was certainly something special.

By the end of the year we had not only completed our outline systems specification, but had chosen to go with Assetwise. We started work on the system in early 2001 and successfully delivered automated decision-making at Bracknell fairly quickly - the first step to our revolutionary Point of Sale Decisioning system. This enabled our internal underwriting to be slicker and quicker with reduced references. But we then hit a roadblock with our plans to extend the system to the point of sale.

When we had purchased the business on which our UK launch was based, legacy computer systems had been involved. It turned out that these were too old to accept either the new technology we were proposing to bolt on in terms of the Assetwise decision engine, or the volumes we were proposing to pass through them. To simplify a complex situation, we had to re-write the front end of the system before we could make real progress towards POSD. From one perspective, having waited so many years to have the opportunity to fulfil this part of my vision, it was relatively easy to be patient and wait another year or so. Already the automation was delivering interim wins in terms of making the burden of processing lighter.

Our volume history does not show that this delay was detrimental to our growth ambitions. On the other hand, it did allow other lenders to catch up and, eventually, overtake us in terms of launching online decision making , although most of the lenders in question eventually launched what I would describe as Decisions in Principle.

While we undertook this systems re-write we took the opportunity internally to make decisions on all of our products through the new engine, starting with mainstream and then adding self certification and, finally, non-conforming. Many felt, and some still feel, that automated decision making is best placed to underwrite prime or niche business only. But we have found that it is equally predictive for non-conforming lending where we know the applicant's credit history is not perfect and can use this to accurately risk-price and determine future performance.

By the autumn of 2002 we were back on track following the systems re-write, and in early 2003 able at last to introduce a select number of intermediaries to the pilot testing phase of our new point of sale decisioning engine. We tested the impact on intermediaries who were not regular supporters, and intermediaries who were.

The most interesting data came from the former category, who started to use the system for much more of their business, such was its ease and simplicity. We had reduced to an average of just 14 questions the information that needed to be keyed in order to get an immediate online decision, and we were maintaining response times around about the 30-40 seconds mark.

We knew it would be important to keep the questions to a minimum, and to make them dynamic. Some lenders make intermediaries go from page to page on the screen, often collecting data that is irrelevant to that particular case, and leaving the intermediaries to wonder when they are going to come to the end of the process.

When an accept decision was delivered we allowed the intermediary to stay online and book funds as well as instruct the valuation on payment by credit card. Often this meant that the valuation report came in before the application form.

We ensured that training was proactive and clear, meaning that we quickly got to 95% usage without the need for the financial incentives that other lenders had introduced when launching their online systems. Our focus from day one on intermediary ease of use had really paid off.

Some performance statistics

The next big stage of the testing process was to eliminate referrals. Again, this was a piece of contra-thinking. We were not going down the same path as other lenders and maintaining the manual underwriting process alongside an automated one. We were shooting for the bigger prize of no doubts, no manual intervention and total certainty. We called it "definitely, not maybe". It meant therefore that we had to eliminate referrals, where the system does not reach a decision and, instead, refers the application for manual underwriting. We had been working on this in parallel to the systems re-write. Figure 4.1 shows our progress in the area of mainstream loans in getting referrals down from an initial 46% to nil by the time we launched to an expectant market in June 2004.

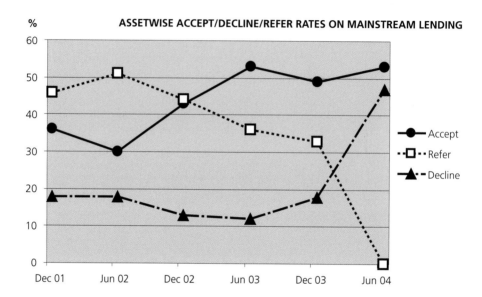

Figure 4.1

The vast majority of "referrals" were longwinded, complicated, frustrating "NOs". A minority were longwinded, complicated, frustrating "YESs". Our Unique Sales Proposition was that we would be the only lender offering binding credit decisions at point of sale without any referrals. Decisions that intermediaries could rely on and use for planning. We therefore had no choice but to eliminate the referrals, and this is what we did. (We do allow a limited appeals process for those few "no" decisions that prove to be the exception to the rule).

There are, of course, those who take a contrary view to ours. Some lenders feel it is a service to intermediaries to deal manually with all referrals. My personal experience in running Private Label and GMAC-RFC, is that referrals rarely do anybody a service. The majority still turn out to be declines after a lot of paper is gathered and emotional energy expended - time that could be spent more efficiently processing better quality applications.

By offering a fast, automated, easy decision we were allowing intermediaries to know exactly where they stood. By not having manual referrals, we would be able to deliver cost savings that could be reflected in the price at which we could make mortgages available. We would also, I was sure, increase the quality of our lending over time through the elimination of manual intervention.

We launched POSD in June 2004, a couple of years later than we had intended, but well worth waiting for. Prior to the introduction of automated decisioning, we prided ourselves on the fact that we were able to give intermediaries a decision in principle on a complete application within 25 minutes. After the introduction of our POSD system, this timeframe reduced to 30 seconds on average.

Moreover, the decisions we were able to give were binding, subject only to valuation and the non-discovery of fraud, as opposed to the DIPs available under manual underwriting. Figure 4.2 shows that dramatic fall in more detail:

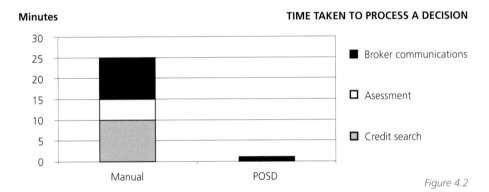

Figure 4.2

We saved about 50,000 hours of work in the first year of POSD related solely to automated vs manual decisioning. No lender, of course, receives a formal application for every decision made so this is reflected in the calculation.

But the benefits of POSD did not stop there. After a DIP had been given in the pre-automated manual world, the resultant application had to be processed. We thought we were being slick in getting an application on average from receipt to completion in two and a half hours of exclusive work on that case, according to our capacity planning model at the time. But in a POSD world the average processing time per application reduced to just 40 minutes, as shown in figure 4.3:

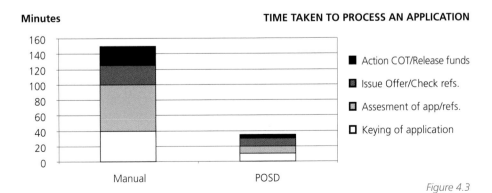

Figure 4.3

In the manual world, the light grey section in figure 4.3 relates to the obtaining of normal references. With some applications, this function took a lot longer. But the average over a large volume of business is reflected in the diagram.

In the POSD world, however, the light grey section relates to audit calls such as checking with employers that the applicant works there, checking with accountants that they do act for the applicants and so on. We calculated that the processing time saved amounted to in excess of 150,000 employee hours, in addition to the circa 50,000 employee hours saved as part of the decisioning piece.

It was thus that, in just a two year time span, we were able to double our level of completions with less processing staff than we had before, as well as halving our cost per completion. These savings were not just reflected in more competitive product pricing, but also in enhanced business volumes as intermediaries started to seek us out as a lender that was always up to date with no processing backlogs.

At no time since we first introduced automation on a pilot basis in 2003 have we had case backlogs because we have automated the application assessment against our credit policy, eliminated most of the paper *and* pushed the decision out to point of sale. I cannot recall any single new development in my business career that delivered "wins" on so many fronts.

I have always, throughout my career, caused problems for my processing departments, due to achieving consistent strong growth in new business. But it is now hopefully a thing of the past. Naturally, it is nice to win any award voted for by the customers you principally serve, in our case mortgage intermediaries and packagers. But the recent awards that have given me disproportionate pleasure have been those that related to service. We are now selected as much for service as for other factors.

As demonstrated above, the most dramatic impact to arise from automation can be found in the decisioning and pre-offer process. However, there are other benefits. For example, the number of days between offer and completion has reduced by 14 between 2001 and 2005, despite a quadrupling of business over that period. The rate at which offers complete has also increased by just over 10% following the introduction of POSD.

These trends are not so easily explainable because we still have similar processes operating post offer as we had before. The answer, we suspect, lies in the fact that bringing forward to point of sale the binding credit decision that was previously made weeks later under the manual process just introduces more speed and certainty throughout the transaction.

How did the intermediaries react?

Our mortgage intermediary customers embraced the system enthusiastically. They were very prepared to substitute certainty and speed for influence and leverage. Within the first year we registered over 23,000 users, and decisions regularly exceed £100 million in value per day. We conducted some research with our intermediary customers to find out what impact POSD was having on their business. The results produced some interesting data, including:

- The result of a binding decision at point of sale meant that more customers were prepared to sign up there and then, in the intermediary's office. In the old manual underwriting world, it was fairly typical for a proportion of customers to take away the application form, and the various quotes supplied by the intermediary, and take the same product through another source

- Having a binding decision within seconds of keying 14 questions was saving valuable processing and chasing time. For those intermediaries who regularly package for lenders, a saving of two hours per case was identified. This has given intermediaries the opportunity to either cut costs or redeploy staff

- Much redeployment has been focused on creating new sales. Freed up time is as good as an uplift on the introducer fee in some instances

- Intermediaries also reported that they, too, were noticing an enhanced offer to completion rate, which was creating more income from the same number of applications

We did some work to calculate that an average intermediary sending in ten cases a month to us was earning an incremental £35,000 just by using POSD versus the pre-automation system. It was obviously necessary to put in quite a few assumptions to recreate the average, so this figure was very much illustrative. But the "hard pounds" way of making this point certainly caused a stir, and some interest from our competitors, when we publicised it.

Those competitors who beat us to market with their online DIP systems had to re-think their credit approach and remove some referrals and some of the previous caveats. They now claim to have binding decisions as well which, if it is true, can only benefit customers, intermediaries and the quality of their books alike.

When you dig deep with some lenders, however, you still see those caveats there which stop it being a truly binding decision. We have caveats relating to the discovery of fraud, but the lenders I have in mind have caveats even if the information keyed in for decision-making purposes turns out to be wholly accurate. Intermediaries just need to keep an eye on this.

The POSD experience

It's not easy in a book to give a truly accurate flavour of a dynamic, interactive online decision making system. But I shall not be put off by that. In the illustrations that follow, nine consecutive computer screen shots take you through that experience. It should bring the process to life.

SCREEN 1

The first screen that is seen and requests your log-in details

SCREEN 2

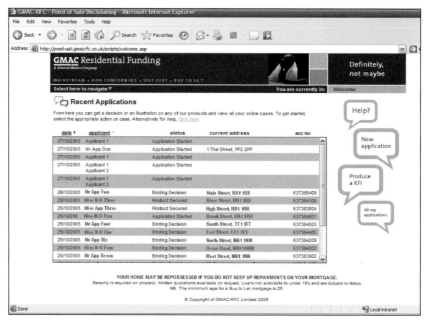

Will show your recent applications to enable you to change details or you choose New Application or Produce KFI

SCREEN 3

Enter product details

SCREEN 4

Application details

SCREEN 5

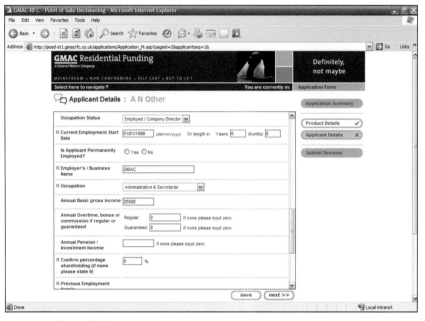

Occupation and Income details

SCREEN 6

Holding Screen while Decision is retrieved

SCREEN 7

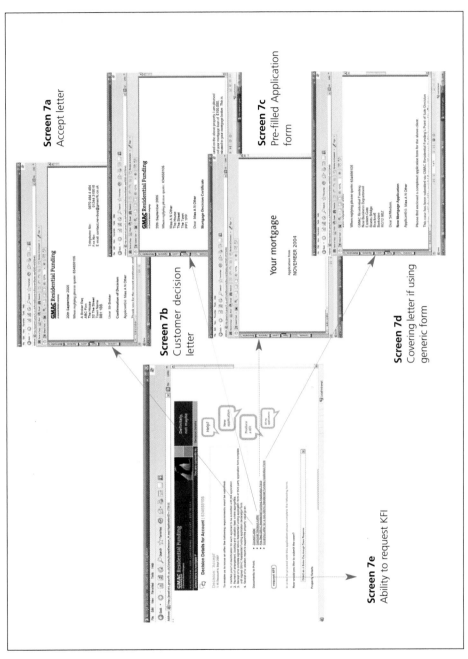

Screen 7a
Accept letter

Screen 7b
Customer decision
letter

Screen 7c
Pre-filled Application
form

Screen 7d
Covering letter if using
generic form

Screen 7e
Ability to request KFI

Documents you can print

SCREEN 8

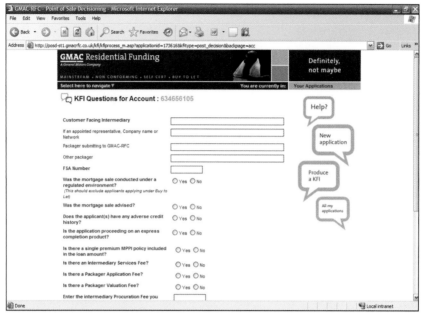

KFI screen

SCREEN 9

Fees screen

The 24/7 debate

Our POSD system is available between 7am and 10pm on weekdays, and 8am to 6pm on weekends. Others are available 24/7, and we've taken some comparative criticism about this. But who is looking for a binding mortgage decision in the wee small hours?

We researched this with a representative sample of intermediaries and published our findings. As expected, some 79% said that they NEVER requested a mortgage decision during the hours when we were closed. Interestingly, one intermediary responded to the effect that he "only" requested decisions between the hours of 10pm at night and 7am the following morning, which just goes to show that there is always one. Bless!

The serious point to emerge from this research is what we heard from our main credit bureau. This credit reference agency told us that it closes down between midnight and 6am. They also told us that their alternative standby site (used for disaster recovery and scheduled maintenance) is not made available to any other mortgage lender during this downtime period. The assumption has to be, therefore, that lenders giving decisions between the hours of midnight and 6am are effectively giving DIPs which are not based on normal credit data. I worry that the few intermediaries using the system in these times may be giving the same weight to the decisions obtained in the early hours of the morning as they give to decisions obtained during normal processing - something that we have repeatedly warned about.

Anyway, that particular debate has largely quietened down. I think that the publication of our research, and the fun we made of it with our fictitious website www.saddos.com (for those who want a fast link to lenders offering access in the middle of the night) has seen off the worst of the competitor criticism. We have no plans to open our system later than 10pm at night, because there is simply no material demand. We certainly have no plans to be open while the credit bureaux are closed.

Arrears levels

The theory put forward by those who prefer to hang on to the more traditional manual underwriting and reference-gathering process is that the experience and instinct of the underwriter will spot potential problems that the computer will not. This is accepted. It is a point in favour of manual underwriting. My case from the outset, however, was that the removal of error, influence and leverage, and the consistent application of a computerised underwriting approach would at least compensate, such that arrears levels would not deteriorate.

Consistency is the key. An automated process always delivers the same decision on the same facts, whereas ten different underwriters could interpret the same facts in ten different ways. Also, a manual underwriter has little, if any, statistical feedback on the decisions made. While many lenders do provide an overall performance level by underwriter (for example, first payment defaults), there is little information on customer profile, or analysis linking the arrears to particular characteristics. This means that decisions biased to individual prejudices and experiences are often not informed or updated.

Even if all this was wrong, as I argued back in 2000, the millions of pounds which we would save by automating the process would dwarf any incremental credit losses.

It is a little early to draw meaningful conclusions on arrears. However, on the statistics we have available to us, arrears levels have not deteriorated. Our two plus vintage arrears levels for business written in Q4 2004 were, for example, exactly the same as they were for business written in Q3 2003. Since the economy has slightly deteriorated in this period, with GDP down, and with interest rates and unemployment up, standing still in this analysis probably means a credit quality improvement.

There are, of course, other factors interacting to cause or prevent arrears, which may be enhanced or suppressed during a short review period. The position needs to be monitored over the longer term. On the other hand, the farther you get away from completion the less likely it is that arrears will have been caused by an initial underwriting factor anyway. All the indicators are that automated underwriting is a very effective risk assessment methodology, providing at least the same (and almost certainly an improved) level of risk management, at much reduced costs, enhanced speed and improved consistency and predictability.

My sense is that, if there was going to be a significant problem arising from the substitution of automated underwriting for the traditional manual process, we would have seen it in the first payment down statistics. Looking long term, therefore, I remain of the view that the predictive nature of credit scoring and profiling will produce a higher quality book than would have been the case had we stuck to the old processes: a position that is further enhanced by our ability to undertake more volume via our automated process, thereby increasing the size of the book and spreading the exposure.

1000 manual checks to find one problem

Under current regulatory rules, it is necessary for there to be an assessment of the capacity to repay. One of the checks that we use as part of our responsible lending processes is a manual "sense check". This is to ensure that bus drivers claiming to earn £100,000 a year do not get through the net in the way that they might have done without any human element at all.

This manual check obviously has a role to play, although the impact on the quality of the overall book is minimal. The reason for this is that we are employing people to check 100% of cases in order to try and catch the *one in a thousand* applicants who might possibly fit into the following category:

■ Prepared to commit a criminal offence and lie about their income *and*

■ Prepared to mis-state their income in a way that is material to their ability to pay *and*

- Choosing the GMAC-RFC loan to depart from a previously consistent track record and credit profile *and*

- Undertaking all of the above in a transaction which actually produces a credit loss for us

As our automated procedures are designed to profile and score an applicant, most of the above problems would be caught in any event. For the small percentage that would slip the net, the likelihood is that there would not be a material increase in credit losses.

We, of course, comply with these rules because we must and, as I say, at the very edge of the margin, this checking will have a positive impact. But its cost, and the need to maintain an infrastructure to support it (in terms of communicating queries to intermediaries etc) is, in my view, disproportionate to the risk presented.

We employ data integrity checks, cross referencing the information contained on the application form with the data on which the automated decision has been based. We also use an affordability model which predicts income using application, bureau and geodemographic data. These checks and sophisticated tools are all contributors to more predictive underwriting.

Quality Assurance

Not everything can be automated. One aspect that we have needed to keep manual is Quality Assurance. These are the manual checks done on a sample of applications so as to learn lessons and discern trends, feeding that back into our automated processes..

To take an extreme example, if the QA checks reveal that borrowers in a particular town are disproportionately mis-stating their income or doing something else that is undesirable, then we will feed this into our automated decision process. This could result in increased fraud reviews for particular post codes or amendments to our bespoke affordability model.

We have always made it clear to our intermediaries that QA checks will be undertaken on a sample basis. We will not overturn an automated decision unless we discover fraud, e.g. mis-stated income or certain other circumstances. But our intermediaries do not know either the sample size or frequency of our QA checks, which remain ever-present. Just because we have automated the pre-offer process in a most comprehensive way does not mean that we have surrendered our power to make a final decision on issuing offers and releasing funds.

Automating the valuation

There is one major element of our pre-offer process which is manual, and that is commissioning, receiving and assessing the valuation report. If that process could be automated then point of sale mortgage offers would be the next logical step.

We think it can happen. During 2005 we ran 17,500 manual valuations through two Automated Valuation Models and there was an acceptable margin of difference. Indeed, an interesting debate ensued as to which valuation was "right" - the automated valuation or the traditional physical valuation.

The use of AVMs in the industry is not new. A number of lenders routinely use them for low LTV remortgages or audit. But why not extend it to all initial valuations?

Many of the same principles apply to this process as apply to the manual versus automated underwriting debate. The thousands of pounds that a lender might lose (or might not lose) as a result of relying on AVMs as part of an automated offer issuance process might be dwarfed by the millions of pounds it might make through incremental business and costs savings.

Momentum has been given to this subject by the comparison work undertaken by the ratings agency, Standard & Poor's. Their broad conclusion was that, taking a portfolio of loans where an AVM had been exclusively used, there was as much chance of an under-valuation as there was of an over-valuation. As a result, S&P published a very helpful paper on 26 September 2005 entitled "Guidelines for the use of automated valuation models for UK RMBS transactions".

S&P said that it would, in future, apply a very modest assumed over-valuation percentage to portfolios of loans that used AVMs (as opposed to manual valuations). The exact over-valuation percentage used would depend on the level of credit rating applied to the portfolio, and the degree of confidence that the AVM supplier had in the valuation being returned.

Both of the two main suppliers of AVMs, Hometrack and UK Valuations, tended to return valuations with an indication of the degree of confidence that they have in the figure being supplied. Although both AVM suppliers used slightly different methods and means of communicating their degree of confidence, S&P aligned them in what they described as five variation levels, to produce the table in figure 4.4.

REDUCTIONS TO AVM-GENERATED VALUATIONS

Variation level	AAA	AA	A	BBB	BB
1	1.07%	0.72%	0.63%	0.54%	0.27%
2	1.74%	1.16%	1.02%	0.87%	0.44%
3	2.95%	1.97%	1.72%	1.48%	0.74%
4	4.16%	2.77%	2.43%	2.08%	1.04%
5	5.37%	3.58%	3.13%	2.68%	1.34%

Reproduced with the kind permission of Standard & Poor's   *Figure 4.4.*

Where the AVM company has produced a valuation with a variation (confidence) level of 1 then, on a BB-rated tranche, S&P will assume an over-valuation of just 0.27%. This increases according to the credit rating. For a top-rated AAA tranche, the over-valuation at variation level 1 is assumed at 1.07%. Even at variation level 5, however, which represents the least confidence that an AVM company has in the valuation being supplied, the assumed over-valuation on an AAA tranche is only 5.37%.

The publication of this table is highly significant for the UK mortgage market. It is, if you like, a "coming of age" for AVMs. As S&P rightly points out in its commentary, if Home Information Packs are introduced by the Government, meaning that a physical inspection of the property being offered to the lender as security for the loan takes place prior to the application being submitted, then this will undoubtedly increase further the use of AVMs by UK mortgage lenders. Even as it stands, most UK RMBS tranches could live with the percentages shown in figure 4.4.

AVMs cannot be applied to every loan. There will be some properties - perhaps those that have not been sold for some years - where no valuation is available. Buy-to-let, where an estimated rental is required, would be another exception. There are others. But we feel that an automated valuation could be acceptable in 75% of cases.

Using an AVM will mean, of course, that there will be no lender's valuation report for the applicants to rely on, at least in the majority of instances. But this may be a good thing. Lenders' reports were never designed to be relied upon by applicants, who should be obtaining their own Homebuyers' survey. The lack of a lender's valuation report may therefore be beneficial by ensuring that applicants do obtain their own report.

I know that some people argue that a point of sale offer may be too quick for customers. I do not agree with that viewpoint. The customers have applied for a loan. The quicker the lender can give them what they have applied for the better. As long as they can then take as long as they like considering the offer, I do not follow the logic that giving them what they have asked for at a slower pace than is necessary will benefit anyone.

Wrap Up

For us, the delivery of Point of Sale Decisioning was a long, tortuous road involving the re-writing of legacy systems and significant cultural change. But all the benefits that we anticipated for this move have come true, and more.

The anticipated cost savings; productivity; superior service to intermediaries, and maintained credit quality, have all been delivered. Intermediaries and their clients know exactly where they stand at point of sale without having to suffer the delays and inconvenience of a long-winded paper chase leading to an uncertain conclusion.

Next in our sights are automated valuations. Giving customers what they have asked for as quickly as we can, gives them more time to consider their options, less expense and more certainty.

In the meantime, those attempting to influence the self certification debate from a position on the sidelines should stop and consider the facts before their statements end up delivering consumer detriment. In my view, there is too much "should-be" thinking evident in media and so-called expert commentary in this area, and too little facts-based sensible analysis.

1 2 3 4 5 6 7 8

INFLUENCING THE INFLUENCERS

As we contemplated the size of business that successful implementation of our strategy might deliver, we knew that we would have to find a role for public policy lobbying. If you are going to grow an organisation into a sizeable institution then you will come to the attention of public policy makers including Government and key Opposition frontbenchers as well as the regulatory institutions. Moreover, public policy makers will have an interest in you, and will also be evolving policies and regulations that affect you directly. These could be negative influences on the business unless we were keeping an eye on and influencing public policy decision makers.

There comes a point when you are sufficiently above the radar to need to engage in the public policy arena, not least to ensure that policymakers and agents of influence know about you and your story. It could be argued that this is even more important when you are a global institution operating in a local market as we do.

In recent years, public policy and new regulatory practice has had a marked effect on the financial services industry. Just as the major utilities found themselves under the spotlight of both Government and regulators in the 1990s, so the mortgage lending sector now faced that challenge. The recent introduction of direct regulation of the mortgage sector by the Financial Services Authority necessitated, in my view, an active dialogue on policy with the regulators and government.

The confluence of where public policy and business strategy collide is where a strategy develops. This is not just a "nice to have" activity, but now a core part of our executive directors' activity-feeding into wider business strategy through the ideas and connections which public policy engagement brings.

When planning our strategy, we discussed the size the company would have to achieve at which point it would be necessary to introduce a public policy committee and board members would have to spend time engaging in public policy work. We decided we would know the correct size of our business when we got there! That occurred in 2003 as we advanced nearly £5 billion and became the 12th largest UK lender. We therefore formed a public policy committee of the board during that year, which I chair.

Committee members comprise one other board director plus a senior manager, alongside a specialist public policy agency and our PR agency, Lansons. The public policy agency, Cicero Consulting, initiate and arrange our contact with public policymakers across the political, regulatory and market spectrum, and come up with new ideas and initiatives.

These might be one-on-one meetings with politicians on particular mutual interest topics. Or we might meet with special interest groups, organise public events to initiate discussion and debate on relevant issues or get together to decide on our response to consultation papers.

Some of our experiences are shared in this chapter. The objective is always to ensure that we contribute and that policymakers know who we are, know of our values and hopefully engage with us on matters that might affect either us or the industry.

The Miles Review

The Chancellor had asked Professor David Miles to investigate why US-style long term fixed rates were not widely available in the UK. I was asked to be a member of the CML working group considering the recommended industry response for the CML Executive Committee to approve. We also engaged with Professor Miles directly as GMAC-RFC, as he consulted various lenders directly.

I thought Professor Miles did a good job with a difficult brief. The idea behind the review had been that long term fixed rates might make the UK mortgage market less volatile, perhaps allowing the Bank of England Monetary Policy Committee to have more flexibility over the setting of short term interest rates - something the Chancellor had very much in his sights at the time.

However, our experience of long term fixes in the US did not support this theory. Fixed rates for 25 years or more were the norm in the US and they were decidedly volatile because they carried little or no redemption penalties. Borrowers in the US do not regard the fixed rates as being particularly long because they know they can, at their discretion, easily switch out of the mortgage.

In the unlikely event of interest rates stabilising over a very long period they could also, of course, exercise the option to stick with the mortgage. Either way, all the options rest with the borrower, thereby creating an uncertain and volatile market for the lender.

I got the impression early on that the review team could see the problems of introducing long term fixed rates in the way that they are made available in the US, namely with little or no redemption charges. On the other hand, a pre-set redemption

Extract from the product brochure describing the 25 year customised mortgage we launched in response to the Miles Review

charge often reflects near worst case scenarios, which can put people off, and which might amount to over-charging, depending on how interest rates subsequently perform. The review team therefore favoured so-called mark-to-market redemption charges where the amount that the borrower pays is related to the interest rate position at the time of redemption.

If interest rates have moved such that the lender could reinvest the redeemed funds without significant financial loss then there would be no charge. At the other end of the scale there would be a charge equivalent to the lender's costs of reinvestment. It is a good example of the mis-match which often occurs between perfect logic and the exercise of consumer choice. There is no way a UK consumer will take on a mortgage not knowing what the redemption charge might end up being, and no amount of persuasion or explanation will change that, however logical the formula might be.

The Miles review applied its brief to looking at consumers' understanding of the risks they were taking on and the issue of lenders offering better terms to new customers than were being made available to the existing customers. In the former category, I felt that the Miles review made a number of important points, which the FSA is trying to address with its Key Facts Illustration. The problem here is that, unlike policymakers, consumers are just not interested in boring financial rigmarole.

They are interested in obtaining the money and either buying the property they desire or, in the case of a remortgage, using the extra funds released to buy something else they desire. The industry can and will spend millions of pounds until it is blue in the face trying to explain risks and various scenarios to customers, but only a fraction will be taken on board. I am involved in this market so I am interested in such things, but even my eyes glaze over at some of the paper we ask consumers to absorb.

So far as the back book/front book argument is concerned, I never fully understood why it was a problem for lenders to offer discounts and subsidies to attract new business. There is not a business in the land, in any industry, that is not spending disproportionate marketing money on incentivising new customers, however that incentive subsequently appears in the market. It is not possible to pick up a newspaper at the weekend and fail to see an article describing how borrowers should transfer from the standard variable rate to a new business rate, so the market is sorting this out in any event.

I felt that there was no need to try and re-engineer this process, which we calculated would mean an average 0.75% increase in the new borrower rate to match a 0.75% decrease in the standard variable rate in order to ensure existing borrowers paid the same as new borrowers. We did not think that it was the role of Government to effectively impose a 0.75% increase for new borrowers for reasons that had nothing to do with the economy or inflation. Moreover, it bumped up against that mis-match between logic and customer behaviour.

Another example of this mis-match working in practice came to my attention during a meeting of the CML working group responding to the Miles Review. Two household-name lenders shared that they had written to a number of their borrowers who were paying the standard variable rate, offering a significant rate reduction by way of a transfer to a generous base rate tracker.

GMAC Residential Funding
A General Motors Company

The 25 year Customised Mortgage

In today's mortgage market, many customers are finding it difficult to find a mortgage product that offers the important combination of rate, longer term security, increased purchasing power and all important flexibility. Many products offer one or two of the above, but how many offer all four?

Our revolutionary new customised mortgage product aims to change this. By offering your clients the opportunity to choose how much of their mortgage is on a **25 year fixed rate at 5.95%** and how much is on a penalty free **bank base tracker rate at BBR + 0.75%**, they can decide not only on the rate they pay, but also the level of security and flexibility available. In addition, the greater the level of payment security a borrower chooses, the greater the income multiples!

If you've never considered longer term products before, then think again and read on. You may be surprised...

Long term security for life

For most people this product will allow clients to pay no more than 5.95% for the rest of their mortgage lives. How would mortgage borrowers have fared if they had fixed their mortgage rate 25 years ago?

The average mortgage rate in this period was 10.25%. A customer with £100,000 repayment mortgage would have saved £85,539.00 in this period had the **25 year customised mortgage** been available at 5.95%.

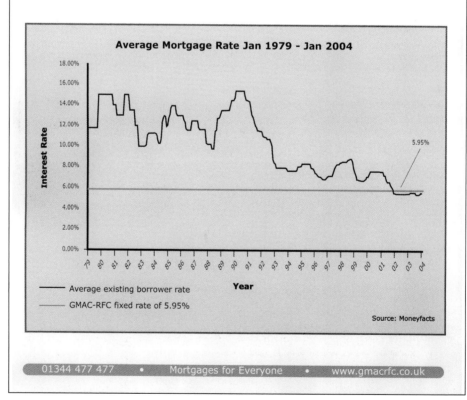

01344 477 477   •   Mortgages for Everyone   •   www.gmacrfc.co.uk

Extract from the product brochure describing the 25 year customised mortgage

All the borrowers had to do was to sign a piece of paper and, in some instances, their interest rate would go down by 1%. Their monthly payments would benefit from a corresponding large reduction.

However, a significant minority of such borrowers - too significant to ignore - had responded along the lines that they did not wish to be troubled by any further communications of that type. They were quite happy to stay as they were and focus on the things in their life which interested them, their mortgage not being one of them. Herein lies a message for all regulators, governments and mortgage strategists.

Markets and consumers do not work to perfect logic. People use local shops, for example, knowing that they are paying more than supermarket prices because that is what they choose to do. I choose a current account that does not pay interest, and which could incur me fees if I do not keep a substantial credit balance, because I choose to have a wider relationship with my bank.

Some mortgage borrowers sometimes choose a particular product or service according to considerations that are important to them. Just because they may not fit the perfect logic of how they should behave, it does not render the subsequent choice bad or inappropriate.

Anyway, the main point of the Miles review was to look at whether anything could be done to persuade UK borrowers to buy long term fixed rates on any kind of scale. We thought not, but it is the role of public policy work to engage with the Government of the day. We were in a position to fund such a product not least because, worldwide, we securitise many billions of dollars of them every year.

So we decided to launch one. We decided to make it as attractive as possible to consumers so that their appetite for a long term deal could be properly assessed. We therefore introduced a number of design features to achieve this end, including:

- The fixed rate element of the mortgage was priced at 5.95% for the full term. The opportunity to fix your mortgage rate at 5.95% for life was at the time, and remains, an exciting option for those who can get their minds around it

- Knowing the concern that people have with predicting interest rates into the future, we offered a variable element at Base + 0.75%, which could be mixed in with the fixed rate element in various combinations. This enabled borrowers who were nervous about long term interest rates to hedge their bets

- There was no redemption charge on the tracker element of the loan and a decreasing 7, 7, 6, 5, 4, 3, 2 percent redemption charge on the fixed rate element for the first seven years only - again extremely competitive

- Income multiples were available in a range up to 5 x single income, and 4.25 x joint. The income multiples varied according to the fixed and variable combination. We had calculated that borrowers taking 5 x income on the long term fixed rate would not pay out materially more on their mortgage than the average borrower had paid out on the average loan in the market over the preceding ten years (the research underlying this calculation was discussed in chapter 4)

GMAC Residential Funding
A General Motors Company

Revolutionary design with freedom to pay back

Unlike many other long-term fixed rates where the borrower is 'locked' in for the full term, **the 25 year customised mortgage** offers unique freedom.

Clients can mix in varying amounts of penalty free tracker with the fixed rate to suit their circumstances. However this isn't the only revolutionary aspect as even the fixed element has a reducing redemption charge over only just 7 years i.e. less than 1/3 of the term!

Up to 5 times income / 4.25 x joint

With longer term rate security, clients can budget ahead knowing that they are protected against any future rate rises. On this basis, the income multiples available on this product step up with the level of fixed rate protection selected, to a maximum of 5 x single income or 4.25 x joint. This could make the crucial difference in bridging the gap between average house price and average earnings.

A borrower on the average salary for the last 10 years of £22,253 would, borrowing on an industry standard multiple of 3.3, at the average existing borrower rate for the last ten years of 7.21%*, would have paid out **23.8%** of his/her gross monthly salary on mortgage payments*. If you apply over the next 10 years the same rate of average income growth that has applied to the ten years previously, a customer on this product with the lowest possible income (£30,000) and the highest income multiple (5 x) would only pay on average **24.7%** of his/her gross monthly salary. These income multiples are both highly beneficial to your client's and responsible lending.

Establish your client's requirements and then satisfy their needs!

For this unique mortgage there's a range of 5 options, ranging from a 100% fixed rate at 5.95% to 100% Tracker rate at BBR + 0.75% for the full term, with three 'mix and match' customised options in between. Please refer to the table below for full details.

Options	Fixed element 5.95%	Tracker element 4.75% (BBR + 0.75%)	Weighted average initial rate	Income multiples available with each option			
				LTV up to 75%		LTV 75% and above	
				Single	Joint	Single	Joint
1	100%	0%	5.95%	5	4.25	4.5	3.75
2	75%	25%	5.65%	4.75	3.75	4.25	3.25
3	50%	50%	5.35%	4.5	3.5	4	3
4	25%	75%	5.05%	4.25	3.25	3.75	2.75
5	0%	100%	4.75%	3.75	2.75	3.3	2.5

The 25 year customised mortgage
Another market leading product from GMAC Residential Funding

Introducer Payment 0.35%

* Data sources, Office of National Statistics and Moneyfacts. Figures shown are on an interest only basis

01344 477 477   •   Mortgages for Everyone   •   www.gmacrfc.co.uk

Extract from the product brochure describing the 25 year customised mortgage

Pros and cons of a long-term fix

Some lenders offer home loans fixed for 25 years, but they will not be suitable for everyone. **Clare Francis** explains

THE government is keen for borrowers to take out long-term fixed-rate mortgages because it believes they will lead to greater stability in the housing market. They are unpopular with consumers, however, because they are more expensive than the shorter-term deals.

GMAC-RFC last week unveiled a 25-year fixed-rate mortgage that it hopes will appeal to more borrowers. At 5.95%, the rate is higher than the best shorter-term deals — you can fix for two years at 4.45% and for five years at 4.99%. But borrowers can opt to have a proportion of their mortgage on a penalty-free tracker that is 0.75 percentage points above the base rate, giving a rate of 4.75%.

Jeff Knight at GMAC said: "This loan addresses borrowers' reluctance to commit to a long-term fixed rate because they can customise it."

Redemption penalties on the fixed part of the deal run for only seven years. The only other 25-year fixes, from Cheshire and Leeds & Holbeck building societies, are less flexible. The Leeds & Holbeck deal levies redemption penalties for the entire term; penalties run for 20 years with the Cheshire deal, although both offer penalty-free windows in alternate years once you are five years into the term.

Leeds & Holbeck's mortgage has a slightly higher rate than the GMAC deal at 5.99%. It is available for loans up to 90% of the property's value. Cheshire's rate is lower: you pay 5.78% if you have a deposit of 20% or more, but 5.88% for mortgages between 80% and 95%

of the property's value.

Ray Boulger at Charcol, a mortgage broker, does not expect GMAC's loan to be widely popular, although he thinks it has the edge over the other two deals because it will lend up to five times single income and four-and-a-half times joint salary. The typical income multiples are three-and-a-half times salary for single applicants and two-and-three-quarter times for joint income. However, you can borrow the bigger amount only if the whole mortgage is on the fixed rate.

Boulger said: "This loan may be popular with people who want to trade up the property ladder but who can't borrow enough using standard income multiples. It shouldn't necessarily be their first choice of mortgage, but it might mean they can get the property they want."

Sunday Times. 22 February 2004. Author: Clare Francis. Thanks to the Sunday Times.

The product was launched in a blaze of publicity, receiving coverage in the national as well as the trade press. Extracts from the product guide appear as illustrations in this chapter. The product created enormous interest, as we expected it would. But it delivered very little new business, which is also what we thought would happen.

We did not know it for sure, because consumer attitudes do change. But this particular product was true to form and we quietly withdrew it the next time that there was a base rate change. Hopefully it did make a public policy contribution, though, in demonstrating that - even with attractive and flexible terms –neither average UK borrowers nor the advisers they use will consider long term fixed rates in sufficient volume to be significant for market planning.

Using research to inform your market

A major part of our public policy strategy has been the research we have undertaken to inform our market on matters of major, topical interest. As the strategy evolved, we decided to commission a major piece of research at least once a year and to present the findings to Government, regulators, public policymakers generally and to our competitors.

The latter always receive our free research with surprise. But contributing to a friendly, orderly, competitive market is an important role for all major lenders.

Our first research initiative looked at non-conforming mortgages, from a consumer perspective. The background was increasing commentary about, and political interest in, non-conforming borrowers.

The impression being created was that these borrowers were disadvantaged, down market and maybe not fully aware of the nature of the commitment they were taking on by way of a non-conforming mortgage. Demands for action or "protection" were beginning to surface as a result of these commentaries, so we decided to conduct research with non-conforming borrowers to assess what they thought about this.

An accurate, demographic comparison between non-conforming borrowers (data generated by NOP World) and general mortgagors was an integral part of the project. IPSOS provided a nationally representative sample of Britain's mortgagors (size 1532), using a face-to-face methodology. The following key conclusions from the research were of great interest:

- Although non-conforming borrowers appeared to be employed in less senior positions compared to general mortgagors, there was not a heavy bias towards unskilled employment as may have been expected before the research was undertaken

- Relationship breakdown directs a significant minority of borrowers into the non-conforming market

- The non-conforming borrower sample had a mean income that was above the national average, and included a proportion that had significant income levels

- All types of individual are involved in the non-conforming market and it is not restricted to the poorest in society

- 30% of non-conforming respondents agreed that their credit rating had improved since they took out their non-conforming mortgage

- Just under half of all non-conforming respondents felt that their overall quality of life would have been worse if they had not been able to buy their current property

- Two thirds of non-conforming borrowers claimed to understand why lenders charge higher rates of interest to borrowers who have low or poor credit ratings

■ Almost six in ten non-conforming respondents claimed that they were prepared to pay an extra 1% - 2% above the standard mortgage rate to secure a mortgage if they had a low credit rating

■ Over half the sample agreed that, although higher rates of interest are charged, repaying a non-conforming mortgage gives people the chance to improve their credit rating over time

Our report, entitled *"NON-CONFORMING MORTGAGES IN THE UK: A CONSUMER PERSPECTIVE"* was published and used as a briefing document for our various meetings with MPs, public policymakers generally, regulators and the press. It received wide coverage and I believe that it truly informed debate at the time, which is continuing. It stands on record as a major piece of independent research which contradicts the idea that non-conforming borrowers can be stereotyped as unduly vulnerable, and unaware of the nature of the borrowing they have taken on.

Non-conforming literacy established

NON-CONFORMING borrowers are more financially literate than stereotypes suggest, according to research from GMAC-RFC.

A survey, conducted by NOP, revealed that more than two-thirds of those questioned understood why interest rates were higher for borrowers with poorer credit backgrounds.

It also showed non-conforming mortgages were not confined to lower-income borrowers. According to the survey, the mean income of non-conforming borrowers was higher than the national average.

One in three borrowers thought their credit rating had improved since taking out their last mortgage. And about half saw non-conforming mortgages as an opportunity to improve their credit rating.

The report into the non-conforming mortgage market included independent analysis by Professor Kevin Keasey, director of the International Institute of Banking and Financial Services for Leeds University Business School.

Mr Keasey said: "It is clear that the response of some lenders to simply exclude potential borrowers who do not fit a strict criteria, can have a negative effect."

Financial Adviser. 2 December 2004

The second major piece of research we undertook related to first time buyers. The Government had made known its concerns at the fact that the percentage of first time buyers had decreased from a figure of 55% a decade ago (source: CML) to around 31% currently.

Part of the Government's Homebuy initiative, offering shared equity loans to key workers, was meant to address this problem. We felt that it would therefore inform our market if we directed some major research into investigating the extent to which the reduction in first time buyer activity was related to affordability, and the extent to which social changes might be playing a part.

A related point concerned buy-to-let. If first time buyers were not purchasing a property, where were they living? If they were choosing to live in privately rented accommodation, to what extent was there a hedge between the first time buyer and buy-to-let sectors of the market? For example was it inevitable that, if first time buyers became fewer in number, buy-to-let borrowers would increase proportionately?

Due to the complex and evaluative nature of the research objectives, motivational research was conducted before the main survey of non homeowners was commissioned. This comprised a series of two hour group discussions conducted in the South East (Richmond) and Sheffield, South Yorkshire.

The non-homeowner sample included men and women living in private rented accommodation between the ages of 23 and 34. To provide cross-generational analysis, an owner-occupied sample was included in the study involving men and women aged between 35 and 45. The motivational research was undertaken by

Brahm Research. A quantitative stage was then used to test the findings from the motivational research using a large and statistically robust sample. Using a face-to-face, in-home methodology, IPSOS interviewed 1126 non homeowners aged between 18 and 34 derived from a nationally representative sample of Britain's population, collected via 160 randomly selected sampling points. Key conclusions arising from this research included:

■ The majority of those researched were comfortable in delaying a property purchase until after age 30, preferring to wait until they "settled down"

■ Around 70% of non homeowners agreed that buying a property signified settling down

■ When asked about the most important influence on buying a property, around 50% gave reasons related to lifestyle: just under half mentioned affordability

■ More people were going to university and emerging later into working life, some with debts. The "settling down" factor has therefore been pushed back, especially among graduates

■ Renting is seen by many non homeowners as giving a range of benefits, including being able to live in a better area than they could afford to buy in

■ Eight in ten non homeowners said that they preferred renting because it meant they do not have to make a long term commitment to a property or specific area

■ Seven in ten said that renting provided flexibility to move geographically within the labour market

The conclusion to be drawn from this research was that the Government's, or indeed the lending industry's, ability to introduce initiatives that would persuade first time buyer percentages to return to previous trend levels was maybe more limited than had been thought. Affordability was only an issue for half of them.

Renting near their social centre, instead of buying outside of their social centre, was high on the list of considerations for many. There also seemed to be a social shift away from settling down too early, with those researched preferring to "live a little", supported by their credit card, before they took on a mortgage.

The average age for marriage is now 31 for men and 29 for woman compared to 25 and 22 respectively as recently as twenty years ago (source: Office for National Statistics). It is perhaps no wonder that the average age of first time buyers is now 34 with more non-homeowners preferring the flexibility of rented accommodation.

Although non-homeowners ultimately expect to buy a property, the availability of quality private rental stock is facilitating this new social trend. Although we could not point to a conclusive, statistically sound "hedge" between first time buyer and buy-to-let lending, it is quite clear from these results that the growth which has occurred in the latter, during a period when there has been a reduction in the former, is not unconnected. We decided that this particular research was of such importance that, in addition to our normal briefings, we should have a breakfast discussion at the House of Commons. This was kindly chaired by Dr Vincent Cable MP, Liberal Democrats Treasury Spokesman. Dr Cable has taken an active interest in this area of policy and we believed it was important to engage directly with him on the issues involved. Professor David Miles had kindly agreed to overlay an academic analysis onto our research and he spoke briefly at the breakfast as did I. Dr Cable then opened the debate up to the MPs, regulators, journalists and public policymakers present. As with the previous research, much positive publicity was generated and, once again, we shared our findings with competitors and the market generally.

It is our assessment that this type of research brings considerable benefits to GMAC-RFC reputationally, and assists its dealings with all sectors of the market. Even if that were not so, however, the contribution our research is making to the quality of debate within the UK mortgage market is sufficient on its own to persuade us to continue on this path.

For those wishing to perhaps commission such research themselves, it may be helpful for me to mention the techniques we use:

- Debate fully internally and externally to find the policy issue that will really engage the interests of public policymakers and the media, making in the process a real contribution to contemporary opinion-forming

- Check as far as possible that that topic is not in the process of being covered by some other organisation or trade body

- Ensure a truly representative sample of individuals researched, so that the conclusions have breadth and real meaning

- Engage one of the big polling companies to demonstrate independence, integrity and size

- Employ specialist consultants to manage the project, and analyse the findings, so that the work burden on directors and employees is minimal while it also enhances independence

- Employ the services of a leading academic to apply his or her own view to the research, adding to its interest, value and newsworthiness

- Present the research in such a way that it is easily read by busy public policymakers (we summarise the content of each page in a shaded box so that, if you just read the boxes, you will get the drift of the research)

- Plan the launch of the research in a way that assists the target audience (for example, if you wish to influence Members of Parliament, do not launch the research in the Parliamentary recess!)

- Gather together the best and most interesting conclusions to be drawn from the research, majoring on these when presenting and issuing press releases

- Endeavour to ensure this work adds to your corporate profile and strategic intent wherever possible

Lifestyle changes threaten FTB market

BY SCOTT PHILIPSON |
First-time buyer (FTB) activity is under threat from fundamental lifestyle shifts, a study by GMAC-RFC has revealed.

The research reported lifestyle factors to be as prevalent as financial concerns for FTBs. Raising a deposit remains the single biggest factor preventing first-timers but a noticeable shift sees social attitudes being equally important.

The research suggested FTB levels may never return to the 'benchmark' of 50 per cent – a new trend which government initiatives and lenders' activity may be unable to influence. A rise in the quantity and quality of private rental stock means that consumers have more choice on how they live their lives, deliberately

Michael Coogan, director-general, Council of Mortgage Lenders (CML)

delaying making long-term commitments towards house purchase.

Professor David Miles, chief economist at Morgan Stanley and non-executive director at the FSA, said: "The view that FTBs are being priced out of the market is too simplistic. This study shows that people don't want to commit to a mortgage and have a different agenda. This reflects changes in society views with the majority of people comfortable in delaying buying a property until beyond the age of thirty."

Michael Coogan, director-general of the Council of Mortgage Lenders (CML), said shedding light on this particular issue is

important. "Property is increasingly being seen as an investment rather than a home. The social dynamics consist of a heady mix of issues, especially the lack of a savings culture. Therefore it's little wonder that raising a deposit is still the single biggest factor," he stated.

Stephen Knight, executive chairman of GMAC-RFC, commented: "We commissioned and sponsored this independent research to gain a better understanding of the influences behind why fewer first-time buyers are entering the housing market. It aims to provide policy-makers with market-led intelligence on the debate. Consumers have a 'live a bit more for a bit longer' mentality and getting on the property ladder seems to have been pushed down their agenda."

Mortgage Introducer. 18 June 2005. Author: Scott Philipson. www.mortgageintroducer.com

House of Commons Breakfasts

I mentioned above the breakfast meeting we had to launch our first time buyer research. We repeated this formula on a non research topic, namely the FSA's financial capability initiative. The FSA wished to increase consumers' knowledge of financial affairs across a wide spectrum of different influence points.

Our discussions with MPs and public policymakers suggested to us that this initiative might benefit from some momentum. We therefore asked the FSA whether they would be prepared to be represented at a breakfast discussion at the House of Commons to debate this issue, and bring it to greater public attention.

Through our continuing MP briefing programme, we had met with John McFall MP, Chairman of the Treasury Select Committee, and Mr McFall had kindly agreed to chair such a discussion. Again, as Mr McFall has been a key player in the overall debate around restoring confidence in the financial sector, we believed it was important to bring our activities to his attention.

The FSA sent two representatives, including one speaker. I spoke briefly and, once again, the debate was opened up between MPs, public policymakers, special interest groups and journalists on this important topic. Publicity ensued and I believe that this public policy initiative was yet another example of the way in which we have helped the quality of debate within our market.

Consultations

Seemingly, everybody wants to find reasons to complicate the UK mortgage market. They issue consultation documents, which often precede commentary or criticism or the latest new idea by the body concerned.

Lenders are requested to commit significant resource towards putting together a response. It is easy enough to bin it, and not make your views known. But you then lose the moral right to criticise and the actual right to influence.

If there is any public policy element to a particular consultation (and there is in almost all of them) we now co-ordinate our response through the public policy committee. Input is received from interested departments within our company, but the formal response is then put together in a consistent format by Cicero Consulting, who also co-ordinate any back up lobbying or influence we wish to exert on the topic in question.

This is becoming an increasingly busy part of Cicero's work on our behalf. For example, in the past couple of years there have been the following consultations we have had to consider:

- The Miles Review: The UK Mortgage Market: Taking a Long Term View

- The Barker Review: Delivering Stability: securing our future housing needs

- The consultation from the FSA on the development of mortgage regulation

- The HM Treasury/Office of the Deputy Prime Minister consultation on the Homebuy initiative: Expanding the Opportunity to Own

- Joseph Rowntree Foundation: Managing Risk and Sustainable Homeownership in the Medium Term: re-assessing the options

- Which? Time for a change: restoring and maintaining consumer confidence in the financial services industry

It is therefore important to have a policy on how you will respond to consultations on market-related matters. The extent to which one organisation can influence will always be marginal.

But the whole point of public policy work is to play a wider role in the efficient working of the market in which you earn a living. So our policy is to continue making comprehensive responses whenever we have something interesting to say.

Liaison with MPs and civil servants

Public policy work also involves meeting a wide range of opinion-formers and agents of influence. We have paid particular attention, however, to MPs, and to civil servants in departments whose work might touch the mortgage market. We have learned a lot from these encounters and, at the same time, we have often been able to convey a different point of view about topical matters that might inform the opinions of this influential group. MPs in particular see, via their constituency surgeries, the impact on individual consumers of actions taken by lenders, and it is good to have that feedback.

A case study example I always quote internally to illustrate the importance of meeting regularly with MPs concerns a decision we took in 2005 to increase the LTV limit on one of our buy-to-let products to 89%. This announcement, which we made exclusively to intermediaries, found its way via the trade press to the office of an MP who was very interested in lending matters. The initial reaction to our initiative by this particular MP was negative.

He felt that a higher LTV would encourage more amateur landlords into buy-to-let which may not be good for either them or the market at large. His office told us that the MP was minded to issue some critical publicity about our initiative. However, having met us, and having formed the opinion that we were a responsible lender, he wanted to first give us the opportunity to state our case.

We were grateful for this opportunity and we shared with the MP's office our background thinking. A maximum LTV was not the same as an average LTV. The 89% LTV facility was only available on one product, which was a long term fixed rate guaranteeing consistency of payment.

There were certain underwriting factors which would mitigate the use of this product. In fact, we put together a comprehensive briefing note covering many more points as well, which we emailed the same day as we received the query.

We were thanked for our input and informed that the MP did not now intend to pursue the matter. Had this MP been an individual whom we had not met, and who was not aware of our values and operating principles, then we might have just suffered the critical blast without any prior consultation. Criticism by an MP may not be fatal, nor might it interrupt new business flows. But any organisation is better off without it!

Meetings with civil servants are less frequent, but they can be just as helpful. A good example of that was a meeting we held in the summer of 2005 with the Office of the Deputy Prime Minister, including a representative from the Treasury. We had a good debate at that meeting about the Government's new Homebuy initiative, which offered a shared equity mortgage under certain conditions to key workers to enable them to better afford a home in their particular area.

We were able to lobby at that meeting for the fact that participation at that time in the Government's scheme was restricted to banks and building societies. Subsequent to the meeting we received a letter confirming that this would be changed by Statutory Instrument to include all regulated lenders.

We are not claiming to have had anything other than the most marginal of influences on this decision because the CML had already lobbied the appropriate departments and so had others. It is the case, however, that the senior officials with whom we met were not at that time aware of the issue.

It is my experience that there is no particular mystique in meeting with MPs and civil servants. They do a valuable job, and the different angle they come from can sometimes be helpful, and a refreshing change to the normal helter skelter of business life. Occasionally, of course, it is a frustration. But the market works by the interaction of various different organisations and interested parties. Much better to meet them, and to share points of view, than to limit yourself to consumers, peers and employees.

Corporate social responsibility

People sometimes say to me in business that they wish we could return to the old values: that things were better in the past. I never accept that. I always think that things are better now, and will be even more so in the future. I think that the whole approach of big businesses to CSR is a good example of how standards and values have improved. It is now inconceivable that a company of our size could trade successfully without evolving policies on CSR. Without such policies, a business would find that its customers, staff and business partners might become uncomfortable. Conversely, the implementation of good CSR policies makes those three target audiences feel good about the company, and it makes the company feel good about itself.

This was an easy decision for us because, although we were a relatively recent entrant to the UK mortgage market, we had developed CSR rules worldwide. It was just a question of phasing these in over the period of our growth so that they were proportionate to our size and influence.

We started off by ensuring that a certain percentage of net income was allocated to selected charities, featuring strongly GMAC-RFC's worldwide "Share the Magic" campaign where, for the same period of time each year, we match employees' contributions to individual charities so that double the money is donated. Following the hearts and minds of your employees' charitable instincts has payback in any number of directions, the most important of which is the money that the charities themselves receive.

As our growth continued we took on a higher profile and in 2002 we decided to add to the existing charitable giving by supporting The Outward Bound Trust, an organisation that gives young people the opportunity to develop self confidence and to learn the value of giving service to others through worldwide expeditions and work projects often designed to help less fortunate people. Our US parent generously doubled our UK contribution, which enabled us to ask for a certain amount of the funding to be allocated to disadvantaged youngsters in the locality of our Bracknell headquarters while leaving the charity free to allocate the rest as they saw fit. This addition to our CSR activities increased our profile further in the business community as we met other corporate patrons. It was also rather nice, on one day in 2002, to open a letter received from HRH The Duke of Edinburgh, who is patron of The Outward Bound Trust, thanking me personally for our involvement. A cut above my usual correspondence!

In 2003 we felt we had enough CSR activity going on to warrant a CSR brochure, the latest version of which appears as an illustration on the next few pages. We find that when meeting with existing and potential institutional business partners, and with public policymakers generally, our CSR brochure is more in demand than our report and accounts or our corporate brochure - another sign of the times.

GMAC RFC

Making a difference

Front page from our corporate, social, responsibility brochure

What next?

Our aim is to continue our work and involvement with the community. We're proud to have been involved with many charities and organisations, some of which are listed on this page.

If you have any questions or comments about our various charitable schemes please contact:

Chris Kujawa
Chair of the Community Involvement Committee & Director of Human Resources

GMAC-RFC Ltd
Eastern Gate
Brants Bridge
Bracknell
Berkshire RG12 9BZ
Tel: 0870 484 4484

Age Concern
Almshouse Association
Barnados
Berkshire Women's Aid
Bisley Village Playgroup
Bracknell Rugby Club
Breakthrough Breast Cancer
British Heart Foundation
Broadmoor County Primary School
Cancer Research UK
Children In Need
Clitheroe Community Hospital
Cystic Fibrosis
Ethiopiaid
First Steps Pre-School
Glebelands CP School PTA
Holly Bank Trust
Home-Start Runneymede
Juvenile Diabetes Research Foundation
Lovington C of E School
Lymphoma Association
Marie Curie Cancer
Meningitis Trust
NSPCC
Paul Bevan Hospice
Princes Trust

Riverside Arts Centre
Royal British Legion
RSPCA
Rushmoor Community Mediation Service
Scope
St Margaret Clitherow
St Stephens PCC
Starmaker Theatre Company
Surrey Border Lions Club
Thames Valley &
Chiltern Air Ambulance Trust
The Iain Rennie Hospice
The Knight Foundation
The Retired Grey Hound Trust
Twyford & District Round Table
UNESCO
Walk The Walk Worldwide
Watford New Hope Trust
Wildridings School Association
Woodley C of E Primary School
Woodley Saints FC

GMAC-RFC in the UK are proud to have been selected by an independent research team and panel of advisers as one of Britain's Top 91 Employers for 2005. They select companies that, through creativity and innovation, have managed to fashion a culture that embodies a pleasant working environment in which the employee is happy and productive.

16 www.gmacrfc.co.uk

Back page from our corporate, social, responsibility brochure

As you would expect from one of the world's largest financial services institutions, we take corporate governance very seriously. We have established the correct balance between accountability and risk management and the ability to innovate and take markets forward. This brochure explains how, through describing our various governance structures.

We also acknowledge that our business in the US and around the world survives and thrives due to a positive social responsibility, which is in accordance with our corporate values and operating principles. It is thus that GMAC-RFC is committed to donating a percentage of its after-tax profits to our local communities, and this brochure explains how we go about that in the UK.

In addition to our community involvement, we have also established the GMAC-RFC Foundation, which focuses on helping mortgage borrowers around the world avoid repossession.

In all markets, GMAC-RFC tries to make a difference. This not only applies to using our global experience to bring new capital solutions to advance the interests of consumers and participants in the markets that we enter. It also applies to our employees, our customers and the communities we serve.

I hope that this brochure will be a refreshing read about an organisation taking a different approach.

Stephen Knight,
Executive Chairman, GMAC-RFC UK

I am pleased to introduce our corporate social responsibility brochure, which will tell you a little bit about us, our corporate governance structure and our commitment to mortgage borrowers and the communities we serve.

02 www.gmacrfc.co.uk

138

Our company **GMAC RFC**

About us

GMAC-RFC is a wholly owned subsidiary of ResCap, one of the world's largest mortgage lenders, and an indirect subsidiary of GMAC Financial Services.

GMAC-RFC is the Group's focus for international mortgage expansion, operating as a significant mortgage lender in the UK, Canada, The Netherlands, Germany and Mexico, as well as its substantial US operation.

In the UK, GMAC-RFC markets "Mortgages for Everyone". This ranges from competitive mainstream loans, that often undercut high street lenders, through niche mortgage products such as self certification and Buy-to-Let, to the non-conforming sector where borrowers are given the opportunity to rehabilitate their financial circumstances.

In 2004, GMAC-RFC UK advanced approximately £6.3bn in mortgages, making the company the UK's 10th largest lender.

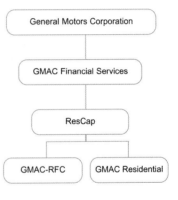

How we run our business

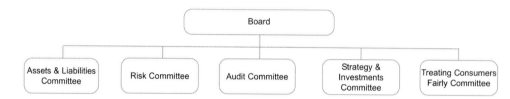

UK corporate governance

We are a responsible lender and manage our business with great emphasis on balancing accountability and risk with the ability to make a difference in all the markets in which we operate. There are five important committees advising the Board in this area.

Assets & Liabilities Committee.
Meets monthly to provide an oversight on behalf of the main Board to ensure that asset and liability positions are effectively monitored and managed. Chaired by the Capital Markets Director.

Risk Committee.
Meets monthly to provide an oversight on behalf of the main Board to ensure that risk throughout the Company is effectively monitored and managed. Chaired by the Director of Risk & Compliance.

Audit Committee.
Meets twice yearly to provide a formal and transparent arrangement to monitor financial reporting and internal controls. It also maintains an appropriate relationship with the Company's auditors to assist the main Board in fulfilling its oversight responsibilities, and to meet regulatory and good governance requirements. Chaired by the Chief Financial Officer for the International Business Group acting as a non executive director.

Strategy & Investments Committee.
Meets monthly to consider acquisitions, investments, joint ventures and similar transactions; to propose terms and make recommendations, as appropriate, to the Board for approval; to enter into negotiations in respect of approved transactions; and to monitor the performance of completed transactions. Chaired by the Managing Director, Strategy & Investments.

Treating Consumers Fairly Committee.
Meets monthly to drive and monitor TCF development and performance on behalf of the Board. Membership includes representation from all major parts of the business. Not only is TCF an important priority for our regulator, the Financial Services Authority, it also represents a fundamental ingredient of our corporate Vision, Values and Operating Principles. Chaired by the TCF business champion.

04 www.gmacrfc.co.uk

140

The day-to-day management of the company rests with the Executive Directors. Our Public Policy and Community Involvement initiatives are handled by two separate groups who report to the Executive.

The Board.
Meets quarterly and is responsible for the strategic direction and supervision of the Company and is chaired by the Executive Chairman.

Executive Directors.
Meet informally on a weekly basis and more formally on a quarterly basis, with the quarterly meetings including other members of senior management. These meetings are chaired by the Executive Chairman and are responsible for executing the Board's strategy in the running of the business.

Public Policy Committee.
Meets approximately six times per year and is responsible for liaison with the GMAC-RFC Foundation and for ensuring awareness of GMAC-RFC and its policies in the UK public policy arena. Chaired by the Executive Chairman.

Community Involvement Committee.
Meets monthly and is responsible for allocating the community involvement budget amongst the various charities and for supporting/promoting charitable employee activity. The Committee is chaired by the Director of Human Resources.

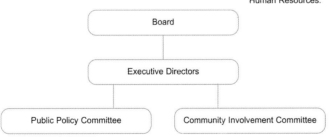

Community involvement

Following our hearts

Our underlying philosophy is to offer fresh innovative thinking in the way we work and live. Reaching out to the communities where we do business makes good sense to us and we are always looking for ways to improve quality of life for others.

With our parent we contributed $75 million last year to charitable causes around the world. Some of this money resulted from our policy of giving a percentage of our global net income back to local communities through our Community Involvement Programme. This focuses on sponsorships and grants for education, housing, health and human services needs. The remainder was raised by employees themselves who are encouraged to support causes dear to them. We follow their hearts by matching their personal contributions – and even their volunteer hours – with cash.

In the UK we have over 700 employees who can choose to get involved in eight keys ways, either through supporting our nominated charities or through a variety of corporate schemes. Other ways in which we're active include visiting local schools to helping with induction days and interview techniques, monthly "dress-down" days, through to recycling.

"Supporting the communities in which we live and work is part of our culture. We provide flexibility in how our employees make a difference, whether it's giving their time, talent or money. Further, we encourage employees to follow their hearts by nominating and supporting charities that are personally meaningful to them. Not only do we make a positive impact on the community, but our employees get further engaged by giving something back."

Chris Kujawa, Chair of the Community Involvement Committee and Director of Human Resources, GMAC-RFC UK

06 www.gmacrfc.co.uk

Making a difference:
to a deserving charity

"Your support has enabled us to achieve our dream of employing a children's worker in our new refuge; to champion good parenting and give traumatised children space in which to heal and grow. You have become an integral part of changing and enriching many lives and we are just so grateful."

Eleanor Pitts, Director of Berkshire Women's Aid

Charity of the year 05/06

Every year, we focus on a particular charity and are currently supporting Berkshire Women's Aid by raising funds in order that they can employ a children's worker. They are an organisation that supports the victims of domestic violence across Berkshire. Some of the ways in which they do this are by providing a 24-hour helpline, refuges and drop-in centres.

To find out more about the Berkshire Women's Aid, visit www.berkshirewomensaid.org.uk

Previous GMAC-RFC charities of the year are:

03/04 - The Almshouse Association
www.almshouses.org

04/05 - The Paul Bevan Hospice
www.paulbevan.org

www.gmacrfc.co.uk 07

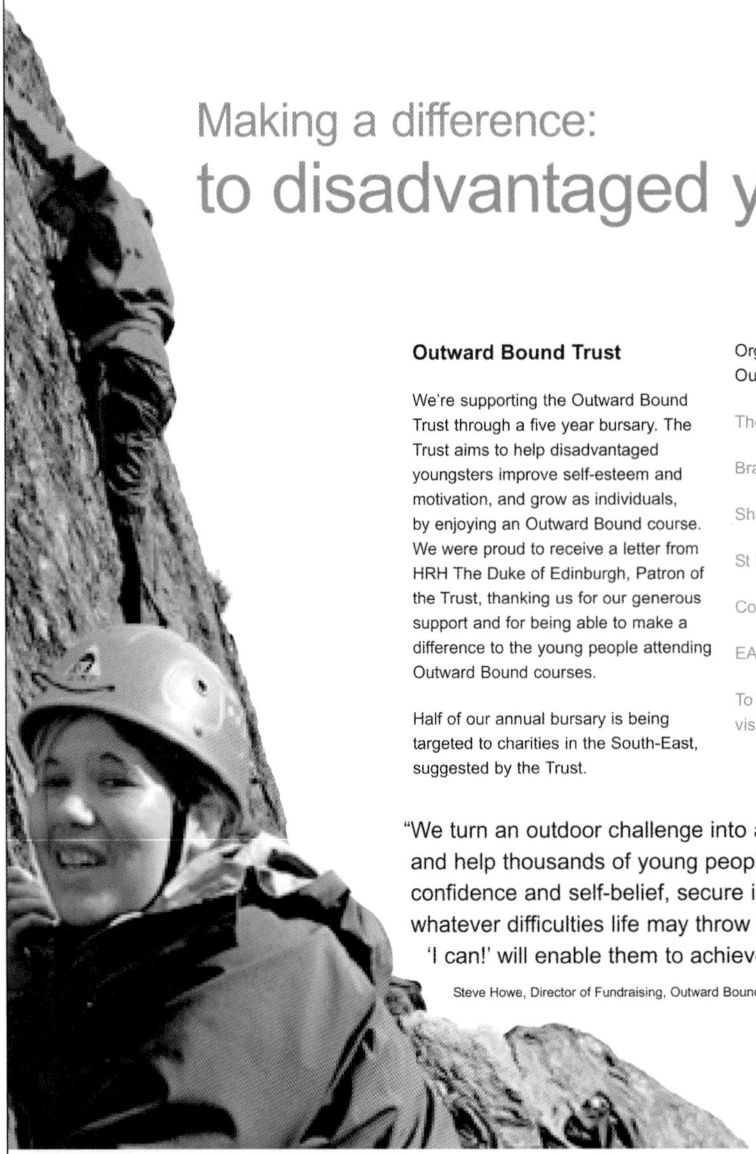

Making a difference:
to disadvantaged youngsters

Outward Bound Trust

We're supporting the Outward Bound Trust through a five year bursary. The Trust aims to help disadvantaged youngsters improve self-esteem and motivation, and grow as individuals, by enjoying an Outward Bound course. We were proud to receive a letter from HRH The Duke of Edinburgh, Patron of the Trust, thanking us for our generous support and for being able to make a difference to the young people attending Outward Bound courses.

Half of our annual bursary is being targeted to charities in the South-East, suggested by the Trust.

Organisations previously sponsored by Outward Bound are:

The Wayz

Bracknell Forest Youth Service

Shelter H2H

St Michael's R.C School

Council for Homeless Young People

EASY Project

To find out more about the Trust, visit www.outwardbound-uk.org

"We turn an outdoor challenge into a life changing experience, and help thousands of young people to face the future with confidence and self-belief, secure in the knowledge that whatever difficulties life may throw at them, the belief that 'I can!' will enable them to achieve their dreams."

Steve Howe, Director of Fundraising, Outward Bound Trust

"When we were building the house I brought my daughters over here when I didn't have to work. I showed them what rooms they were going to have and they were more excited than I was. They're still enjoying it. I told them, after they get older, it's something they're going to have one day. Now they see that I'm maintaining and keeping the bills up and they'll know how to maintain a home."

Freddie Lawton, Savannah, Georgia. Habitat for Humanity beneficiary.

Habitat for Humanity

More than two billion people around the world live in slum housing. Habitat for Humanity is an international charity dedicated to building affordable housing for low-income families throughout the world. To date, they've built over 200,000 properties in 100 countries. Habitat relies on volunteers working together and GMAC-RFC became an official partner in 2003, building houses in the US, Canada, India and Mexico.

Volunteers commit to a full day's work and could be involved in any aspect of the property build, from the foundations to the roof. They're not expected to take the time as holiday and will receive their usual pay.

To find out more about the charity, visit www.habitatforhumanity.org.uk

Making a difference:
through building
affordable housing

GMAC-RFC employees at a recent build

www.gmacrfc.co.uk 09

145

Making a difference: through the little things that count

Match Funding

We match any funds donated to a registered charity – either through sponsorship or personal donation – up to £2000 per employee per year. It can be a national cause or a local playgroup.

In the past year, employees have raised substantial sums for Scope by trekking up Mount Olympus; for Surrey Border Lions Club through a pram race; for St. Margaret Clitherow school through a stall at a Christmas fair; for the Lovington C of E School through an auction of promises and for the British Heart Foundation by running the London Marathon.

"I cycled 350km in India for the charity International Childcare Trust. I try and do something each year for charity, as I feel children should be given the best chance to succeed whatever their backgrounds, and for GMAC-RFC to double donations, makes this all the more possible."

Wesley Budd, Marketing Communications Coordinator, GMAC-RFC

"I'm passionate about helping dogs that have been rescued following abuse and that's why I give a monthly donation to The Dogs Trust. With GMAC-RFC matching my monthly donations I feel like me doing "my little bit" is doing a little bit more!"

Jill Flower, HR Co-ordinator, GMAC-RFC

"Thank you for your kind donation in matching the funds raised by one of your employees. This was not only a lovely surprise, but has allowed us to begin putting plans into place for the much needed refurbishment of one of our school classrooms."

Bisley C of E Primary School

10 www.gmacrfc.co.uk

Summer School at Starmaker Theatre
Company 2004

Return on Involvement

Any employee who makes an exceptional contribution to the community through volunteer work can be nominated for our half-yearly Return on Involvement award. This is an international award and the successful employee receives a plaque and a corporate donation of £3,000 for their registered charity.

In 2004, we were proud to have two employees chosen from the UK, as recipients of this award. One of them was Michelle Palin, in our Learning and Development department, who is the Membership Secretary of the charity Starmaker Theatre Company in Reading. This charity provides training and guidance to young people in all aspects of theatre and the performing arts.

"I have been involved with Starmaker for over 17 years and currently give 35 hours of my time a week to them. I look after the membership, run the website, organise all social events and even do sound and lighting for the productions. I get a huge amount of personal satisfaction from the work, especially seeing 100 children doing something positive with their spare time."

Michelle Palin, Trainer GMAC-RFC

Making a difference: by going one step further

Making a difference: through applying for a grant

Volunteer Match Programme

An employee who has a working relationship and volunteers at a registered charity, can apply for a grant on behalf of that charity. Grants range from £320 to £2,240, depending on the number of volunteer hours.

Lynn Cobb, Completions Assistant, successfully applied for a grant for the Rushmoor Community Mediation Service, which helps those in dispute with their neighbours try to resolve their problems. Common problems include noise, parking, property, children and pets. Lynn gives about twenty hours of voluntary work per month, which is almost 240 hours per year.

"Coming from an area where neighbours were constantly at each other's throats, I strongly believe that people should be encouraged and helped to live happily with each other. This is something I want to do and it makes me feel I'm giving something back to the community I'm living in. It's such a pleasure to see people settle their differences amicably instead of taking matters to the court."

Lynn Cobb, Completions Assistant, GMAC-RFC

12 www.gmacrfc.co.uk

148

Share the Magic

Share the Magic is a global scheme which runs over two weeks in the second half of the year. During this time, the company will match annual donations made through employees' bank accounts and/or one-off donations outside of the annual Match Funding allowance.

In addition, we prepare containers of sweets with the Share the Magic logo and sell them. The money raised in the UK goes to our Charity of the Year. People buy the sweets to give to someone who they think has done a good job during the year, whether in the UK or in one of our other international offices, making this a truly global event. Blank labels on the containers mean people can write messages to thank people such as:

"Thank you for being understanding and for your support during the difficult times last year"

"Thank you from the other side of the Atlantic for organising my trip to your offices"

"Thanks for all the lifts into work"

"Your help on the project ensured its success. Thank you"

Making a difference: **by**
showing appreciation
of others

Gift of Time

During the first quarter of each year, employees are invited to volunteer three – or more – hours of their own time to a charity of their choice. In return, we donate £100. We believe that volunteering in the community highlights the need to give to others.

For example, employees have helped the Friends of Clitheroe Community Hospital by visiting patients, cleaning out kennels for the RSPCA, working in a local cancer charity shop and sorting out the accounts for a Bolton hospital.

"Working at a centre for homeless people made me appreciate that becoming homeless can happen to anyone. I covered shifts on Christmas and New Year's Eve and felt like I was doing something a bit special at a difficult time of year."

Jo Broccolo, Regional Sales Executive, GMAC-RFC

Making a difference: by giving three hours of our time

"I agreed to donate three hours of my time to the RSPCA as I already donate money each month to this charity and wanted to do more for a centre in my local area. I enjoyed my time there although I did realise that cleaning out kennels could not be a new career direction for me!"

Helen Malone, Underwriter, GMAC-RFC

"We are deeply concerned that the recent rise in interest rates may cause problems for people who have already borrowed heavily. In many cases, only a small increase in mortgage payments could turn manageable credit to unmanageable debt. Free and impartial advice is the most important thing we can give those who run into financial difficulties. By funding the Citizen's Advice Bureau Specialist Support Unit, GMAC-RFC is really helping people to avoid the devastating effect of serious debt."

David Harker, CEO of Citizen's Advice Bureau

GMAC-RFC Foundation

We believe that we are the only lender in the world to have established a Foundation specifically and solely aimed at preventing mortgage repossessions for all borrowers, not just ours.

The GMAC-RFC Foundation was established in 2003 with very substantial initial funding. Its main purpose is to reduce the amount of borrowers who get repossessed by working with partners whose role is to assist borrowers in financial need.

Although operated out of the US, the Foundation seeks globally to assist borrowers. In the UK, the Foundation has donated a substantial sum to Citizen's Advice Bureau to support better debt counselling and assistance in the UK.

The Foundation looks to help all mortgage borrowers and not just customers of GMAC-RFC and its funding activity is in addition to the localised community involvement.

Making a difference: by going the extra mile

Also in 2003 GMAC-RFC had formed its worldwide charitable foundation - the first of its type to focus on one objective only, namely to prevent borrowers from being repossessed. The GMAC-RFC Foundation is separate from, and additional to, normal CSR work and charitable giving.

It makes donations around the world to organisations who have a clear line of sight between their work and preventing borrowers from being repossessed, whoever their lender may be. In the UK, we secured the first ever contribution made by the Foundation following its formation - a significant cash sum to the UK Citizens' Advice Bureaux to fund debt counsellors to whom members of the public can turn for free advice when faced with debt or repossession problems.

The CSR work continues, and we look for new ways to expand it. The point of mentioning CSR is not to claim any high moral ground for GMAC-RFC. We no doubt do more than some, and less than others, in contributing to charities and communities. The point in mentioning it is because, these days, if you are planning a strategy for growth then you must also have plans to phase in increasing CSR and public policy work, because those are requirements for membership of the bigger players' club.

Wrap-up

Size and market position will often determine the extent to which you are above the public radar. As the UK's 10th largest lender, we assume that we will be noticed from time to time. We therefore seek to influence the backcloth against which that visibility takes place and to see if we can, in some small way, affect the outcome of policy for the greater good.

In so doing we can hopefully improve our marketplace by contributing research, other special initiatives and responses to consultation papers. At the same time we wish to demonstrate the highest standards of corporate social responsibility to all our audiences. The way the market currently operates, these are minimum standards for a major lender.

| 1 | 2 | 3 | 4 | 5 | **6** | 7 | 8 |

PRIVATE LABEL: THE FINAL YEARS

A brief history

Most people who read this book will have heard of Private Label. Some may even have read my previous book, covering its history from launch to 1997, from where this chapter picks up. For those who have never heard of the company, however, here is the briefest of histories.

I launched Private Label in 1987 as the UK's first "packager" (although that description had not been invented then). In 1988 B&C had made an unrefusable offer and purchased Private Label from me.

B&C was acquiring a portfolio of financial services businesses and had already bought John Charcol, MSL (now part of HML) and many others. Unfortunately, B&C then suffered difficulty in an unrelated area so, in 1989, mortgage broker firm John Charcol and Private Label extricated themselves from B&C and formed Mortgage Group Holdings. Both companies then became wholly-owned subsidiaries of MGH.

MGH and its subsidiaries prospered for the eight years through to 1997. I was a director of John Charcol, and John Garfield (one of the founders of John Charcol) was a director of Private Label. All was going well until the lead up to Private Label's 10th anniversary party on 17 October 1997, which is where the story now picks up.

1997

■ Buying it Back

Just before the party, John Garfield had told me confidentially that he wanted to sell his business and retire. Given that I was not ready to retire, and had more plans for Private Label, it became increasingly clear that I would have to buy the business back again.

Due to having earned and exercised performance-related share options, in addition to the shares I had received following the B&C transaction, I was now the equal largest shareholder in MGH, alongside John Charcol founders John Garfield and Charles Wishart. If the numbers being discussed as a possible sale price for John Charcol were ever realised then a share swap, by which I gave up my shares in MGH in return for re-acquiring Private Label, seemed achievable.

Some, on the inside of this transaction, having reviewed the amount for which I subsequently sold Private Label for a third and final time approximately one year later, felt that I had got the better of that deal. When I look at the price at which John Charcol subsequently changed hands twice in the next few years, however, I think the deal was about right.

We completed the buy-back on 9 December 1997. It was relatively painless. I resigned my directorships of all MGH companies, including John Charcol. MGH representatives resigned from the Private Label board.

We had, of course, to find a public positioning for the split. John Charcol was not yet ready to offer itself for sale and wished to inform the market it was up for sale,

An emerging conflict of interest has led John Charcol, the mortgage adviser, and Private Label, the mortgage wholesaler, to part company. **Jason Mitchell** reports

John Charcol splits from Private Label

JOHN Charcol, the mortgage adviser, and Private Label, the mortgage wholesaler, are to become separate companies after a nine-year alliance.

The amicable break-up has been agreed by both companies and has been achieved through a share swap. The businesses felt a conflict of interest was beginning to emerge.

Mr Stephen Knight, Private Label's chairman, and other senior management at the mortgage wholesaler have given up their stakes in John Charcol.

In return, Mr John Garfield, John Charcol's chairman, and its top management have transferred their shares in Private Label.

Mr Knight will become the largest shareholder in a new company called Private Label Group. Mr Garfield will have a large stake in Mortgage Group Holdings, made up mainly of John Charcol. Both men will remain on each other's boards as non-executive directors.

Mr Garfield said: "Private Label's new leads-generation service for IFAs and Independent Mortgage Collection means that it is becoming more involved in the retail side. We felt there was the potential for a future conflict of interest."

John Charcol, founded in 1974, has ten UK branches and plans to open a further 15 during 1998.

Mr Knight said: "The companies came together to achieve a critical mass; but each of the companies is now able to achieve that in its own right."

Stephen Knight: new opportunities

Financal Adviser. 18 December 1997

when it was ready. So we decided to say that the split was down to Private Label moving closer to retail (with its new lead generation proposition) and John Charcol moving closer to wholesale (with its increased product design and packaging activities).

This positioning was accurate. It had cropped up as an issue during our discussions with an investment bank during the summer as being one reason why full value for both MGH subsidiaries would be more easily achieved by being separate. It was not the main reason for splitting: the main reason was John's wish to sell. But it was certainly a factor. We did not lie: we just put forward the secondary reason.

So, as I went into the Christmas 1997 break, I owned the company again. At 10 years old, this was not the fledgling business it had been when I sold it first in 1988. As the 1997 accounts revealed, turnover was almost £8m for that year, with pre tax profit at £1.1m. The year 1998 would definitely be exciting, and different.

1998

■ Early challenges

A key priority for the new year was to secure the continuing commitment of the senior management team. Godfrey Blight and Simon Knight already had shareholdings in MGH, for which they had personally subscribed. These shares were converted at the time of the buy-back into equity holdings within the newly-formed Private Label Group.

We then put in place a share option scheme for Godfrey, Simon and Barry Searle (who joined the PLG board on 1 January 1998) so that they could acquire additional shares and thereby benefit from any future sale of the company. We were not at that time contemplating a sale, and would certainly not have predicted that, by the end of the year, we would be in new ownership once again. We were at that time just establishing the foundations for further growth.

The key to maximising both our growth prospects, and the value of our company, (or so we thought at the time) was diversity. This is why we had established a lead generation company in 1997, called IMC. This was the "move closer to retail" mentioned at the time of the buy-back out of MGH. The launch and subsequent closure of this lead-generation business is a story on its own, which I cover later in this chapter.

The biggest issue on our minds in early 1998 was the move by some lenders to have mainstream and niche lending undertaken by separate companies. Private Label had always covered both areas under one roof, but its main focus was on mainstream products. So this was a serious development.

The first lender to move in this direction was Britannia Building Society, who had been the largest lender on our panel by volume of business generated for some years. Britannia announced that it would in future only make mainstream products available via its branches, without any accompanying procuration fee to brokers or packagers. The thinking behind the Britannia move was to separate the mutual side of its business from the rest. Intermediary-sourced customers were to be differentiated and would not benefit from mutuality. As a mutual, of course, Britannia was effectively owned by its members. The non-mutual businesses were to be run in a way that contributed profit to the mutual side. The reality for us was that, no sooner had the ink dried on our buy back, our biggest lender withdrew from our biggest market.

To cater for intermediary business, Britannia was launching a new subsidiary, called Verso. Our main contact at Britannia, Ian Jeffery, was transferring over to Verso, and Ian knew what we would need to make this move palatable to us - an eye-catching exclusive product.

The Verso launch product we agreed with Ian had never, at least to my knowledge, been offered before. It was effectively six products in one,

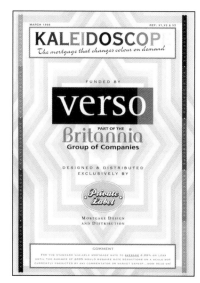

which is why we called it *KALEIDOSCOPE, the mortgage that changes colour on demand.* As our multi-colour launch brochure explained, the base deal was a seven year fixed rate at 6.99%, which in 1998 was pretty competitive.

By adding various rate differentials, however, the product could be turned into a high income multiple option, a self certification deal, a 100% product or an any

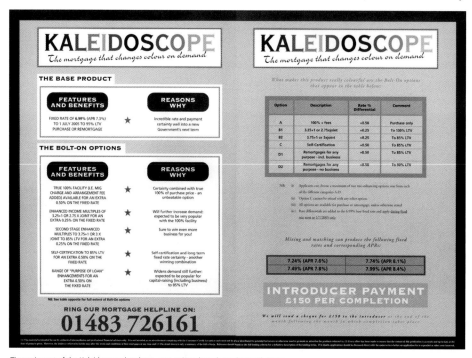

The main part of the Kaleidoscope brochure - our unique launch product with Verso

purpose remortgage - all niche areas in their own right where *Kaleidoscope* would really score. Instead of separate products to address each niche, we presented it as one multi-purpose product.

It seems strange now, in today's highly competitive market, for any purpose remortgages, self certification or high income multiples to sell at a significantly higher price to reflect their niche value. But at the time there was not nearly so much supply around for this type of product, and no equivalent deal available in the market at the time that offered all these options under one product umbrella.

We had understandably been nervous when our largest lender said that it would be offering its cutting edge mainstream deals via its branches only. We were right to be nervous, for, as it turned out, it was the beginning of the end for the Private Label model, albeit three years later.

But the innovative Kaleidoscope product certainly delayed any adverse impact on our volumes. It took off from day one. People liked the options, all based around a long term fixed rate. Hundreds of millions of pounds worth of business were generated under this product.

■ Bradford & Bingley follow suit

Shortly afterwards, Bradford & Bingley did the same thing. It's a trend that has now become well established. Bradford & Bingley had always been a solid performer on our panel. Never the top lender, but always in the £100m - £300m per annum completions range, with an interesting selection of mainstream products.

One such was The Destiny Fix which we had launched as our 10th anniversary celebratory product at the end of 1997, featuring a two year fix followed by a selection of discount and cashback choices. What was good about our lender panel at the time was that, if one lender was unable to fund a particularly esoteric product design that we wanted, it was probable that another lender would.

However, like Britannia, Bradford & Bingley was determined that its packager and intermediary relationships would be managed by a different subsidiary (in its case Mortgage Express), again concentrating mainly on higher margin niche products. As with Britannia, however, Bradford & Bingley had been loyal to us in spelling out its plans and working with us to achieve some exclusive launch products for the new arrangement.

A&L signs distribution deal with Private Label

By Sophie Tullis

Alliance & Leicester is moving into third-party distribution for the first time in a deal with Private Label which it expects to bring in £100m in new business.

The bank says it wants to expand distribution in the face of a flat mortgage market.

Alliance & Leicester director of sales Stephen Jones says: "We have gained market share and we want to look at how we can sustain that growth. When the market is static or in decline you have got to fish in more ponds."

Alliance & Leicester is the first lender Private Label has signed for two years. The last to join was Halifax Mortgage Services Limited in June 1996.

Private Label has been looking for a mainstream lender to replace Britannia Building Society since the society became a niche lender after launching Verso.

Private Label executive chairman Stephen Knight says: "Britannia was a very significant lender and moved into the niches. Bradford & Bingley stepped in but we felt we needed to add to the mainstream. We wanted to replace Britannia in the mainstream although we still do good business with Verso."

A&L is not ruling out other distribution deals with packagers. Unlike other mortgage banks, Alliance & Leicester managed a 20 per cent increase in net lending for the first six months of this year.

Private Label expects to do £100m in completions with Alliance & Leicester as a result of the deal.

Money Marketing. 3 September 1998

The final version of the record-breaking £1bn produce that dominated our volumes over several years

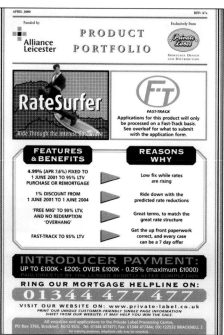

Our best Alliance & Leicester product

In the case of Mortgage Express, the main business generator was in the buy-to-let market - something that we had actually been slow to move into. But we quickly caught up, with a range of new products funded by Mortgage Express.

■ Alliance & Leicester is launched

We mitigated this reduction in our mainstream funding capacity by launching products during 1998 with Alliance & Leicester. Our negotiations with this lender had been going on for many months, mainly because they would not sign our normal funding contract and asked for a bespoke version to be agreed. In this, we were appointed A&L's agent - something that our other lenders had specifically excluded from their contract terms. We used this status responsibly and no issues arose.

We offered a series of competitive products with Alliance & Leicester, none more so than Ratesurfer. Although it came chronologically a little later in the relationship, it was a fix followed by a discount designed to "ride through the interest rate wave", and we had a lot of fun with the graphics and Hawaii 5-0 musical introduction to this product at one of our sales conferences.

■ HMSL becomes number one

The change of direction by Britannia and Bradford & Bingley left the field open for HMSL to dominate our mainstream volumes, even though Alliance & Leicester had just launched with us. Born out of the purchase by Halifax plc of the UK lending arm of BNP (affectionately referred to in Yorkshire as "Bank Near Pontefract", but actually standing for "Banque Nationale de Paris"), HMSL had hitherto been offering us only one mainstream product.

It was a product, though, that had been defying gravity. Today, when mortgage products have a shelf life of a matter of weeks, this particular deal, in its original and successor guises, stayed in our range for four years and generated in excess of £1bn of business. The Mortgage of the Century, as it was called, consisted of a 2% discount for three years with two cashbacks, one at the front, and one a few years' in. We marketed the product on the basis of a 10% total giveaway based on a £50,000 loan, and the total package was considered of far greater benefit than the five years of redemption penalties which underpinned it.

Mortgage of the Century was replaced by Mortgage of a Lifetime with slightly adjusted benefits. That product, in turn, was replaced by Mortgage of the Moment. Each successor product reflected minor tweaks designed to refresh and update the deal. Never before or since has one product generated so much business for so long via a third party organisation like Private Label. Truly a marketing phenomenon.

■ Three market approach

So far as 1998 was concerned, therefore, the moves by Britannia and Bradford & Bingley had been net beneficial. The mainstream business had simply passed to HMSL and Alliance & Leicester, while Verso and Mortgage Express - effectively new lenders to our panel - had allowed us to more aggressively attack the niche self cert, buy-to-let and 100% sectors of the market.

At the same time, the fact that we had exclusively launched Kensington Mortgage Company into the sub prime sector in 1995 had given us a certain amount of "first mover" advantage for that type of business, even three years later. Brokers continued to seek us out on Kensington cases even though they could by then use other routes, because they associated us with having been an integral part of Kensington's launch.

Kensington had chosen us to exclusively launch them into the UK because we could help them with product design and in breaking down distribution barriers. There were still some insurance companies and large brokers, for example, who refused to consider non-conforming products.

At the design stage for the first Kensington launch range we had asked for terms such as very high commissions, discretionary rates and rule of 78 redemption calculations (where the redemption charge is largely fixed, and related to the initial loan) to be avoided. We wanted an upmarket feel to the product range, which fortunately aligned with Kensington's approach. We had therefore, I guess, played a part in shaping the sub prime market as it is today.

It was no surprise that 1998 turned out to be a record year for volumes, thanks to our assault on these three different product sectors.

■ The Mortgage Code

Business in 1998 was also greatly influenced by the market adopting self regulation, for the first time bringing new rules and codes of conduct. The new Mortgage Code itself had been introduced in 1997 by the CML.

I always thought that it was an excellent initiative, flexible enough to react quickly to unforeseen circumstances, but authoritative enough to ensure compliance by the majority. In the end, of course, all it did was pave the way for statutory regulation, although it did set up a register of intermediaries and introduced many of the disciplines now required under the Financial Services and Markets Act.

Under the first phase of the Mortgage Code, only lenders were covered. In 1998 intermediaries were to be added. I was part of a CML working group chaired by Colin Harris which was attempting to come up with some recommendations that would allow the CML Executive to determine the final rules. It was certainly an interesting process.

A couple of debating points in our working group warrant a mention - disclosure of earnings and packagers. Not much has changed all these years later.

Many brokers were upset about having to disclose the fees that they received from lenders. Others were ambivalent, claiming that it had not caused any significant problems when disclosure was introduced for investment products. Connected to the emotion of this debate was the role of packagers. If brokers had to disclose their earnings then why, so it was argued, should not packagers similarly disclose?

The problem was that the Mortgage Code was introduced to regulate lenders and intermediaries (the latter defined as those who advise customers). Where organisations were both intermediaries and packagers, that was awkward but definable nonetheless.

Since we were unable in our working group to devise a satisfactory way of separating the two sides of such a business, we concluded that these organisations should be considered intermediaries first and foremost, and disclose everything. Where organisations were stand alone packagers, however, acting for lenders and coming into no contact with customers during the advice process, the position was different.

The Mortgage Code specifically excluded such organisations. Lenders use all kinds of outsourcing companies including call centres, product design and marketing consultants, and third party administration companies.

If they choose to use the services of a packaging company that typically offers all three types of service in one, that does not change the logic. Requiring lenders to disclose the contents of confidential outsourcing agreements could be anti-competitive, since it might standardise such payments and prevent healthy competition.

If a lender chose to outsource such services rather than pay for them in-house, this was a commercial decision that was of no interest to the customer. Certainly, so far as Private Label's products were concerned, there was no suggestion that the share of earnings passed by lenders to Private Label resulted in a less competitive customer rate. Indeed, the reverse was often true. Thwarted by the logic of this line of argument, those emotionally in favour of packager fee disclosure then started talking about "influence". By talking to an intermediary about a particular lender's product, the packager was "influencing" the advice that the intermediary subsequently gave to the customer.

This line was taken up by several trade newspapers until I pointed out some of the marketing material we were receiving from their advertising departments, which claimed "influence" if their particular publication was selected for an advertisement! Did they fancy disclosing to all new advertisers the rates they had offered to previous advertisers? I didn't think so.

The reality is, of course, that influence is not capable of being regulated, neither was there any intention within the Mortgage Code to cover the interaction between an unregulated outsourcing firm and a mortgage lender. It was and is quite clear that mortgage intermediaries can take into account any influences to which they choose to subject themselves when preparing client advice, so long as they take full responsibility for the subsequent advice given.

To help this debate along, I commissioned a written opinion from a leading City firm of solicitors on a number of aspects relating to the Mortgage Code, but particularly earnings disclosure. What basis in law would there be to apply the Mortgage Code to organisations who were neither lenders nor customer-interfacing intermediaries?

The advice was that any such extension of the Mortgage Code to cover outsourcing firms, in particular requiring such firms to disclose the contents of confidential contracts, could be anti-competitive and challengeable. I shared this legal advice with the CML and do not know the extent to which it influenced the outcome. But when the rules were eventually published, they were in line with the points of view I had put forward within the committee.

Although I felt the situation was quite clear, it turned out subsequently that some lenders were turning a blind eye to the non-disclosure of packaging fees by organisations who were both regulated intermediaries and packagers. At the same time, packagers were being regularly asked by some lenders to obtain a Mortgage Code intermediary reference number even though they were not intermediaries as defined by the Code.

The subsequent use of these reference numbers as "umbrellas" for cases introduced by various different types of intermediary, including those who had not registered under the Mortgage Code, plus the general confusion which reigned over broker-packagers was, I fear, one of the background reasons why it was felt that the Mortgage Code had to be replaced by statutory regulation.

But there we are. The Code still did a great job in many respects, and it was a good experience to work on it with colleagues from around the industry.

■ Mortgage Code implications for Private Label

My work on this committee was separate to my day job. Nonetheless, I felt that there were two specific implications for Private Label. The most important related to fee disclosure.

As I debated this whole area time and again during the committee work, I conceded that the practice of packagers collecting a gross payment from the lender, and subsequently splitting it out (largely on a discretionary basis) between its own earnings and the payment to be made to the intermediary, had the potential to cloud the debate. As the leading organisation of its type, I wanted Private Label to set a precedent by introducing clarity.

We therefore said to our lenders that we wished to no longer handle intermediary procuration fees. These should instead be paid directly by the lender to the intermediary whom we had identified on our submission sheet.

We would invoice the lender separately for our share of the mortgage-related earnings. In this way, we would get separation between the fee that was paid to the regulated intermediary, and the earnings that came to Private Label for the provision of outsourced services. The disclosure debate would go away, for us at least, and there would be transparency about the fee received by the customer-advising intermediary.

We presented this proposition to HM Customs & Excise and received a ruling that, so long as the application was introduced to the lender by us (irrespective of whether there was an intermediary in-between us and the customer), and so long as our earnings were represented by a share of the non-VATable mortgage fees, commissions and interest rate, then our fee did not attract VAT. Armed with that written ruling we persuaded our lenders to introduce this service, and I was surprised that many similar organisations did not follow suit, although this practice started to be introduced more widely some years later.

The VAT rules on outsourced services are under review again as this book goes to press, so maybe we would not have got that ruling today. What we can say is that our concerns over a possible loss of profile with intermediaries when the lender was paying them instead of us were unfounded. The intermediaries continued to focus on us as the product deliverer: the mechanism by which they got paid proved to be just that. Today, with the new Mortgage Conduct of Business rules making it very

Private Label made sole packager on DBS panel

Knight: 'The best advice'

By Sophie Tullis

DBS is warning its members to be wary of mortgage packagers when the Council of Mortgage Lenders' code of practice for intermediaries comes into effect in May.

The advice follows a review of its best-buy mortgage panel, including the appointment of Private Label as the only packager on the panel.

DBS expects to increase the amount of mortgage business going through its panel to 85 per cent from 73 per cent over the next year, as a result of the review.

According to DBS, it is appointing Private Label because it offers added value to members and is the only independent packager which has signed up to the CML code.

DBS Mortgage Services commercial director Colin Preston says: "We are hoping our IFAs will re-examine their relationships with packagers in light of the code.

"Some packagers perhaps offer higher fees to IFAs at the expense of the product but others are wonderful because they present added value."

The move follows DBS's decision to take responsibility for members' compliance by registering them for the voluntary code under the DBS banner rather than individually.

The network is investing over £1m in becoming code-compliant. It is holding over 40 meetings for members in February to talk to them about the code and how to register.

Private Label chairman Stephen Knight claims: "DBS wanted to ensure the best possible advice is given. Our products were unavoidable."

Preston says: "Private Label has a 10-year track record of designing market-leading products and being the only company of its type to be a full member of the Council of Mortgage Lenders."

Money Marketing. 5 February 1998

systems-intensive to differentiate on Key Facts Illustrations between payments to packagers and payments to their brokers, the majority of lenders are disclosing the gross amount paid away on all cases. Full circle then.

The other implication of the Mortgage Code that particularly affected Private Label was our membership of the CML. I was actually at dinner with Mark Boléat, then the Director-General of the BSA, when he first started to talk about the formation of a new trade body called the Council of Mortgage Lenders.

The idea was that the interests of the mutual building societies on the one hand, and of the banks and converted societies on the other, were diverging and needed two different trade associations. I felt that this was probably right and expressed my support. I said that as Private Label was doing the job of the lender when interfacing with intermediaries in relation to our exclusive products, we would want if possible to become a full member of the CML from the outset.

The CML was duly formed and we did become a member - one of the first in fact. We paid our subscriptions based on the total lending we were generating, just like any lender-member. It was open to competitor organisations to follow suit. Nobody did. They might have succeeded in an application for full CML membership had they wanted to pay the subscription and play a full part in the CML's work on behalf of the lending industry, as we did. But only HML, the third party administrator, followed our lead. Our packager competitors kept their hands firmly in their pockets. This situation happily continued for some years, with Private Label as one of only two non-lender, full members of the CML, until a storm blew up, publicity-wise. DBS, then the largest intermediary network, said that it

Packagers hit out at CML ban

Mortgage packagers are accusing the Council of Mortgage Lenders of double standards over its decision to bar them from membership.

The CML decided two weeks ago to only allow lenders to join in future despite already having packager Private Label and a number of other non-lenders on board.

The CML decision is sensitive because packagers are worried it will give members a competitive advantage as it is perceived to give an added stamp of respectability. The CML is offering associate membership to non-lenders.

Mortgage Next managing director Martin Maynard says: "I am surprised. How can they exclude non-lenders and retain Private Label? This is one rule for one and another rule for the rest. I don't understand how they can justify that position."

CML director general Michael Coogan says: "It is a policy decision that existing non-lender members can stay. It is equally unfair for those who have been in the CML to have their membership revoked.

"There is clearly different treatment and we are going to be talking through the implications with the institutions involved."

Others to be barred from CML membership include life offices and estate agents.

Money Marketing. 9 April 1998

was appointing Private Label to its panel of mortgage suppliers and had taken into account in reaching that decision that we were a full member of the CML. All hell broke loose. Many of our competitors then demanded that the CML either make them full members or remove Private Label.

The CML were in a difficult position. They had moved on and were now representing 98% of the lending industry's assets. They had won awards for trade body expertise and had clarified in their rulebook as to who could or could not become members. Our competitors no longer had the option to become full members, although they could become associate members at a reduced subscription.

The CML had decided not to apply this rule change retrospectively to Private Label and HML. As we had always paid our subscriptions based on the full amount of our lending, and had played an active role in supporting the CML, such a move would not have been justified.

The CML did ask us to ensure that our membership was not used in a promotional sense, with which we were happy to comply. Of course, the problem then died down and nobody referred to it again. Principle always becomes an issue when profit is threatened.

■ Blood in the water from the John Charcol sale

Once the Private Label buy-back had gone through, John Charcol had set about preparing itself for sale. As the UK's then highest profile independent mortgage broker, the company naturally attracted a lot of suitors. I believe I am right in saying that over 40 information memoranda were issued to interested parties by KPMG, acting on behalf of John Charcol which, if it is true, is an extraordinary number. I had also heard that the bids from the lowest to the highest were more than £20m apart.

Eventually, there could of course be only one winner. This turned out to be Warburg Pincus, who acquired 75% of John Charcol for a significant cash sum. My old friend, John Garfield retired to Ibiza, where he largely stayed for seven years until he reappeared recently to buy John Charcol back. But that is another story, and his to tell.

As a result of the John Charcol sale, there were many potential buyers who had returned home empty-handed. We therefore started to get calls. Until then, I had not focused on the fact that we were, following the sale of John Charcol, the UK's largest independently-owned distributor of mortgages.

Despite our initial "not for sale" reaction, the enquiries kept coming. Eventually, I sat down with Godfrey, Simon and Barry to talk about the future. Although we had not re-purchased the business to immediately sell it again, it is true that we were facing what we regarded as a glass ceiling on our future progress.

Third party companies like ours are only as good as the weakest lender on the panel. You can go into a broker with the best sales techniques, and sell the best product in the market from lender A. But if, last week, lender B - totally unconnected with lender A - had given poor service via your company then the broker will very often not listen to the new sales pitch. No sooner would we get one lender's administration up to date than another would fall over. We had been trying very hard to persuade our lenders to rely more on credit scoring, and less on old-fashioned paper reference-gathering, but progress was painfully slow.

We could break this cycle if only we could take the loan to completion ourselves, controlling every aspect. If we could then sell on the loans to the market post completion, we thought that there was unlimited future potential for this model.

Coupled with the move away from mainstream lending that Britannia and Bradford & Bingley had started, which we believed others would follow, I remember well a lunch at the Savoy involving Godfrey, Simon, Barry and myself at which we agreed the terms on which we might be prepared to sell our business to a lender willing to give us this power. We also agreed our minimum price, and the fact that we would all continue to stick together as a team.

■ GMAC-RFC comes calling

Then the dinner with Bruce Paradis took place that I mentioned in chapter 1. There was no talk of acquisitions or investments over this dinner. As far as I was concerned, it was just a general strategic discussion. Nothing more was heard from GMAC-RFC for a month or so afterwards until a group of their senior people in the UK, led by the then Europe Chairman, Chris Nordeen, wanted to come and meet us to talk about joining our lender panel.

Again, the conversation did not cover acquiring our business. We talked about what it would take for GMAC-RFC to be appointed to our lender panel. It was true that we had been considering the appointment of a second sub prime lender to complement Kensington and had had false starts with The Money Store and SPML.

We invited GMAC-RFC to match the terms then being offered to us by Kensington. This stalled the negotiations a bit because we had an interesting remuneration structure with Kensington, including payment for abortive work. Eventually, and reluctantly, GMAC-RFC agreed to match this.

Then the question of acquiring Private Label was raised. There seemed to be a fit in terms of business style, model and values between the two companies. I therefore met with Godfrey, Simon and Barry once again.

We agreed that, notwithstanding the attraction of GMAC-RFC, we should not sell to the first bidder. Instead, we should obtain the right advice, prepare an Information Memorandum and have a proper sales process. If we could get more control of the lending up to and including completion, positioning us as a lender, and selling completed assets rather than the pre-offer packages, then this could be an exciting new chapter for us.

We asked several of the established players in the M&A world if they would act for us in the sale, but I could not accept their fee structures. A seven figure commission for selling my tiny company? I could not relate to it.

Instead, I asked my solicitor, Peter Smith of CMS Cameron McKenna, if he could recommend anybody. He could, and we engaged the services of John Herring, who was at that time running a small advisory business. John had acquired his M&A experience at Kleinwort Benson and had done such a good job for one particular client that the client had set John up on his own.

Private Label Group Limited   **Information Memorandum**

---

1.   SUMMARY

1.1   Summary business description

Private Label is the largest privately-owned distributor of mortgages in the United Kingdom. Its business comprises the design of mortgage products and the provision of related services on behalf of a panel of lenders and the distribution of such mortgages through intermediaries to their clients. Since it was established in 1987, Private Label has enjoyed almost uninterrupted growth in profitability on the back of a constant pursuit of excellence in service, innovation and professionalism. The costs it saves lenders are ploughed back into the products. It consequently enjoys very strong relationships and an excellent reputation with lenders and intermediaries alike.

1.2   Key strengths

1.2.1   Management team

Private Label's management team, lead by the business's founder Stephen Knight, is the key driver behind its success. It is a stable, highly experienced and innovative team which includes experts in the fields of mortgage design, sales, marketing and processing.

1.2.2   Leading UK distributor

Private Label completed some £550 million of mortgages in aggregate in 1997. This level of completion is comparable with a top-ten UK building society.

1.2.3   Operational efficiency

Private Label is an extremely tightly-run business and adheres to the highest standards in all aspects of its operations. It is not regulated by any organisation, it has never had a PI claim, there has never been cause for an auditors' management letter and it has never had an unpaid invoice.

1.2.4   Sales and marketing

Private Label has the most productive mortgage sales force operating in the UK market, backed by tried and tested sophisticated marketing techniques.

1.2.5   Innovation

Private Label has an excellent and award-winning reputation for product innovation achieved through comprehensive research combined with management expertise.

1.2.6   Pre-offer processing

Consistent with its policy of providing an unrivalled service, Private Label's processing centre ensures that a very high level of applications proceed to mortgage offer and in a time frame which is two-thirds of the industry norm.

The Executive Summary of the Information Memorandum by which we offered Private Label for sale

1.2.7   Cash generation

Private Label is operated under strong financial controls and is highly cash generative - this has allowed the business to invest in its development on a continual basis. At 31st December 1997 the group had net cash balances of some £1.3 million; these are expected to grow to £2 million by 31st December 1998.

1.2.8   Independent Mortgage Collection Limited

Independent Mortgage Collection Limited ("IMC"), launched in September 1997 for subscriber recruitment and March 1998 for lead generation, represents one of the largest groups of independent mortgage advisors and it has already established itself as a brand recognised by financial journalists. IMC endorses and promotes Private Label's products direct to the consumer, thus increasing overall demand and is an added-value lead-generation company for mortgage intermediaries.

1.2.9   Niche market opportunities

Although Private Label specialises in designing and distributing market-leading mainstream mortgage products, it has also developed exclusive sub-prime mortgage products on behalf of Kensington Mortgage Company. A similar niche market has been developed in the self-certification and 100% sectors with Verso, a subsidiary of the Britannia Building Society.

1.2.10 Accelerated growth opportunities

Private Label's growth and profitability could be significantly enhanced by the ability to complete and service mortgage loans itself. The resultant reduction in the time taken to complete would   open up new distribution opportunities, whilst the sale of loans post completion would allow a much wider funding base than the seven lenders with whom funding contracts are presently held, increasing supply dramatically.

This development would greatly expand Private Label's capacity and product differentiation and the control of all aspects of the mortgage process up to legal completion would further increase market share through enhanced service and speed. In such circumstances, Private Label has the potential to become a dominant force in the UK in originating mortgages and the directors believe that the business faces no immediate threat from its current competitors.

The Executive Summary of the Information Memorandum by which we offered Private Label for sale

Private Label Group Limited　　　　　　　　　　　　　　Information Memorandum

1.3　Summary financial information

Private Label has achieved strong growth in profits since its inception and that growth is forecast to continue:

Year to 31st December	1996 Actual £m	1997 Actual £m	1998 Forecast £m	1999 Forecast £m
Mortgage loans completed	343	548	566	602
Turnover (including interest income)	6.2	8.2	10.0	9.1[3]
Profit before tax	0.8	1.1[1]	2.0[2]	2.4[2]

1. *Before c.£150,000 set up costs of IMC.*
2. *Before directors' bonuses.*
3. *The fall in 1999 turnover is due to a change in the payment of brokers' fees by lenders (see section 5.1 below).*

1.4　Business philosophy

Private Label operates its business through strong adherence to its stated values:

> To exceed customers' expectations
> To go the extra mile for its customers
> To continually revisit established thinking in its markets
> To innovate
> To maximise profitability
> To be entrepreneurial
> To push out frontiers
> To be the best
> To look at all opportunities
> To have respect for the individual
> To maximise each staff member's potential
> To add value
> To have a "can do" attitude

These values underpin Private Label's overriding mission statement:

> *"To profitably maximise all opportunities for innovation, service excellence and growth in the UK mortgage and financial services market, maintaining the company's reputation for professionalism"*

The directors believe that these values have been critical to the Company's success.

The Executive Summary of the Information Memorandum by which we offered Private Label for sale

In record time John and his team produced a comprehensive Information Memorandum that certainly showed Private Label in an impressive light. We issued this to GMAC-RFC and to a couple of other organisations which had by then shown interest, the most significant of which was Countrywide Credit Industries, the largest lender in the US. Unknown to us at the time, Countrywide was a leading rival of GMAC-RFC, something that eventually helped us in the bidding process between the two competitors.

Countrywide came over to see us and then invited Godfrey and I to visit them at their headquarters in Calabasas, California. They spared no expense as they flew us out first class and put us up in the Beverley Wilshire Hotel, in Beverley Hills. They were an impressive group, and I particularly enjoyed meeting Angelo Mozilo, who is such a legendary figure in the US mortgage industry.

They did not quite have our sense of humour, though. During one tour of their premises, when we were invited to walk along seemingly never-ending corridors with rubber-clad floors (to protect the computer environment), I remarked to Godfrey that I had not seen that much rubber since his last party. Not even a smile from the non-British contingent. At least the GMAC-RFC executives occasionally laughed at my jokes!

We returned to the UK genuinely unsure who we would choose between Countrywide and GMAC-RFC in the event that both bids were for the same amount. We had a greater connection with GMAC-RFC by way of corporate style and values, but Countrywide's volume machine was impressive.

The debate became academic, though, because GMAC-RFC emerged as the clear winner with a bid that valued our company very highly. As we realised the extent of GMAC-RFC's international ambitions, in contrast to Countrywide's at the time, we realised that fate had allowed us to make the right choice. Our business was always run with prudence and governance. We had from day one employed a firm of accountants to prepare monthly management accounts, which a separate firm, Ernst & Young, then audited. All payments due to us arose out of contracts with lenders and had time constraints attached to the payment of invoices.

There had never been a bad debt. The due diligence therefore took just two days, and the sale and purchase contract negotiations only about six weeks. I said at the outset that we would not renegotiate any of the core terms once we had accepted the GMAC-RFC offer, and neither did they.

The only problem we had throughout had been on the penultimate day before completion when the lawyers and the M&A team from GMAC-RFC wanted to go on through the night. I refused and told everyone to go home to their beds. They explained it was normal practice in such deals to work through the night in order to get them done, but I said that I was never much persuaded by "normal practice".

When they saw that I was determined to go home and get a night's sleep they asked if they could contact me on my mobile should any big queries arise. I said "certainly not", switched my mobile off and left it there. When I returned the next day I found both sides very tired and arguing about points that were really simple and straightforward. After some head-banging, we completed the deal on 17 November 1998. Private Label had been sold for the third and final time.

General Motors buys Private Label

By John Lappin

Mortgage packager Private Label has been bought by US giant General Motors in a deal which will let it increase services to IFAs.

General Motors' mortgage subsidiary GMAC-RFC has paid an undisclosed fee for the company. Private Label's current directors, including chairman Stephen Knight, will remain on the board. Knight also becomes a managing director at GMAC-RFC.

The deal means Private Label will be backed by a global finance company with assets of around $110bn as it embarks on a growth strategy.

Knight says: "Private Label's ambition is to become the biggest originator of mortgage loans in the UK, using the American definition of originator, namely, a company that specialises in generating loans for the balance sheets of others."

He says Private Label will add to its service by taking over loan admin after completion. It

also wants to speed up the delivery of mortgage offers and completions to IFAs.

GMAC-RFC entered the UK mortgage market two years ago. Its first significant acquisition came in March this year with the purchase of mortgage servicing company MSL from Birmingham Midshires.

GMAC-RFC managing director and RFC Mortgage services chairman Chris Nordeen says: "We stated when we entered the UK market that our commitment would be substan-

tial and this relationship helps us move forward with our plans. Through our experience in securitisation, lending and investment, GMAC-RFC is uniquely positioned to provide capital for the UK mortgage lending industry via organisations that share our long-term strategic vision."

Nordeen says he does not see the need for significant changes at Private Label as it is already successful. He says Private Label fits with GMAC-RFC's distribution needs.

Knight: Ambition to be UK's biggest mortgage originator

Money Marketing. 26 November 1998

Following the sale of the business there were staff to present to, customers to visit and press to brief. It was a whirlwind of meetings and Christmas could not come soon enough. The GMAC-RFC people were just great, as they have been ever since. We were supported when we needed or wanted support, and left alone when we wanted to be left alone. I went into the Christmas break extremely pleased with the year's work. Mortgage completions for 1998 represented a new record, and our pre tax profit had passed the £2m mark for the first time, a virtual doubling of the previous year's number. But we could not afford to hang about. We appointed GMAC-RFC to our lender panel and set about attacking the new year with new products.

The Private Label vendor directors comprise four of the five executive directors on the GMAC-RFC UK statutory board in 2005 - still working closely together seven years after the sale of business. From left to right: Simon Knight, Godfrey Blight, Barry Searle and Stephen Knight

We had asked GMAC-RFC to trust our promise that the four vendor directors - Godfrey Blight, Simon Knight, Barry Searle and myself - would stay for at least five years notwithstanding the cash we had received, and the earn out we were due to receive. They did trust us and here we are, not five, but nearly eight, years later.

1999

■ Growing the business as a GMAC-RFC subsidiary

All good years need an early major product success, and we certainly had this with the *Discount, Cashback & Droplock* product funded by HMSL. In addition to the 3% upfront cashback and 2.75% upfront discount, the product guaranteed the opportunity to transfer to a fixed rate during the 5 years following the ending of the discount.

It captured the mood of the market at the time. The upfront incentives were irresistible, and intermediaries felt good about explaining what a *"drop-lock"* (the option of subsequently fixing the mortgage rate) was. We generated nearly half a billion pounds worth of business from this one product. Combined with the HMSL-funded *Mortgage of a Lifetime* it put HMSL way ahead of the other lenders on our panel in terms of volume generated.

We were always looking for innovative, interesting and "cheeky" marketing initiatives to bring ourselves to the attention of intermediaries and get noticed in the market generally. Timed to arrive on 14 February 1999, we therefore sent every intermediary on our database - all 14,000 of them - a Valentine's card with a chocolate inside.

The card referred to our *Discount, Cashback & Drop-Lock* product. Not only did this go down well with our customers, it also got mentioned in the trade press. You have to be different to be noticed.

As well as being one of our most successful ever, this product also gave us our only Ombudsman query: not bad for 14 years of highly proactive mortgage marketing. The query that was raised with the Ombudsman related to an aspect of the product design about which we had thought long and hard, namely the guarantee of a fixed rate offer from the lender in years two to six.

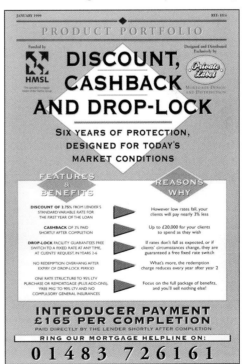

Definitely new product of the 1999

This offer was what it said on the tin, namely the obligation for the lender to quote a fixed rate. It was not a guarantee of any particular fixed rate, and we were careful to make clear that the fixed rate that would be offered had no linkage to any benchmark, including the fixed rates which the lender might at that time be offering to new customers.

The whole point of this product was that it gave customers a total 5.75% year one incentive - something that would be unheard of today. The majority of that incentive was in cash up front. The *"drop-lock"* was an additional, but secondary, design feature.

If customers did not like the fixed rate they were subsequently quoted by way of the drop-lock option, then they could stay on the variable rate and apply again a little later when perhaps the lender might have a fixed rate available that was more to their liking. Seeing the potential for this to be misunderstood, we printed the following wording very clearly on the product guide:

"An offer condition will confirm the applicants' entitlement to contact HMSL at any time in years 2-6 inclusive and be quoted a fixed rate into which they can then transfer with no switching fee or redemption charge payable in respect of the switch. The terms of the new fixed rate, including any redemption charge applicable, will be determined by the lender at the time. The Drop-Lock facility can only be exercised once during years 2-6 inclusive".

The lender also put similar wording on its mortgage offer. The product was then sold to many thousands of borrowers, without query. There was this one broker, though. I guess there's always one. He said that he had heard our salesman say that the fixed rate that would be offered by the lender would always be the same as the fixed rates the lender was making available to new customers at the time. He had therefore passed this information onto the customer, and this had been a key factor in making the customer decide to take this particular product.

The broker took this up with the lender, which had originally been HMSL, but whose business was now being managed by Birmingham Midshires. The lender contacted us and we pointed out to the broker that:

- All Private Label salesmen had been issued with written instructions on how to sell this product, and it would have been a breach of those instructions for the salesman in question to have said what the broker said he did

- We talked to a cross section of brokers in that particular salesman's region and there was no evidence to suggest that he was mis-selling the product, corroborated by the fact that no queries were raised by any other broker he served

---

IFAs have a not so secret admirer

IFAs that continually suffer the embarrassment of never receiving Valentine cards can get ready to celebrate receiving one this year.

Private Label, the mortgage design and distribution company, is sending Valentine cards to the 12,000 IFAs on its database. The card has a romantic exterior brandishing a loving message so IFAs can display it and fool fellow workers into thinking they have a genuine admirer.

Sadly, the interior carries an advert for the new range of discount, cashback and drop-lock mortgages Private Label offers.

IFAs will be cheered by the fact that the card contains a little chocolate and more probably by the fact that they can say: "Yes mother, I did receive a card this year."

Money marketing.
11 February 1999

- Even if the broker had misheard what had been said at point of sale, the product guide clearly contradicted this (and the broker had confirmed that he had received the correct product guide)

- Even if the broker had not read the product guide, the mortgage offer reiterated in the same terms the basis on which subsequent fixed rates would be made available

- Did the broker really feel that, having given away 5.75% in cash and discounts during the first year, the lender would be making available another new business subsidy to the same borrower 12 months later?

There were no satisfactory responses to any of these points. The broker and the customer carried out their threat to refer the matter to the Ombudsman. The complaint was against the lender as the regulated entity. The appropriate fees were paid, a case manager allocated and an investigation started.

I honestly felt that, at first glance, the Ombudsman's case manager would throw this complaint out. The idea that an allegation of something said informally during a sales call more than a year before, between parties that did not involve the customer, could override what was said in a product guide, and in the mortgage offer, seemed incredible to me.

Yet the case manager doggedly pursued this point until the file became very thick. To support the lender in this transaction, we needed to trace the Private Label salesman concerned.

This was not easy. Not only had he left the company some time before, but he had also moved house. Letters to his previous address were returned unanswered. In the end we had to painstakingly go through all of his contacts to see if anyone knew where he was.

We finally got hold of him and he confirmed that he had not made the statements attributed to him by the broker. Then, and only then, was the complaint thrown out. Despite no corroboration for the idea of mis-selling, and notwithstanding written material to the contrary, it was apparently necessary to be satisfied that the salesman denied the allegation.

The problem with a pendulum is that, while it may eventually settle in the middle, it takes ages to do so. It you want to bring about balance a little earlier than that, then you have to adjust it manually. That is what I feel is necessary in connection with the Ombudsman service.

I think it is a great idea that consumers have access to such a service to stop themselves being exploited. I also think it acceptable for that service to be weighted in favour of the consumer. But does it really help all consumers for the complaints process to be so weighted that the simple allegation of something said many years before, in contradiction of everything that had been given in writing, can cause many thousands of pounds worth of costs in responding to it?

Both we and the lender had to make staff available to read this correspondence and respond to it. In our case we had all the effort to track our salesman down and while our staff were involved in these tasks they were not providing a service to the rest of our customers. The total cost, including opportunity cost, of responding to this complaint is a charge that will no doubt appear on all other mortgage borrowers' bills by way of the interest rate they pay. When unsubstantiated complaints are made, it is a cost and a disservice to all mortgage borrowers if they are pursued in this manner.

■ The sales conference is a proven formula

Back to real business! The annual Private Label sales conferences were known at the time to be unique. We spent many months, and well into six figures, producing an event which would communicate and entertain. Our payback was that we sometimes achieved as much as one third of our full year new business target in the weeks that followed the conferences.

They were an ideal medium to get the more complex product designs in which we specialised across to the intermediary sector. Whether measured by new business or creativity, the 1999 sales conferences were our best ever. As these also contributed to my subsequent decision to invest in a business specialising in bringing a show business feel to corporate presentations, a sharing of tactics and techniques here might be beneficial to the reader.

Our timetable to start planning our sales conferences was normally six months in advance. This is when our outsourced production team would visit venues and ensure that we could create the right atmosphere. We then started regular meetings to develop content and a theme.

We had previously used, for example, awards ceremonies and sports videos with celebrities providing the voiceovers or hosting the events. On one occasion we had even employed a young Rory Bremner, now a major TV celebrity, to help us. Anything to achieve the communication effects of a piece of entertainment rather than the atmosphere of a corporate presentation. The audience is much more receptive to messages when presented in an enjoyable and entertaining way.

For the 1999 conferences we chose a game show theme. With the help of Terry Morrison, a scriptwriter and performer that we had used for many years, we started to put together the creative aspects of the presentation. The bits that we could not include at that early stage were the products we would have available to sell.

Typically, we would feature in our presentations at the sales conferences products from our existing range to analyse in greater depth. One of the main reasons the Private Label sales conferences were so well attended, however, was the fact that we always had brand new products to launch, which we would then make available on favourable terms for a short period to those who attended the sales conferences.

We were always taken to the wire on this part of the process. We would ask our lenders to be more generous than normal with the product profitability model in return for the high profile that a launch at the sales conferences would deliver. Mostly our lenders were keen to launch the "star of the show" product and achieve the longest and largest treatment from the stage.

With the 1999 conferences we were pushed closer than we had ever been before by a particular lender who, in a game of bluff and double bluff, did not actually sign off on the product we had requested until the night before the first conference. We only had time to produce the barest of handout material, and we had to work through the night to get this particular product incorporated into the presentation.

It was, however, the deal we had requested and it went down a storm. Everybody benefited from the pressure this build-up to the annual sales conferences always generated, mostly the end customers who got some great deals.

We had four brand new, exclusive products to launch at the 1999 sales conference roadshows, each in different sectors and all market leaders. We chose three products from our existing range to give longer treatment to and were then able to finalise the show.

We had rehearsed maybe 10 times to ensure that we were word perfect, and had engaged our normal production company to build an impressive stage plus lighting/sound system. (Never use the venue's own system, unless you've booked the Albert Hall!). The initial visual impression, and the subsequent sound production quality, must be at least equal to any show your audience might visit in the West End in order to maximise absorption and retention.

Once our audience was seated, the technique we always used was to get the lights dark, and the sound loud. It's difficult to be distracted if you cannot see much immediately around you, while the sound arrests your senses. Of course, if the content then fails to entertain, your audience might feel uncomfortable, and even leave. So you have got to get their attention from moment one and keep it.

We kicked off the show with a version of "Play Your Cards Right". The audience were encouraged to shout out whether the next, unturned card was "higher" or "lower" than the previous card. Instead of using normal playing cards, however, we had diagrams and charts to do with our own business.

For example, we invited the audience to guess whether the Private Label sales figures were higher or lower than the previous year (they were higher). We asked whether the application fee scale was higher or lower (it was lower). We had fun with such things as application turnaround times (lower) and Tony Fisher's hairline (higher).

As the answers were shouted out, it got everybody relaxed and in "entertained" mode. They temporarily forgot about business, with the result that they were more receptive to the first product presentation that then followed. After a couple of product presentations we then introduced another entertainment interlude to re-introduce relaxation, and so on.

We always finished with a prize draw, again involving audience participation. Runners up got champagne, but winners received luxury holidays, tickets for major sporting events and so on - always something worth having. We never knew the value that the intermediaries who attended these conferences attached to the various component parts, namely the new products with their exclusive incentives for conference attendees; the entertainment value; the prize at the end; the chance to meet industry colleagues or whatever. What we always knew, however, was that, if we put in the planning and rehearsal time, the sales conferences would be an invaluable contributor to each year's sales targets, while enhancing our reputation as a company. The year 1999 was a record for Private Label by all measures, and this was due in no small part to the sales conferences held in the Spring of that year.

As a post script to the success we had enjoyed with our sales conference formula, I invested in, and became Non Executive Chairman of, a company called Entertainment in Business. My partners in this company were Terry Morrison and Norman Pace.

I had known Norman, who had enjoyed much success in the 1970s and 1980s as one half of Hale & Pace, for some years. Terry had been a friend for even longer. I had received permission from GMAC-RFC to become non executive chairman of this business and some of my industry colleagues were surprised to see me on the front page of *The Sunday Times* striking a silly pose with Terry and Norman at the launch of the company.

Paul Hackett

A funny thing is happening at AGMs

LIGHTS, camera, action . . . annual general meetings will never be the same again. Half of the comedy double act Hale and Pace is going into business this week to help directors to liven up shareholder meetings and staff presentations, *writes Rupert Steiner.*

Norman Pace and partners are launching Entertainment in Business with £250,000 in seed capital from private investors. It will specialise in delivering business messages as entertainment, because traditional ways are proving less effective.

Pace explained: "We have just spent too many occasions standing in the wings at corporate events ready to do our after-dinner act when the chief executive just died on stage delivering a couple of gags he thought were funny while shaving that morning.

"Staff and customers get bombarded each day with thousands of images, principally from the entertainment industry. That is their reference point, and business needs to harness that. In the new world you have to entertain to inform."

Pace will own 10% of the business, with the remainder split between Stephen Knight, who runs his own mortgage-lending business, and Terry Morrison, a writer and performer. Clients already signed up include Charlton Athletic football club and the Institute of Groundmanship.

Pace setter: Norman Pace (right) is stepping out as part of a business triple act with Stephen Knight and Terry Morrison

Sunday Times. 16 June 2002. Photographer: Paul Hackett. Author: Robert Steiner. Thanks to Sunday Times
© Robert Steiner/News International Syndication, London 16 June 2002

The idea behind this venture was to demonstrate to other organisations what success they could have with corporate presentations and events if they used showbusiness techniques rather than death by PowerPoint. It was certainly a fun thing to do, but I found that regrettably I could not devote any time to it and I subsequently sold my stake.

I still passionately believe in the concept, though. The number of images with which we are all presented each day is on the increase, meaning that we process each one in a quicker and more superficial manner. If you really want to get your corporate points across you have to entertain, where resistance is lower and absorption higher.

■ New website launched

At the 1999 sales conferences we also launched our new website. The UK mortgage market was initially very slow to embrace the internet, and new technology generally. It has speeded up in recent times. Nevertheless, we felt it important to have an interactive website up and running, which we achieved via a white label arrangement with IFOnline, as it was then (Trigold as it is now).

We became one of the UK's first packagers to offer application submission online. The problem was that this was still 1999 and, at that time, nobody was interested in applying that way.

Then, our Director of Marketing, Tony Fisher, noticed that we had received 30,000 hits on this website over a short space of time. This was far in excess of our expectation. Upon further investigation, however, these internet users appear to have been mainly from Russia and America, plainly mistaken as to what they might view on a website entitled "Private Label".

How sad is that? Also how disappointing to seek a certain type of visual material, and get details of mortgage products in response!

■ Increasing business with GMAC-RFC

Stage one of the integration of our business with our new parent occurred as planned during the first half of 1999, with their establishment as a panel lender and the launch of their sub prime product range. Business was ticking over nicely, so the time was right to launch an exclusive product.

It was an idea I had put to several of our other lenders, but which they had turned down. There could therefore be no objection if GMAC-RFC stepped in to fund it.

The product idea turned out to be a controversial one. When I had been a non executive director of John Charcol during the 1990s, I had seen Bank of Scotland meet a very specific applicant demand with a product that did not require customers to state their income on the application form. This appealed particularly to upmarket customers, who often had complex and/or confidential income arrangements.

Preferring not to self certify an actual figure, customers would find this unique product appealing, as would applicants in the public eye, who would prefer not to disclose earnings. Of course, if you dispense with income details altogether, you have to put in compensating factors. We proposed several in this product design including:

- ■ Applicants had to demonstrate a clean, recent credit performance on other debt, without which they would be rejected

- ■ Telephone checks were made to employers or accountants

- We offered a restrictive loan-to-value

- Initially, there were no discounts or incentives

- Each case was given a sense check (did the applicants' personal status sit logically with the overall lending proposal?) before proceeding

It was our prediction that we would reject at outset two thirds of applicants, but that the third that got through would be of high quality. A full product proposal was therefore put to our colleagues at GMAC-RFC.

It turned out that this was a pivotal product in our relationship with GMAC-RFC, although we did not realise it at the time. Like many securitising lenders, even today, GMAC-RFC was at that time reliant on its capital markets team to approve retail products.

If the capital markets team did not believe that a product could be sold or securitised they would turn it down. I disagreed with that approach.

In any conduit-style lending organisation, the input of capital markets to product design is invaluable. They should always be at the table with an important vote. But it should never be the casting vote. The sales and marketing departments, constantly in touch with the customer base, should have an equal vote, as should credit risk, finance and other interested departments.

In the event of a stalemate, the CEO should exercise judgment and flair. The traditional capital markets-led scenario ends up leading to a potential disconnection with the retail marketplace, in my view.

That was exactly the situation at GMAC-RFC in the UK. The capital markets team turned down our product proposal, saying that it could not be exited. I said that I thought this analysis was wrong, at which point they contacted several lenders, who could feasibly be potential portfolio purchasers. These lenders all said that they would not touch a product where the income was not declared, thereby "proving" that it was not sellable.

My view was that all this proved was the long-established tradition that you cannot sell "air". If you ask someone whether they will buy something you have not yet got, do not be surprised if they turn you down! I therefore said to Chris Nordeen that I thought the capital markets team was wrong.

I argued that, when we had established a large enough portfolio of low LTV, performing loans, institutions would fall over themselves to acquire or invest in these assets. We could securitise them or sell them in portfolios.

Chris offered the compromise of a pilot with this product. We would only increase the tranche size beyond the amount agreed for the pilot if we were successful in selling our first portfolio. Thus, the "STAR" product was born. Standing for Simple, Transparent, Accessible and Realistic, this product really captured the imagination of the market, as we thought it would.

We quickly built the target portfolio. The loans performed well and the LTVs were low. Rejections were indeed about two-thirds of the cases put to us. Also, as predicted, there was no shortage of lenders wishing to buy the first portfolio, including those who had refused the product when it was just a theory. We achieved what would by today's standards be a very high premium.

We then rolled out the "STAR" product more widely and kept it in the range for five years, introducing incentives and responding to market conditions along the way, but always embracing the credit enhancement principles noted above, namely that you have to substitute tighter criteria if you give up income details, and always reject the far-fetched.

In total, over five years, there were over £2.5bn of "STAR" completions which we sold in portfolios and securitised. It was always our most popular product for portfolio buyers because the average LTV was lower than on mainstream business, the average loan size was higher and the arrears level showed no material difference to our mainstream book.

"STAR" was fulfilling a real purpose, namely allowing those who had reasons

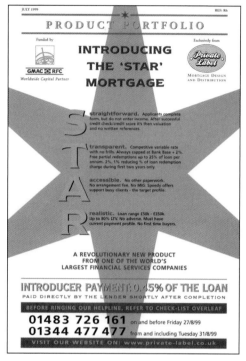

The controversial but very successful "STAR" product - out first with GMAC-RFC

for keeping their income details confidential, to exercise this choice in a competitive market, while providing for extra credit checks, above and beyond those applied to mainstream products, in order to produce better arrears performance. Regrettably, the regulator's interpretation was that the product did not meet the 2004 MCOB Rules because no income was stated, and had to go. But were customers, choice and competition best served by its withdrawal? I don't think so.

Either way, our success with "STAR" not only helped to deliver a fantastic 1999, but also laid down a marker in relation to future product design ideas and how they would be approved within GMAC-RFC. They all went through a little easier after that!

■ A brief foray into lead-generation

We had formed IMC in 1997 to help us diversify and increase new business. It would allow Private Label's exclusive product designs to be featured in ads and articles in the national press, and create a new stream of new business and profits for our group. I had been interested in lead generation since the launch of Mortgage Intelligence. Indeed, I had made a tentative bid for Mortgage Intelligence just a few months after it had launched.

I was clearly under-valuing the business at the time, given the price that it received shortly thereafter from Close Brothers. So, instead, we decided to launch our own lead-generation company.

An advertisement promoting IMC to intermediaries

With hindsight, I'm not sure how we came up with such a clumsy name. Our legal advice suggested initially that we could only have as subscribers independent financial advisers. We wanted to make clear that we were focused on mortgage products only and would be offering a collection of products and lenders. Good explanation, poor execution!

Working with the appropriate business suppliers, it proved to be a relatively simple task to break the country down into about 300 territories, each containing approximately 60,000 households. Unlike Mortgage Intelligence at the time, we did not "sell" these territories to intermediaries for a lump sum. Instead, we invited them to enter into a longer term agreement with IMC, varied by notice, by which they would subscribe typically £150 per month for the exclusive rights to receive all leads generated in a particular territory.

Because Private Label had by then established such a strong reputation for itself in relation to product design and innovative marketing, the territories were snapped up fairly quickly. Indeed, "big name" brokers like John Charcol, Chase de Vere and DBS bought several territories each. In fact, some territories were so popular we had to invite sealed bids, effectively selling them to the intermediary bidding the highest subscription. The bidding process was new, and bizarre. Some intermediaries bid thousands. Some bid pennies. One said that he would buy my last book, "The Art of Marketing Mortgages" if we allocated him one particular territory. A cheeky but poor offer!

Examples of ICM's national press advertising

By the Spring of 1998, we had sold enough territories to be able to launch with a national press advertising campaign. We chose the advertising agency CCHM to lead this, and their innovative use of real pictures accompanied by eye-catching doodling was well received all round.

We used every ounce of ingenuity we had. Our best marketer, Simon Knight, was made Chief Executive of IMC, and he generated as many leads from PR as we did from advertising. We undertook direct mail, we bought databases and took display slots in the Yellow Pages.

We had market-leading exclusive products advertised by a top London agency in all the main national press publications. Inevitably there were some territories unsold at any given point in time and we passed the leads generated in those territories to the nearest subscriber, in addition to the leads to which they were entitled, to further boost business for IMC's intermediary customers.

We introduced new software that got a lead into the hands of the subscriber within a few minutes of the initial call. We issued customer-friendly explanatory booklets to the callers, and we followed up leads with the subscribers.

In total, we generated over 20,000 leads in the short eighteen month life of IMC, and we felt that we had done enough to make all subscribers happy. Most were, but, unfortunately, too many were not.

Consumers who respond to advertisements are often window-shoppers, yet many subscribers had got it into their heads that these would be customers that only needed a perfunctory signing-up process to seal the deal. Some thought that we had guaranteed to generate a certain number of leads for them, even though the agreement specifically said that we had not.

Some subscribers did not bother to follow up leads for several days after the initial call, and then complained that the prospect was cold when they got there. Quite a few made contact with customers and dissuaded them from proceeding with the product advertised, about which

IFAs move quickly to snap up Private Label's territories

PRIVATE Label said 300 of the 353 territories in its new lead-generation service have been snapped up by IFAs with two months to go until advertising starts.

In October Private Label launched Independent Mortgage Collection, its new lead-generation company, following the apparent success of Mortgage Intelligence, a similar service which was last year bought out by Close Brothers.

Both services were designed to generate leads for mortgage applications by advertising, principally in the press.

The country is divided into a number of territories which are "bought" by financial advisers.

In the case of Private Label, only IFAs or independent mortgage brokers may apply.

These pay £150 plus VAT per month, in return for all the leads generated from individuals in the area in question.

IMC plans to spend £500,000 a year on advertising, and will use Private Label's existing call centre and processing facilities to make mortgage applications and processing more efficient and cheaper to territory holders.

The move, the company said, would allow more resources for lead generation.

Mr Stephen Knight, chairman of Private Label, said out of the 300 territories now "sold", 107 of them were the subject of multiple applications.

He said Private Label accepted sealed bids from those interested, to decide the victor.

"We had some weird and wonderful bids," Mr Knight said.

"One was for £1, some bid in the thousands."

One wit offered to buy Mr Knight's new book, The Art Of Marketing Mortgages, if he got the territory.

This bid, Mr Knight assured Financial Adviser, was refused.

John Charcol, Chase de Vere and DBS have all applied for territories.

Financial Adviser. 22 January 1998

NEWSWATCH

IFAs storm mortgage lead-generation launch

John Charcol and Chase de Vere have each snapped up 10 territories in the run-up to the launch of Private Label's lead-generation business, Independent Mortgage Collection.

Over 300 of the 353 territories, which each consist of about 60,000 households, have already been taken by IFAs. IMC refuses to say how much the highest bid has been although the lowest was just £1. All the money will be ploughed into an advertising campaign which kicks off in March.

Money Marketing. 22 January 1998

they had enquired, instead placing the case with whoever their favourite lender was at the time.

One particular incident represented the beginning of the end for me so far as being in the lead-generation business was concerned. Within the same week, I received both a letter of complaint, and a letter of praise, about the same lead! As these letters were from two different subscribers, I was intrigued to discover how they had both tried to close the same lead.

It turned out that the caller had initially given his home address, which generated a lead to the subscriber who "owned" that particular postcode. The IFA in question made contact with the individual and formed the view that he was a time-waster, prompting a complaint letter to me from the subscriber, claiming that this was a typical example of the "no hope" leads that we were passing out.

Undaunted by the poor service he had received from the first IFA, the customer called IMC again, this time giving the postcode of his business address. That had generated a new lead for a different subscriber. Once again, the IFA in question followed up and he, too, determined that the customer was not really suitable for the mortgage being advertised.

However, this particular IFA, through undertaking a proper fact find, had uncovered a need for pension advice which had resulted in the establishment of new personal and company pension plans. The sale of these pensions, apparently, had generated more than five figures of commission for the IFA, prompting a letter of praise to me about how good IMC's leads were.

It dawned on all of us that, however hard we worked, there would be a core rump of subscribers who would never be happy, largely because their expectation was out of line with reality. Coupled with the fact that we were at that time at the start of the trend by which fewer and fewer customers were responding off the page, I felt that there was no future in continually being in dispute with your customers, albeit a small minority.

About eighteen months or so after the initial launch we therefore called it a day. We stopped collecting subscriptions, but honoured our long term advertising plans, enabling us to carry on passing out "free" leads for several months afterwards. This gesture enabled us to ensure no long term reputational damage for Private Label.

We had not lost money on IMC, but we had not made much either. Our best guess at raw lead-to-completion conversion was 3% - too low to base any profitability expectation on completed business. There is no doubt that some IFAs increased their overall business levels with Private Label as a result of their involvement with IMC, including business that did not derive from the leads themselves.

Their greater familiarity with our product range through participation in the advertising campaign had positively contributed to our revenue. In addition, the national press coverage that we got for the Private Label products being advertised by IMC also gave the business an additional boost. All in all, however, when you are in the business of providing service to customers, it is a good idea to get out of any business line that promotes the potential for conflict. It is thus that we withdrew from the lead generation business and would never enter it again in that form. There are those who are making personal fortunes today from lead generation on a completely different model, offering an internet lead for sale to intermediaries for a relatively small fee, using technology to control the volume of leads tailored to buyers' needs. I wish that I had thought of that formula for IMC, because that does seem to work. But I never said I was smart!

■ Moving in with our sister company brought unexpected benefits

One of the background factors we had all recognised in the sale of Private Label to GMAC-RFC was the potential for cost savings. If the Private Label Processing Centre was moved out of its existing Woking premises a few miles along the road to the GMAC-RFC headquarters in Bracknell, where there was spare space, there would be a net benefit to the group. We were coming to the end of our tenancy at Woking in any event and needed expanded square footage, so this was an obvious move.

Based on a detailed (and subsequently flawed) study as to where people lived, we calculated that we would lose maybe half a dozen members of staff from our then total of 120 as a consequence of this move. But the study had not taken into account the very personal choices people make when choosing to work locally.

An extra mile can be the straw that breaks the camel's back if it extends, for example, over a couple of junctions that involve minutes' of traffic queuing in the morning and evening. As a result, while the move to Bracknell went successfully in all other respects, we actually lost a third of our staff and suffered some processing issues as a result.

That did not last long. We replaced the staff and moved forward. But there's a useful lesson there for anybody planning a similar move for their own business. In our case, the benefit of having our people based at Bracknell, where all the GMAC-RFC people were based, outweighed any disadvantages, since communication, computer facilities and general administration support were rapidly upgraded to those of a bigger company.

But there turned out to be an even bigger prize in this move, which we had not anticipated. This was the confidence the GMAC-RFC credit risk managers were able to build up in the Private Label processing teams through the close access. As this contact and confidence grew we were able to introduce something that was then unheard of in the packager part of the market, and which is still very rare today, namely delegated underwriting, from lender to packager.

Quietly, we put a number of Private Label "Personal Mortgage Consultants" through the GMAC-RFC underwriting tests. As they passed, so we eliminated the extra step that all third party mortgage companies find so frustrating, namely second-guessing by the lender.

Because the Private Label team could make decisions every bit as good as the GMAC-RFC underwriters, so the service on offer to intermediaries leapt forward. No lender referrals. No delays. The Private Label contact person was the decision-maker. After delegated underwriting came delegated offer issuance. We had thought that lenders putting their underwriters on-site at our Processing Centre was a major step forward. But in fact it was a tiny movement compared with being able to underwrite the business yourself, and issue the offers. We were in complete control and able to prioritise and communicate more assuredly with intermediaries. The business we placed with GMAC-RFC soared as a result, and presented a very stark contrast to the service we were able to offer on behalf of every other lender on our panel. Coming swiftly after the successful "STAR" launch, it is easy with hindsight to see why greater integration of the GMAC-RFC and Private Label businesses then became inevitable.

■ Another record year

Thanks to all of the above, mortgage completions in 1999 increased by 25% year-on-year to £703m, continuing to be the lending equivalent of a top 10 building society. Turnover was up at £9.1m, and this reflected a full year of operating under the arrangement where the procuration fee ultimately destined for the intermediary did not pass through our hands. If the figures were adjusted to reflect a like-for-like comparison with 1998, then the increase in turnover would have been even bigger.

Pre tax profit increased to £2.2m in 1999, while cash balances increased to £4.4m. We also successfully overcame the alleged Millennium computer issues, which turned out to be a non event. Satisfied with another good year's performance, I flew off that year for a celebratory Christmas break in my favourite place at that time of the year - the Caribbean.

2000

■ Cocking it up t'North

One of my first acts for the year 2000 was to negotiate and execute an acquisition. We had met some months earlier a small packaging firm operating from the North West with whom we had discussed the possibility of joining forces.

They seemed to like the idea of becoming Private Label in the North, and the hope was that their loyal broker database would be happy to continue dealing with them in their new guise. We agreed terms and re-launched them as the Private Label Northern Operations Centre, channelling all of our business in that area to our Northern colleagues to add to the business they were already doing.

The first lesson we learned was that the reason these previous brokers were theirs and not ours was because there was something desirable about the nature of the local service they were receiving which they were not getting from a high volume company like Private Label. It turned out, therefore, that by offering our high volume service we retained too little of what we had thought at the time would be an additional distribution database. Good lesson there for potential acquirers.

It is also fair to say that, whatever the initial attraction, the key individuals found that they did not get along. It happens. It was no-one's fault. However much you plan, it's living together that's the test. And this acquisition failed that test.

We felt that the situation could not continue so we ended the relationship. Subsequently the original owners re-launched their company at the original premises, and they still operate as a successful local packager today. It was difficult at the time, but useful lessons were learned.

■ Our best ever product range

Despite this distraction, our product designs were bearing fruit as never before. In the summer 2000 issue of Private Label News we were able to boast a total of ten products that were each number one in their particular sectors at the time, funded by five different lenders from our panel.

We were riding high. We had launched buy-to-let and 105% LTV products with Mortgage Express and were increasing sub prime volumes with Kensington and GMAC-RFC. Procuration fees were increasing and we were making our service enhancements count.

It was all going so well, until we received the call we had been half-expecting. HMSL announced that it was intending to broadly follow the lead that Britannia and Bradford & Bingley had set two years earlier and transfer its third party business to a

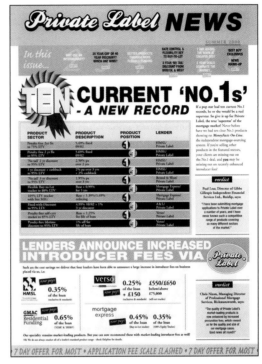

Our summer issue containing ten number one products

subsidiary, which would focus mainly on niche products. Back to first base again. Halifax plc had acquired Birmingham Midshires a few years previously. Following a strategic re-think it was decided that Birmingham Midshires would be re-launched as a niche, specialist lender. As we know from subsequent history, that strategy has been expanded as Birmingham Midshires has now entered the sub prime arena.

Although Halifax was very friendly about it at the time, the core of our relationship with that lender had always been market-leading mainstream deals backed by the Halifax name. In the final quarter of 2000, therefore, we had to have a long, hard strategic re-think. Fortunately, our record-breaking year had given us the time and financial success to be able to do this.

■ The decision is made

We could have looked for more mainstream lenders to add to our panel. But it seemed obvious that eventually Private Label would be forced into the niche areas of the mortgage market for the majority of its business, which is indeed where most

In the second in our series on specialist packagers, **Karen Bayne** looks at Private Label which is receiving acclaim for its products and services

PRIVATE Label has been earmarked as "the most innovative of packagers" by smaller mortgage brokers.

Mortgage advisers praised the company for designing market-leading products which adapted to changes in the market place.

Simon Jones, associate at London-based IFA Savills Private Finance, said: "It has mastered the art of bringing the lender a new idea for product models and negotiating exclusive deals.

"It is first in the field for providing a packaging service for the smaller broker – especially on loans under £100,000."

Patrick Bunton, senior manager at Bath-based IFA London and Country Mortgages, said: "It knows the broker market well and uses its bulk purchasing power to secure good headline rates. While it is of limited use to big brokers, the 'small guy' on the high street gets access to products he would not get as a smaller broker."

Ray Boulger, technical manager at national IFA John Charcol, praised the provider's lifetime tracker product.

He said: "This is the best rate on the market at 0.65 per cent above the Bank's base rate. It taps into an expanding area as borrowers will become increasingly attracted to a product where they can benefit when base rates fall below 5.5 per cent in the coming years."

Commentators ranked the provider highly for product range and service.

Andrew Clothier, mortgage specialist at Wolverhampton-based Kensington Investment Management, said: "It has improved over the last six months and applications can be completed within two to three weeks.

"The fact that it has underwriters on site means that there is a straightforward and speedy line of communication for advisers."

He recommended the buy-to-let tracker mortgage, funded by Mortgage Express.

Mr Clothier said: " The rate is 6.99 per cent – 0.99 per cent above the bank base rate. It is available on purchases and remortgages up to 80 per cent of the value of the property for five years and there are no restrictions on the number of properties, up to a maximum of £1m."

According to Mr Clothier, the closest competition comes from rival packager Exclusive Connections.

He said: "It offers a similar product also funded by Mortgage Express. The initial payable rate is 6.5 per cent – a discount of 1.25 per cent off the lender's variable rate. But it only lasts for two years."

But advisers bemoaned the withdrawal of the two-year fixed product. Private Label replaced the product with a 2.25 per cent discount last week.

Patrick Bunton said: "Funded by G-Mac, it was one of the stars of the range, with a rate of 5.95 per cent and no extended penalties.

Leeds & Holbeck also offers 5.95 per cent for two years but borrowers have to take its buildings and contents insurance or pay an extra 0.2 per cent."

Mortgage best-buys, page 53

Excellent publicity as we powered on in 2000. Financal Adviser. 13 April 2000

packagers operate today. We felt that we needed a strong mainstream presence in order to fully maximise our growth potential with major distributors, and we were keen in any event to turn ourselves more into a creator and trader of assets, as opposed to an originator of pre-offer packages. The experience of underwriting and issuing offers on behalf of GMAC-RFC had further strengthened this view.

We therefore decided that the HMSL move would be the catalyst for a fundamental change to how we did business. At the end of 2000, we wrote to all of our lenders and gave notice that we would be discarding the Private Label model by Q4 of the following year (2001). Going forward we wanted to be operating under a model where we issued the offer and completed the loan in the GMAC-RFC name.

We offered our lenders the option of the through lending model, or the alternative of us selling completed portfolios of mortgages to them. To make this change transparently clear, I included the following words in my chairman's report published with the 2000 Private Label Group accounts:

"We believe that by taking more control of the manufacture and delivery of the products within our range, trading them post completion rather than at offer hand off, we will be able to make quantum leaps forward in terms of our market penetration and influence, whilst also delivering new services to our intermediary and institutional customers. This approach will also better suit the market conditions that lie ahead".

Private Label then closed the year 2000 with new business flat. Pre tax profit increased marginally to £2.25m and we ended the year with a record £5.1m in cash at bank and in hand. We knew that 2001 would be our last year operating the traditional Private Label model.

2001

■ New brand assists transition

As marketing director by then of both GMAC-RFC and Private Label, Simon Knight felt that Private Label had to do something early in 2001 to prepare for the transfer of all pre completion business to GMAC-RFC by the end of that year. He therefore devised a new brand for Private Label which used the GMAC colours and showed us as "a GMAC company". His prediction (which subsequently turned out to be correct) was that the next move, effectively losing the Private Label brand altogether, would be seen as a small step from the new position, but too large a step from the original logo.

We announced our "face lift" in a new style Private Label News issued in February 2001. In that edition we also announced a couple of mainstream products funded by GMAC-RFC.

The launch of these products had strategic

Private Label
A GMAC company

News   February 2001

Same name. Same team. New style.

Our logo's had a facelift. The new image is not only crisper and more modern, it also reinforces that we are part of one of the world's largest financial services groups. The same well established Private Label management team will continue to provide you with market leading, exclusive products from a range of lenders in an intermediary-friendly manner in order to give you a competitive edge. But - fourteen years on from our original incorporation - we've now updated our style a little which we hope you like.

Our new, interim logo on our way to full integration

rather than financial motives, designed as they were to further assist the transition from Private Label to a fully integrated GMAC-RFC company, while positioning GMAC-RFC as a provider of "mortgages for everyone". This move certainly raised eyebrows in the market, particularly since most of the lenders Private Label dealt with were moving in the other direction.

■ The lender panel diminishes: GMAC-RFC increases to 70%

As we moved into 2001, we sat down with each lender in turn to discuss the new way forward. We saw Bristol & West first. Then Verso. Then Kensington, Alliance &

Leicester, West Bromwich BS and the rest of the panel. We quickly realised that it was going to be difficult to achieve two giant leaps at the same time.

Giant leap number one was to end the Private Label relationship in the way that had worked so well for many years. The second leap was to then persuade the same lenders to adopt a completely new model, that is to buy completed assets from GMAC-RFC. Rather like the rejection and selection debate discussed in chapter 2, it proved impossible to achieve in one stage. We had to have a clean break first.

Subsequently, not too long afterwards, I am delighted to say that Britannia, Bradford & Bingley and West Bromwich from the original Private Label panel returned to the table, and they remain among the largest of the GMAC-RFC portfolio purchasers some five years later. So the concept clearly had value - it just took time to select the new way forward.

As the year progressed, we were ending new business with one Private Label lender and replacing it with products funded by GMAC-RFC. By the summer, 70% of our business was GMAC-RFC products.

The end was most definitely in sight. In fact, by the autumn, we only had two other lenders left funding new products for us (Mortgage Express and Birmingham Midshires). So we agreed to stop passing business to them after October 2001.

Wrap up

So, that's it. We generated our last applications as Private Label in October 2001. The offer pipeline took until early 2002 to complete. Even now, Private Label remains a live company receiving renewal income from business generated many years ago. But it stopped trading four years ago. Did I feel sad about the closure to new business of my creation some 14 years previously? Not a bit.

I had a great time creating this company, and leading it on a rollercoaster ride. Along the way, some fantastic people have joined me and helped the company develop in a way that reflected their style as much as mine. Some 39 of them are still with me now, most having put up with me for 10-20 years each.

The simple truth is that the core Private Label business model of designing and distributing exclusive mainstream mortgage products funded by household name lenders, had run its course. Private Label was the first company of its type, and grew to be the largest.

It has a permanent role in the history of the evolution of the UK mortgage market. It spawned "the packager sector" and had several market firsts to its name. But the new model is better, and the merging of the Private Label skills and experiences with the global lender GMAC-RFC has played a part in taking the latter to top 10 lender status in the space of a few short, hectic years.

THE EVOLUTION AND FUTURE OF PACKAGERS

"So, you're a broker".
"No, there's a broker in-between us and the customer. We won't be seeing customers or giving advice".
"Then you're a master broker".
"No, we'll act for the lender, with whom we'll have a funding contract".
"Well, that kind of makes you the lender, doesn't it?"
"No, because we'll not be raising the funds ourselves, or entering into mortgage contracts with borrowers".
"Could you run this by me again?"

The original packager model

Even today, packagers sometimes complain that it is difficult to explain to others what they do. But at least there are other companies in the same boat. Back in 1987, when I was launching Private Label, we were on our own.

There was no other company like us. It took me the best part of a year, from initial concept to ultimate launch, to get just one lender, and just four insurance companies, to understand what I was proposing.

A year after that, however, we had two lenders and eleven insurance companies. So it quickly caught on. A few years after that, other similar organisations started to appear. The packager sector, now estimated to be contributing more than £20 billion of lending each year, was born.

The word "packager" arrived much later though. It was not a word we used to describe ourselves in the early days. Private Label called itself a "mortgage design and distribution company".

Several other descriptive names have been tried since, such as "outsourcer"; "branded mortgage arranger"; "aggregator" and so on. But "packager" has stuck, even though it does not actually mean anything, and has certainly contributed to regulatory confusion. Anyway, we go with the flow. "Packager" it is, and the UK's first packager was launched in 1987.

The original objective behind the launch of Private Label was that we reckoned we could do a better sales and marketing job than most lenders' sales and marketing departments. We knew we would not be able to convince lenders of that just by claiming it to be so. We therefore went in search of a lending organisation that would allocate us a tranche of funds, and agree a pricing model with us, so that we could go and prove it, and get paid per completion.

I had already presented my concept to Mortgage Systems Limited, then the UK's largest third party administrator (now incorporated into HML). They were keen to take on the administration and look after the loans post completion. Indeed, Michael Kelly (MSL's founder) and Barry Field (its legal director) joined the Private Label board to boost our search for a funder.

The initial distribution was available. What I described at the time as the "marzipan layer" insurance companies - those who were not quite big enough to get onto the distribution panels of the newly launching centralised lenders - were feeling threatened about their ability to access competitive mortgages. At the time, wholesale funded centralised lenders were very much the flavour of the day, undercutting the slow-to-react building societies and fast claiming a large market share.

Building societies had dominated UK mortgage lending for 200 years. In some years they had claimed over 90% of total mortgage advances. From a standing start in the mid 1980s, however, centralised lenders had quickly claimed significant market share. Building societies were shocked when, in the final quarter of 1988, statistics showed that centralised lenders had taken 50% of all new lending. Wholesale funded lending was therefore very

Extract from Private Label's first promotional brochure in 1987

much the fashion, and much in demand.

We could offer the smaller insurance companies something better than their aspiration of gaining access to the distribution panels of the new, centralised lenders. We could offer them the same sort of pricing model, but with products customised to their requirements and branded in their name. They had to do the printing and pre-offer processing, but we sold this as a benefit.

The insurance companies sought to attract new business and sign up appointed representatives in light of the sales adviser polarisation rules introduced under the Financial Services Act 1986, whereby advisers had to choose to be independent financial advisers or operate as tied sales reps. We offered the companies an

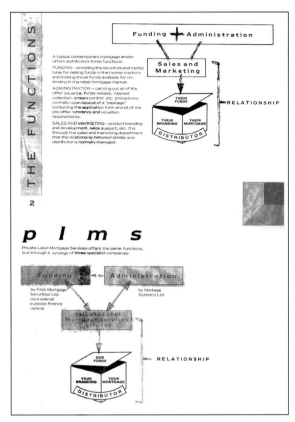

Extract from Private Label's first promotional brochure in 1987

in-house, off-the-shelf, ready-to-use mortgage scheme. It would be a scheme that we had put together, but which they would put their label on. Hence the name of our company.

Our first funder was FMS, itself a joint venture between several financial institutions including Bank of Scotland and Morgan Grenfell. FMS dedicated a special purpose lending company to each of their schemes, because there were different products in each of them, and it was easier to securitise that way. We were allocated a company with the exciting and innovative name, FMS Number 3.

But we did not care. We had our first tranche of funding and, anyway, the branding on the forms and marketing material was in the name of the insurance company distributors.

We launched with the initial four insurance companies and then set about recruiting some more. We even had the idea that we could offer branded schemes to building societies to top up their lending with some of the new wholesale-funded money, but that did not work.

The illustrations on these pages show extracts from our first ever promotional brochure, reflecting the convoluted way we had to try and explain this new concept to the insurance company audience.

As ever, the products did the talking. We had used the product model to create some highly competitive rates, and interesting criteria angles. Other medium-sized insurance companies had noticed this and called us up. So did some large ones. Within a few months, we had more insurance companies applying to become distributors than we had available resources to serve them.

As a small company, funded by my life savings and the equity in my house, we were not in a position to quickly inject new funds. The banks were not interested in lending it to us because we had only been trading for a few months. The venture capital boys wanted too big a stake of my company.

We therefore hit on the idea of charging the second wave of insurance companies a fee. Yes, not only were we paying no procuration fee, but we were actually charging insurance companies to access our product designs and branded packages.

They did pay, between £15,000 and £25,000 each. Nobody complained: the insurance companies were getting something unique.

We used the cash to bring in some more people and the business went from strength to strength. We added a second lender, Paribas, in 1988 and a third lender, Leeds & Holbeck Mortgage Corporation, in 1990. Insurance company distributors had by then reached 15 in number and Private Label's annual lending was already the equivalent of a medium-sized building society.

The initial joining fees paid by the insurance companies were self evidently one-offs. Our regular earnings derived from the lending itself. We received from the lender the customer-paid arrangement fee, then about £195, plus a 50% share of general insurance commissions and trail earnings of 10 - 15 basis points per annum on outstanding mortgage balances, paid monthly in twelfths.

It was very tight in the early days and I took no salary, no expenses and had no company car. But as we went into the early 1990s I was so glad that we had structured our earnings in this way (with a large renewal content), because, when the recession hit, two of the main structures which had underpinned the original Private Label proposition crumbled away.

As interest rates began to soar, building societies started to undercut the wholesale funded lenders again - a reversal of the previous position. The building societies had access to retail deposits which tended to stay put in a recession as investors fled to safety. Building societies were paying so little for these funds that the investors were "enjoying" a negative real rate of return: in other words, the interest rate they received net of tax was less than the rate of inflation.

The resultant building society mortgage rate was less than the centralised lenders could afford, dictated as the centralised lenders were by money market rates. As quickly as they had become fashionable, the centralised lenders became extremely unpopular and, one-by-one, those initial players quickly disappeared off the scene.

As this was going on, the insurance companies were also involved in recessionary cut backs. They felt that they could no longer undertake themselves the pre-offer processing of mortgage applications for no fee. They did not have to do the "packaging" when they were passing mortgage applications to building societies, so they told us that they would no longer do it for Private Label. We therefore had very quiet years in 1992 and 1993 as we reacted to this swift market change. But we still made a profit from those renewal earnings. It gave us time to re-group.

We largely swapped our centralised lender panel for new building society appointments including bigger lenders such as Britannia, Bradford & Bingley and Bristol & West. We set up our own pre-offer processing capability so that we could receive unpackaged applications.

We changed the nature of our remuneration so that we received everything upfront on new business, to defray the cash flow strain caused by the new investment in people and systems. We also launched Private Label version 2- the packager model that readers will more easily recognise today.

New packager model is born

Since we could now accept unpackaged applications, there was no need to restrict our distribution to insurance companies. We had no need to rely on the staff and systems those institutions had in place to perform the pre-offer packaging process. We were undertaking that work now, so we opened up our products on a generic basis to the broker market at large. It was around about this time that we started to see others attempt to copy our strategy.

Because of our historical links with insurance companies, we still received the majority of our business from that sector in the early years. However, as the desire for branding on the part of the insurance companies drifted away, we focused mainly on the products themselves, clearly identifying the lender in every instance. An illustration from Private Label News appears in chapter 6. This will give you a flavour of how we were then marketing ourselves - markedly different from the highly conceptual presentation that we used initially, as illustrated in this chapter.

The first competitors we were conscious of were The Mortgage Operation and Advance Mortgage Funding. The latter represented an alliance of packagers, each using the same name with their home town in brackets afterwards. Advance Mortgage Funding (Lichfield) became Pink Home Loans.

Staff who previously manned insurance company "mortgage desks" were a prime source of new packager launches. The insurance companies were cutting back, but helping brokers place mortgages was what the desks specialised in. So why not do it independently and create a business out of it? Another source of packager launches was salesmen and relationship managers leaving the exiting centralised lenders. John Rice, Managing Director of RAMP remembers it well:

"The expertise that had been built up among personnel in the insurance company mortgage desks, as well as among Business Development Managers of centralised lenders, provided a rich pool from which packagers emerged".

Some lenders were initially reluctant to deal with packagers. Indeed, some maintain that stance even today. The specialist lenders were first to recognise the role of packagers plus some mainstream lenders like Bristol & West.

As the market picked up, the reason why brokers and lenders might want to deal with the packagers changed. On the lending side, packagers were proving to be good sources of distribution. Instead of dealing with hundreds of different brokers, the lender could deal with one packaging source. It was particularly cost effective.

On the broking side, packagers offered a choice of lenders. Because of the concentrated amount of business going through one source, packagers often had power and influence over lenders that an individual broker could not exercise. This was useful on many occasions when trying to get marginal cases through, or getting queries and complaints resolved flexibly.

Also, many brokers liked talking to packagers who, like them, were keen to get the cases completed so that everyone could get paid. Too often the bureaucracy of the lender's staff caused frustration among brokers, helping to drive up demand to deal with the more responsive and commercially-minded packagers.

Packagers began to increase the fee they required for their services, as paid by the lender, and started to share some of this fee with brokers. Packagers also started to evolve some of the add-on benefits for using their services which still very much survive today.

One common application form, acceptable to all lenders, is a good example of this. If the initially chosen lender rejected the application, but another lender on the packager's panel could be persuaded to accept it, there was no need to go back to the client and change application forms.

In Private Label's case, we got all of our lenders to also accept a generic valuation report form as well, confirming that the valuer owed his duty of care to "all lenders on the Private Label panel". We could therefore switch the valuation over as well.

We never did this on behalf of the brokers. Even pre Mortgage Code and statutory regulation, we stressed to the broker that, by offering a switch, we were simply presenting them with a choice. We required specific confirmation back that this choice was something that they and their clients wished to exercise.

One application fee scale, one common application form and one seamless switching process offered great service to the busy mortgage broker. By and large, they are what packagers still offer today, in addition to a whole range of new technology-inspired benefits. Very valuable they are, too.

One thing that differentiated Private Label from its contemporaries was that it was still designing its own products. Right up to the last month of trading, October 2001, Private Label undertook the vast majority of its business on products which it designed and which were exclusive.

Another contrast was that Private Label had a relatively small lender panel because it wanted to be more important to fewer lenders. From the lenders' perspective, there were not that many who were prepared to understand the cost savings of dealing with a packager and credit these to the product design model so that the resultant customer rate was competitive.

Private Label's competitors of the time tended to work with lenders' standard products and to specialise in offering a wider range of lending choices. This was a perfectly sound and differentiating model, which enjoyed good success.

I know that some people today feel that the packager sector evolved at the same time that sub prime lending launched in the UK. That was certainly the catalyst for an expansion of packagers from a handful to several hundred. But it was not the origin of the packager sector. For many years before that, packagers existed, offering mainstream and self certification products to insurance companies and brokers.

Sub prime is here

I describe briefly in chapter 6 the launch of the UK's first major sub prime lender, Kensington Mortgage Company. I am aware that there were some sub prime first mortgage lenders operating in the market prior to Kensington's 1995 launch. However, some of them were offering terms that did not qualify them in my view for the description of sustainable or serious first mortgage player. Kensington was different.

Kensington, in the form of founder Martin Finegold, first approached us at the end of 1994. Eventually, after much persuasion, we agreed to participate in the launch of Kensington so long as we were able to eliminate all of the "nasties" that had previously been associated with this end of the market (Rule of 78 redemption charges, high discretionary rates, very high procuration fees and so on). Kensington were very happy to go along with this and we exclusively launched Kensington products in the autumn of 1995 and Kensington went open market in 1996.

The customers were getting a great deal. The gap between the ordinary mortgage rate, and the terms being offered by those previously prepared to lend to sub prime borrowers, was huge. The Kensington rates were in the middle of that gap, trending nearer to mainstream.

Nonetheless, the earnings that were available to packagers with sub prime were at least three times the level then being enjoyed on mainstream loans. Today, that ratio has increased, to at least five times mainstream earnings. It is no surprise, therefore, that mainstream lending through packagers has largely disappeared and sub prime has become the main focus.

Seeing Kensington's success, other lenders decided to launch into the sub prime market. Indeed, GMAC-RFC, an early funder of Kensington, launched its own sub prime lending operation in the spring of 1998.

By then, The Money Store, SPML and others had launched into the sector, all with a US background. The sub prime market is more mature on the other side of the Atlantic and there is no doubt that, with the Americans' greater experience of how this market can perform, the US lenders took their UK counterparts by storm with this new style of lending.

These emerging lenders all required packagers to distribute their products. Sub prime was still a relatively new concept and brokers did not understand it. Even up to the late 1990s there were some brokers and insurance companies who refused to handle sub prime business. But packagers persuaded brokers that they would be better off handing an enquiry to them, rather than telling the customer to go away, because the packager would almost certainly be able to find a solution, and the broker could earn handsomely from this.

It is thus that many more individuals in the industry decided to give up their jobs and start packaging companies. There were, quite literally, hundreds of them launching, based on business plans which involved focusing on sub prime only, enjoying the significant margins available.

This partnership, between packagers and sub prime lenders, then became self-perpetuating. As packagers became more specialist in sub prime lending, so lenders increasingly turned to them. As lenders increasingly turned to them so the position of packagers became more powerful, and so the spiral continued.

There is nothing wrong in this. It is often how markets work. Packagers did a great job in helping to steer brokers through the maze of choices that were starting to characterise the sub prime market. It seemed that no two lenders categorised borrowers in the same way, thereby rendering a direct comparison between two sub prime lenders' product ranges quite difficult.

Packagers became adept at this, and brokers came to appreciate their specialism. For most brokers a sub prime application was still outside of the norm, so if a problem could be handed off to a packager to solve then this freed the broker up to deal with his more mainstream cases.

As Roger Morris, Managing Director of EM Financial puts it:

"In those days, packagers took all the provided information and assessed the main requirements of the client. They then searched through the thousands of products available to them from a number of lenders with a view to finding the best fit".

John Rice, Managing Director of RAMP adds:

"Packagers had the ability to aggregate a multitude of product offerings; they could cascade horizontally across lenders as well as vertically".

Private Label never provided that service, which is why sub prime never came to dominate Private Label's volumes. When its access to mainstream products started to disappear under margin pressure, that is when Private Label exited the packager sector in search of a solution under which it could become a lender.

It was not in my original plan to become executive chairman of a lender, but, having done so, I was happy to offer a type of lending solution to other packagers, via the correspondent and branded arrangements discussed in chapter 2.

I think there is more that can be done down that route, as I discuss a little later in this chapter.

Disturbing the packagers' stranglehold

When Birmingham Midshires entered the sub prime market it launched an astonishing attack on packagers. Having started the UK's first packager, and having been a strong supporter of the packager concept, I protested. The responses I received were along the lines that BM wished to open up a broker direct distribution channel for sub prime mortgages and felt that it had to disturb the packager channel in order to do so.

I did not agree with this approach then, and I do not agree with it now. The elegant way in which to increase market share is to boost yourself, not knock down others. The attack on packagers by BM was aggressive, both in terms of PR quotes and the trade press advertising campaign. I am surprised that the trade magazines agreed to carry advertisements like these:

EXAMPLE 1

HEADLINE: "Sub prime. Won't deal with greedy packagers? Neither will we".

VISUAL: Sinister person behind bars with sign showing "Danger do not feed"

COPY: "In our book, there are only two things worse than a greedy packager.
Being forced to use one. And being forced to pay their excessive fees.
It's unfair to you. It's unfair to your clients. And we want nothing to do with it.
That's why we'll package our mortgages for you. Completely free of charge.
So, if you'd rather know more than pay more, give us a call".

EXAMPLE 2

HEADLINE: "Sub prime. It's time to cut out the middling man".

VISUAL: Man with box on his head

COPY: "Bad packagers make sub prime worse for everyone. Why?
Because they're not exactly transparent. And they slow up the whole process.
So, unlike some lenders, BM Solutions won't force you to use them.
In fact, from now on, we'll package any of our sub prime mortgages for you.
More interested in the product than the packaging?
Just call our dedicated sub prime number".

BM claimed that it was not criticising packagers generally, only those packagers which did not meet that lender's "seal of approval". It can claim some success in its strategy, in that it did open up a broker direct channel for sub prime business that did not exist before. Moreover, it can claim with some justification that it did support certain packagers, and it is true that there was a footnote on some of their advertisements listing, and thereby promoting, the packagers that it did endorse. It was surprising, though, that the packagers concerned gave their permission for their names to be included in this campaign, but it did bring to them a notoriety of sorts.

There are therefore arguments on both sides of this debate. But I felt that the image of a packager behind bars, in particular, was unnecessary. Coming as it did at the time of consultation regarding statutory regulation, I believe this campaign had the potential to seriously damage the image and reputation of packagers. What it did demonstrate, quite clearly, was the power and status that packagers had by then acquired.

Channel conflict

Lenders offering brokers the opportunity to deal directly on a simplified range of sub prime products brought with it the issue of channel conflict that still exists today. Previously dominating the sub prime sector, packagers were naturally reluctant to see lenders bypass them and offer products direct to brokers. They felt this was disloyal and undermining, and such moves were very often accompanied by emotional telephone calls and letters from packagers to lenders.

As I argued in chapter 2, if you try and say that a particular demand will not be satisfied in order to "protect" others, it never works. You don't protect anybody by stifling demand. You protect by seeking at all times to attract (rather than contract) business, accentuating the positives and adding value.

There happened to be brokers in the market who preferred dealing directly with lenders. Telling them they could not, and forcing them to deal with packagers, was not the answer. We were the first lender to give packagers the opportunity of presenting themselves as the lender, through the correspondent and branded lender arrangements. That was a positive step to increase choice.

At the same time, for those intermediaries who were not persuaded, GMAC-RFC, too, joined the ranks of those lenders who offered brokers the opportunity to deal directly, if they preferred, as described in chapter 2. If packagers want the benefit of dealing with a major lender, with all the image, service and product competitiveness that this implies, then they must understand that a multi-channel distribution policy is the only viable option for such lenders.

I do not ever recall at Private Label seeking to stop lenders offering competitive products through other distribution channels. I always reckoned that we could design better products anyway. We welcomed the competition.

We felt, as most packagers should feel now, that there was a very good case for dealing with a packager, and that there was a sufficient number of brokers able to be persuaded in that regard. There were some who could not be persuaded. But that is how it is in the real world.

The channel conflict debate becomes most heated when the lender offers different products through each channel. Therein lies one of the key market dilemmas for packagers and lenders. For the main cost-saving benefits offered by packagers are in fact for the benefit of brokers rather than the lenders. Yet it is the lenders who pay for them.

Technology has eroded pre-offer costs for lenders, as covered in chapter 4. Yes, packagers deliver concentrated volume business and that is certainly worth a financial consideration. However, not the 2% difference which can separate the broker and packager fee on sub prime business.

When lenders deal directly with intermediaries, therefore, they can reflect a lower procuration fee in the product design model. That means that the products are often cheaper. However, the brokers do not get the benefit of the full range of packager services by dealing directly, and that could end up costing them. But if they choose to deal directly with the lender nonetheless, there is an uncertain future for lenders who still debit that direct product model with packager costs that are not actually payable. This is what lenders are doing when they offer the same product range through both channels.

Moreover, I think that, increasingly in the future, sub prime competition is going to come from building societies and mainstream lenders moving along the risk curve. They will offer sub prime pricing at even keener rates than are available in the market today. Those who burden their product design model with large procuration fees of up to 3%, as currently exists in the market today, will either be moved by the market into very toxic areas of lending, or be in the position of trying to sell rates that are one or two percentage points higher than are available elsewhere.

Our policy is to have two different product ranges, each reflecting the cost of distribution, and each designed to have their own in-built advantages. We believe that packagers are best placed to maximise their future prospects by promoting the best sub prime terms they can, at the minimum viable remuneration they need in order to make a good profit, and then justify this business based on the powerful range of services that they offer.

This will often mean a packager choosing a lender's "packager products" instead of its "broker direct" range. But I think that the packagers and the market will flourish using this approach. When I researched this chapter with a group of leading packagers, I asked them what they considered to be the principal threats to their future prosperity. A majority said "lenders dealing directly with the broker". But, although I agree with a lot of what they say, and their wisdom has certainly enriched this chapter, I do not agree with them on this issue. The biggest threat to packagers is lenders choking off a distribution channel, or loading the interest rates available through that channel, in order to somehow "protect" packagers from having to persuade brokers that their services are superior to dealing directly with the lender. This approach would never survive the regulator's interest, nor the inexorable march of mainstream lenders towards the sub prime market.

How technology has changed the landscape

One way in which packagers have clear differentiation is the manual versus automated underwriting debate. While point of sale decisioning has delivered tremendous operational and capacity benefit to the lending industry, as well as delivering an instant decision to customers at point of sale, it has brought with it some disadvantages.

It is difficult to argue with or persuade a computer. Some brokers, and their clients, want the opportunity to argue their particular case. Increasingly, therefore, packagers are promoting the fact that they offer manual underwriting.

Lenders are doing their bit to help packagers promote themselves in this regard, by supplying onsite underwriters who can make subjective decisions. We have a completely separate brand, High Street Home Loans, that serves smaller and satellite packagers with exactly this service.

Lenders are starting to realise, including ourselves, that automated decisioning may not be best suited to the packager sector, which has built up years of experience and goodwill with human underwriters. It is therefore a massive opportunity for packagers to "sell against" the world of automation so far as underwriting decisions are concerned. Even though we are pioneers in automated decisioning, we encourage that approach. There can never be anything wrong in offering choice. Some intermediaries will be persuaded that, instead of applying to the lender directly online for an automated decision, they should instead refer their applications to a packager who will nearly always come up with a series of choices. There will be other intermediaries who prefer to retain the control of dealing directly, and they will often access a different product range that is priced to reflect the use of technology. This is real competition, from which the customer benefits.

I do not subscribe to the view that customers are self evidently disadvantaged if they do not receive the cheapest rate in any particular sector. Very often, the customer makes an active choice for service or convenience over price.

It is perfectly valid for a customer to choose the local service of a small broker, and equally valid for that broker to choose the services of a packager to look at solutions for that particular application. Those solutions, coming as they do via the packager channel, will be priced to reflect that level of service. It is not bad advice for such customers to be served by their channel of choice.

Technological enhancement has brought other opportunities for packagers, beyond the manual versus automated underwriting debate. Linkage with lenders' websites is a good example of this. By using the website of one packager, brokers can have fast links to a number of lenders' KFIs. They can apply online to a packager for a decision in principle and have the packager respond with various solutions. The top packagers now offer online case tracking, and online submission to a variety of lenders. One website offers all solutions and this is a very powerful selling tool on behalf of packagers. As Paul Fletcher, Director of Zebra Homeloans puts is:

"The packager can act as the friendly interface between the intermediary and the lender and bring a simpler approach to the business. The prospect for an intermediary of entering online data several times to various lenders to produce DIPs is daunting. If the packager can save the intermediary that most precious commodity of time, then the service offered will be valued".

Obviously, the more that technology drives the interface between packager and broker, the more difficult it will be for the smaller packager to survive. That does not mean they are going to be extinct, however. The average age of a mortgage intermediary is well over 40, and many of those market participants are not entirely comfortable dealing with all aspects of technology.

A healthy level of demand could exist for some time to come for the personal service offered by a small packager. But over the long term, the attractions of technology are hard to resist.

At Private Label, all those years ago, we used to offer brokers a couple of choices if their first choice lender rejected the case. But using technology, the top packagers can now offer a fantastically better service than that. As Michael Clapper, Chief Executive Officer of Enterprise Group comments:

"One issue that remains for most packagers is the need to demonstrate beyond doubt that no product or lender bias is included in their solutions. This is an area that the regulator will pick up on in the future and procedures and systems must be robust. At Enterprise, we built our own sourcing system which provides factually ranked solutions (from 7 to 300) based on any client priority requested".

Technology can therefore deliver via a packager something that a lender could not deliver on its own, namely a vast array of choice across a number of different lenders, all ranked according to the priorities identified by the broker.

On the case

Case tracking is another good example of where packagers have scored with the use of technology. How much more convenient for brokers if they can track all of their cases, with a variety of different lenders, through one source rather than chase all the different cases individually?

I remember well comments by several industry observers to the effect that the the growth of technology would remove the need for packagers altogether. In fact, pretty much the reverse has happened. Packagers, being entrepreneurs at heart, have embraced technology in a way that gives them market advantage. For those who like healthy competition, and more choice, it is a most welcome development.

But packagers need to keep investing. Technology never stops coming up with new solutions. As it becomes possible to eliminate valuation reports in the majority of cases, such that point of sale offers are available online within seconds of applying, then there is no case to track.

Technology will have to be used in a different way, to provide a service that cannot be predicted today. Packagers who invest heavily in technology will often find out what that new service will be long before lenders think of it.

Regulation

All packagers I researched felt that regulation had made fundamental differences to their business - some beneficial, some detrimental. They all point to the increased costs of validating broker status and having to introduce procedures to recognise a new Treating Customers Fairly regime.

Fee disclosure and polarisation of brokers, particularly those that join networks, are suggested as regulatory-driven factors that offer both opportunity and threat. But all welcomed the fact that some brokers are using packagers much more post-regulation, as the packagers can produce the paper trail that will be required by regulators to show that various products were considered.

The biggest unsolved issue in relation to regulation, however, is the state of limbo in which packagers find themselves concerning their own status. Some packagers serve customers directly and are therefore regulated as a broker.

Others have chosen to be regulated in relation to one or two particular activities, such as providing quasi-underwriting services on behalf of lenders, issuing offers and so on. Yet others, so-called "pure packagers", have no choice but to stay unregulated (although these are few in number because of the wide definition of "arranging"). At the time of going to press it is something that needed to be resolved by the FSA.

When I was a member of the CML working group investigating what recommendations we would make to the CML Executive Committee relating to the extension of the Mortgage Code to the intermediary sector, I was against the inclusion of packagers in rules that were meant for intermediaries involved in customer advice. There was no sense or logic in including organisations that provided outsourced services to lenders. I still take that view and argued in favour of it when responding to the various FSA consultation documents. However, the landscape has changed. The FSA decided to regulate bits of what packagers do, but not other bits.

We now have this patchwork packager regulation, with some lenders saying that they will not deal with unregulated packagers as if the packagers have a choice. If you are not carrying out a regulated activity, you cannot be regulated! But that does not mean that you are undertaking an activity which is of no economic value to lenders and brokers.

Given where we are today I now take the view that packagers should be regulated. The FSA should define the various types of packager which exist in the market today and come up with a regulatory regime which enables those statutory duties to be transparently discharged in a way that gives comfort and clarity to all. I therefore agree with Paul Robinson, Chief Executive of Solent Mortgage Services when he says:

"I believe that all packagers should be regulated. There should be no such animal as an unauthorised or unregulated packager".

Learning from the lenders' experience, the packagers I researched acknowledged that costs were a major deterrent when it came to mortgage regulation. Estimates vary as to how much the introduction of statutory regulation has cost lenders. The chairman of the Intermediary Mortgage Lenders' Association said at the annual dinner in September 2005 that the total cost to the lending industry of statutory regulation was £200m. The chairman of the Building Societies Association had suggested earlier in the year a higher figure than this, some £500m.

I think something towards the latter figure is likely to be more accurate than the former. What statutory regulation has done is to be so prescriptive in IT-related areas that millions of pounds has had to be spent getting KFIs, for example, to produce information exactly in the order required by the FSA, whereas a more generic approach could have cut those costs by at least two-thirds. David Wylie, Managing Director of C2 comments:

"One thing which is constant across all packagers is that regulation has increased costs, and this must be accounted for either by increasing market share or by cutting costs elsewhere. Increasing margins is the least likely model to succeed".

In other words, if new, regulatory costs are on the horizon for packagers, then some room will need to be created to accommodate them. This will either be through greater efficiencies or by finding ways to serve more customers. It is another point in favour of those who argue for the future survival and prosperity of the largest packagers only.

The need under regulation to create and maintain records demonstrating that appropriate choices have been given to customers is regarded by some as a further regulation-inspired opportunity. Packagers are well placed to provide a variety of choice from their own lender panel, and can get this together in a way that reduces the administration required of the broker. The biggest and most controversial points made in the regulation debate, though, are to do with fee disclosure and the power of networks. I will take these on under separate headings.

Whilst I think that regulation of packagers is probably inevitable, it should be from the perspective of logic and clarity. The one stumbling block is the resources available to the FSA. The regulator may feel that, until it can fully scope the resources it will need to regulate lenders and intermediaries (we are, after all, barely a year on from M-Day) they will not volunteer to take on the regulation of packagers beyond the activity-led approach taken so far. Time will tell.

Meanwhile, regulation as it exists today is certainly popular with some. Roger Morris of EM Financial says:

"Regulation was the best thing that ever happened. It allowed us to reinvent ourselves. Regulation made us look at our processes and prompted us to evolve our business. These investments and changes allowed us to capitalise in a market where many ill-prepared packagers failed to adapt".

Fee disclosure

The general consensus is that packager fee disclosure has not presented any disadvantages. Paul Robinson, Chief Executive of Solent Mortgage Services again:

"I see disclosure of fees as a good thing and this has not had an impact on my company. We can justify why we are paid packaging fees by the lender in the service we offer to our intermediaries".

Michael Clapper, Chief Executive Officer of Enterprise Group adds:

"We have not seen any negative consequences of disclosure. I do not believe that disclosure of fees will have an impact on the role or future of packagers, other than to provide more transparency and less 'deals behind closed doors'".

You have to listen to the guys who are running successful packagers, but I wonder whether the impact of fee disclosure has been beneficial or as neutral as might appear at first glance. Those 'deals behind closed doors' are sometimes good for the customer.

At Private Label, we often used to try and negotiate customised remuneration to help us bring particular products to market. I remember well an occasion when we surrendered all per completion earnings on a particular product and invested them in a market-beating customer rate. Our earnings on that particular product derived solely from the non refundable reservation fee we charged. We brought an exciting, high volume product to market that had, in our view, a tremendous strategic impact on the way that certain distributors viewed dealing with a packager.

We were demonstrating that we could bring a "best buy" product to the market just when it needed it, and we made money through the other business we did with the distributors who signed up because of that product. But we did not want that move known to everybody, because our brokers might have asked us to do it next time, and the time after that.

In other instances, we saw particular opportunities arising for the lender out of the use of interest rate derivatives, for example, which permitted us to ask for a share of the incremental earnings our idea had generated. Those occasional extra payments enabled us to not only invest in the services that we were able to offer customers through their brokers, but also to undertake exercises of the type described above, where we surrendered all earnings from the lender in order to get a particular customer rate. This is the way of business and it works to consumer advantage. But it can only be achieved if the details are kept secret.

Yet another example of this was our launch of Kensington Mortgage Company back in 1995. When we realised the profile of borrowers we would be attracting under this new sub prime product, it was clear that we would be involved in a lot more reject work than would be the case with mainstream loans. Instead of loading the fee that we received from the lender so that completing customers paid for the expenses generated by aborting customers, we asked Kensington for an additional fee per application.

We said that if our application form was completed and entered onto the system then we wished to be paid for that work by Kensington, not by the completing customers. Kensington were free to audit our systems at any time they wished in order to ensure that we were not being dishonest about the number of applications submitted and keyed to our system, but this is the way in which we wanted to approach the matter.

For a long time, we had a negotiating impasse on this issue. Kensington had not factored in such a fee to their calculations. But equally, we were determined to stick to our guns that this was the fairest way of dealing with the extra rejections that occur on sub prime work. We won the day, and our contract with Kensington reflected this payment right through to when we stopped accepting new applications in 2001. We also insisted that GMAC-RFC matched it if they wanted to join our panel.

Now, I'm not so presumptuous as to say that Kensington would not have eventually launched into the mortgage market, and gained just as much success, had it not linked arms with Private Label. However, I can only deal with the facts.

These are that Kensington did exclusively launch with Private Label and we were instrumental in breaking down some barriers for them in terms of the willingness of some distributors to participate in the sub prime market. Attaching our reputation to this new product gave Kensington, I believe, a faster launch than they would otherwise have achieved. Had we not been able to negotiate this fee, and keep it secret, the launch may never have taken place.

I do not believe that Kensington repeated this particular payment with any other distributor, and I know that GMAC-RFC did not. It is much better for the lender if one certain payment is made per completion, and the sort of auditing requirements a lender would need to establish with the packager to check that correct payments were being made are onerous at today's volume levels. Nevertheless, this is yet another example of something that would not have been possible had fee disclosure been in the public domain, because everyone would have asked for it and that would not have been viable.

Disclosure has therefore brought with it blandness and consistency. By and large, packagers are not able to exploit with lenders their own particular ideas and opportunities, because lenders cannot afford to pay one packager differently to another similar packager, because it is all in the public domain.

Packagers only have one way to leverage their efficiency and that is to try and win business by giving up more of their earnings to their introducing brokers on the back of operational efficiency. I believe that could be anti-competitive.

Ironically, fee disclosure in the way that is currently operated in the market has not been brought about by regulation. There is in fact no requirement for lenders to disclose the fees paid to unregulated packagers.

The requirement is to show the procuration fee paid to regulated entities on the KFI. But most lenders were not prepared to incur the IT development cost of differentiating between types of intermediary so as to split out that part of the procuration fee which is due to a regulated entity, whilst shielding the part that is paid for outsourcing.

We actually did incur that IT development cost and we were prepared to introduce it. However, we could only find two or three other lenders who were going down that route. It is thus that all fees paid away are disclosed by us as well.

Another way in which fee disclosure has probably worked to the disadvantage of packagers is the ability it has given brokers to demand an increase in share of the packager margin. Some would argue that this is healthy and reflects normal market supply/demand interaction. But ultimately, it could reduce customer choice because some packagers just cannot survive by paying the amount that brokers are requesting from them. Moreover, there is an active market of brokers playing one packager off against the other to get the highest procuration fee without obvious regard for the customers' best interests.

Vic Jannels, Group Managing Director of All Types of Mortgages, and a director of the Professional Mortgage Packagers' Alliance picks up a related point:

"There must be created a level playing field between what is paid to the packager versus the real cost to the lender for dealing with that direct client".

This is a fair point. When using a packager, lenders save costs that they would otherwise have to incur. The costs saved are nothing like the incremental procuration fee paid since, when it is not packaging itself, the lender loses the application fee income. Moreover, with automated, binding decisions made at point of sale by the computer, the actual cost to a lender of bringing an application through to offer is relatively small.

In fact, the main benefit to a lender from using a packager is on the distribution side, being able to access all of that packager's distribution through one point of contact. The point remains valid, however, that whatever cost savings there are do not have to be disclosed by the lender as an offset to the packager fee. This would be a problem if consumers took the slightest notice of these disclosures.

But they do not. We all knew this following the introduction of commission disclosure on investment products more than a decade previously. The consumer has not the slightest interest in who is being paid what and cannot in any event relate those payments to what is somebody's true worth, and what is not. All they know is that they do not have to make the payment, so if this disclosure proves that somebody who works in mortgages is better or worse paid than them, then that is something they probably expected anyway.

The financial services industry has spent millions of pounds complying with fee disclosure regulations, yet the number of customer cancellations or queries relating to the information they have received amounts to a fraction of one percent of all transactions undertaken during that period.

I think that regulation has achieved many good things, and I am on record as commenting that the FSA has done a great job with a difficult brief. But consumer benefit proportionate to the IT costs in the area of fee disclosure is not, in my view, one of the great victories.

The growth of networks

This is the other impact of regulation that most packagers researched commented upon. The typical customer for many packagers was the small, independent broker who occasionally had a sub prime or niche application. These brokers appreciated the service that their favourite packager could supply. They would be told which lender could offer the best terms for that particular application, and they would have experienced specialists guiding the case through to completion, using their knowledge of the market and relationship with the lender concerned to ensure no difficulties for the customer.

Then regulation put a huge cost and administration burden on the small broker, with the result that some were forced to join networks in order to have the compliance side of the business taken care of. The networks, not unreasonably, insisted that their own lender panel was used for all new business thereafter.

This was not just to create leverage in order to extract better customer products, particularly exclusives, although they were major considerations. It was also to make compliance monitoring practicable. A network would not be able to offer realistically priced compliance monitoring services if they potentially had a hundred lenders to follow up with and review. It was thus that many packagers lost broker customers that they had served for many years, and this was definitely a blow.

But, wherever there is disadvantage, there is also opportunity. The managers of networks soon received complaints from new recruits that the lenders the networks were able to offer could not match the same products or services the brokers used to enjoy with their favourite packagers. In what I believe was a major turning point in favour of packagers, networks started to realise that they could not do without them.

The leading packagers then started to be appointed to the supplier panels of the major networks. The appointed representatives could deal with any lender on the panel or any lender on the panel of the appointed packagers. It is a point well made by Michael Clapper, Chief Executive Officer of Enterprise Group:

"Just as there is a threat to those packagers that don't secure sufficient distribution, there is real opportunity for those that do. Once appointed to a network's panel, exclusively or not, there is less competition cost and this saving can be redirected towards service and product enhancement".

Tony Hughes, Director of Pavillion Securities agrees. He identifies being appointed to network packager panels as being the most important opportunity for packagers in the future. He says:

"The principal opportunity for packagers is being appointed to network packager panels, giving access to the network members to a limited number of packagers".

There is no room on every network panel for every packager. Those who do not make many, or any, panels are going to have to seek their distribution from independent brokers and/or by going directly to the consumer. For the biggest and most successful packagers, however, the polarisation of the broker community brought about by statutory regulation has brought net benefits so far as network panels are concerned.

Satellite packagers

This is a relatively new development for the market. Satellite packagers comprise mainly brokers who have turned themselves into packagers in order to benefit from the higher procuration fee, but who are not given direct packaging rights by many lenders. Instead, they receive their packaging rights from other, larger packagers who monitor their work.

In principle, I cannot see anything wrong with this. If a packager wishes to diversify its distribution in this way there is no reason why appointing satellite packagers should not be a valid choice.

It does mean, however, that the "host packager", if I can describe them in that way, must have effective monitoring techniques to ensure that the satellite packager is discharging its responsibilities in exactly the same way as the host packager would have done. Lenders will hold the host packagers responsible for the work of the satellite packagers, so it is essential to ensure that audit trails and supervisory visits are in place.

The future existence of satellite packagers would have been vulnerable if lenders had had to pay more when they were involved. But if it is a question of packagers splitting their own income then there is no real difference between this and the case of the regulated mortgage broker asking for a larger share of the packager's earnings.

The question always remains, though, did the consumers benefit in their chosen weighting between service and product? If so, then why shouldn't satellite packagers survive? If not, then their existence is going to be under threat.

Professional bodies

There are now two major trade bodies looking after packagers. The Professional Mortgage Packagers' Alliance represents more than 20 packagers. The more recently launched RAMP represents a further dozen. Those two trade association roles did not exist before packagers became important. But the role they perform now is generally considered to be valuable and effective.

Our contact at PMPA is Vic Jannels, one of the original founder members. RAMP is represented by John Rice. Both used to work for me. I am not sure whether that is good because I have been able to help them, or bad because I have given them a reason to leave. Probably a bit of both.

The good job they are both doing is raising standards and awareness. They represent their members well in the media and to lenders. They have been able to negotiate exclusive products and terms because of the concentrated volumes they represent. Indeed, one new lender, Beacon Home Loans, declared on launch that it would only be distributing its products through RAMP members. PMPA also has its own exclusive deals. Tony Hughes, Director at Pavillion puts it this way:

"Packager alliances are a major opportunity, improving access to exclusive products".

Michael Clapper of Enterprise Group concurs:

"RAMP and PMPA are two bodies which are now adding real value to packagers, lenders, brokers and their clients through additional regulatory safety and exclusive schemes negotiated by the bodies themselves, on behalf of their members".

If PMPA and RAMP continue to develop in ways that promote higher and higher standards, I can see a role for them to play in helping the FSA achieve the appropriate regulation for packagers. It is interesting how markets create an opportunity that businesspeople then fulfil.

It is only because packagers have maintained their influence and status, shrugging off much of the criticism that has come their way, that bodies like PMPA and RAMP have a job to do. It will be interesting to see if they merge or remain separate.

If they become lenders of course - and both bodies have floated this idea - they will just become commercial players like the rest of us. Their trade body status will go and others will have to come and fulfil that role.

The future

As I see it, the future for packagers has the same ingredients as the future for mortgage lenders and all other players in the market, namely uncertainty; threats to those without robust business plans; opportunities for those that are preparing well, and a real chance to build substantial organisations, rather like the mortgage bankers we see in the US.

Branded lending, which promotes the packager's own brand, and which delivers control of the application through to completion will be an important status to acquire. Building from this, I can see some packagers establishing their own warehouse lines, either becoming regulated lenders in their own right or using the umbrella of a lending organisation like The Money Partners have done in partnership with Kensington.

In the case of the warehouse line approach, the security for bank borrowing is largely provided by the mortgage assets being generated. There is a small requirement for additional capital, but this may not be too onerous for a large packager set-up. This is the way that mortgage bankers have evolved in the US, albeit without the same type of regulation we have in the UK, and I see this as an important opportunity. So does John Rice:

"If lenders outflank packagers to go direct to the intermediary or consumer, what stops packagers outflanking their suppliers by going direct to the funding markets?"

Some packagers see the future enshrined in more IT investment, producing better and more sophisticated services and choices for intermediaries. Others feel that close association with certain lenders could drive the way forward.

Most of those researched do not necessarily agree with me that building societies and mainstream lenders pushing along the risk curve, and introducing sub prime for their members and regular brokers, is a particular threat. Paul Robinson of Solent Mortgage Services comments:

"I think there will always be the need for the role of a packager. Building societies and mainstream lenders do not have the relationships in the B2B market that most packagers have. Companies like us that have been around 15 or 20 years have built their distribution on relationships, and I don't see this changing".

David Wylie, Managing Director of C2 agrees:

"Packagers have demonstrated that against all odds they can adapt and thrive. The entry of building societies and mainstream lenders into the BC market will, although bringing additional pressure to bear, ultimately not endanger the packager. We would see this as a further maturing of the market and the raising of consumer awareness where such products are in existence".

There's something in this. The more building societies and mainstream lenders get into sub prime, the more the product will become "mainstream". That is a two-edged sword, however, because this will have the effect of commoditising the products and bringing down margins to a level that might not be able to sustain the current level of packager payment. The increasing willingness to outsource right across the economy generally is another factor in favour of packagers, according to Vic Jannels, Group Managing Director of All Types of Mortgages Limited. He says:

"A major potential benefit for packagers will result from the desire of all parties in the mortgage food chain to consider outsourcing requirements. Lenders will find that their market suffers peaks and troughs. A packager will provide a steady distribution outlet with minimal cost to the lender, who does not have to recruit and dispose of staff simply to manage these variations in market forces".

Tony Jones, Managing Director of Pink Home Loans also has strong views about how packagers need to prepare for the future:

"The future of packagers is in their own hands. The market will continue to evolve rapidly and packagers must ensure that they continue to add value to their customers. Some may specialise in pure packaging operations, but this is a dangerous strategy as it is likely that lenders will use their own or outsourced systems to achieve economies of scale. Other packagers may seek to broaden their offering through providing network services; if they choose this strategy they will need to ensure that, when consolidation occurs, they will be one of the winners".

A pattern for future success is therefore starting to emerge:

- Increased investment to provide enhanced services to brokers

- More control of the lending

- Closer associations with lenders

- Stressing the power of outsourcing

- Greater status through regulation and/or association with packager alliances

- No one model dominating

These are all good possibilities, in varying shapes and sizes, which could contribute to the future success of packagers. The critical point so far as I am concerned is one that does not appear in that list. It is the reason why so many brokers want packagers to sort out their problems for them, and why so many packagers are able and happy to do this.

It is why, against all odds, so many packagers have survived and thrived, even when nasty attacks have been made on them. It is the "secret sauce" of the packager world which institutionalised lenders may never fully appreciate. It is put better than I ever could by Paul Fletcher, Director of Zebra Home Loans:

"Most intermediaries and packagers are owner-operator organisations and this proprietor-to-proprietor relationship is powerful and persuasive".

Brokers and packagers are both owner-managers, trying to make a living by their own enterprise. The vast majority of those working for lending institutions have not risked their own money and are working for a salary. Therein lies your secret sauce.

Wrap up

Packagers have actually been around for more than 18 years, starting with Private Label's launch in 1987. The first group of packagers distributed mainstream products. The packager sector only really exploded in terms of increased supply when Kensington launched into sub prime in 1995.

Packagers have evolved the services they offer to brokers. Technology now plays a massive part in that. Regulation can help, or it may hinder: it depends on how and if the regulator extends its supervisory control into the packager world.

Packagers should worry less about channel conflict and concentrate more on accentuating the positives, of which there are many. New lenders coming into the sub prime market might be a threat, but they also represent an opportunity of more funding for this mature, outsourced market.

Will packagers survive? Never bet against a good entrepreneur.

WHAT NEXT?

One of the most popular chapters in my previous book "The Art of Marketing Mortgages" was the one largely written by other people. I take no offence at this: the customer is king! In fact, as you will read in the pages that follow, I have built on and expanded this concept.

Last time, I asked 14 industry figures to let me have their views on "What Next?" in the mortgage market. This time I have asked 22. All eminent figures and real experts. I hope you will enjoy reading their views, provided in the latter part of 2005, as much as I have.

It is perhaps a sign of the times that only three of the original 14 are still doing the same jobs they were doing in 1997. However, I was delighted that those three, Adrian Coles, Michael Coogan and Robin Phipps have all contributed again.

Sadly, two of the original 14 contributors - Jim Gilchrist of Scottish Life and Sheila McKechnie of Which? - have died, and are sorely missed by the financial services sector as well as those close and dear to them. I knew Jim better than Sheila, and I miss him as an industry colleague and friend.

One contributor, Mark Wood, announced after writing his copy that he would be leaving Prudential for pastures new, but he graciously agreed that his piece could remain.

The 22 contributors are all individuals so well known to most people in the mortgage world that they need no introduction from me. They are very generous to share their views in this way and I offer them all warmest thanks. Their contributions differ in length because we have reproduced their words verbatim.

RAY BOULGER

SENIOR TECHNICAL MANAGER, JOHN CHARCOL

With the market awash with capital the current strong competition, including from some new players, will continue but a combination of commercial necessity and concerns about complying with the FSA's "Treating Customers Fairly" principle will mean that in 2006 many lenders will be looking closely at their retention policy. As borrowers become increasingly savvy, and intermediaries take a larger slice of the market, the proportion of lenders' books on SVR or equivalent has been dwindling for years and is now under 15%, although for some major groups the figure is around 10%. Consequently there is now little fat in the back book to support too many loss-leading offers to attract new business.

The handful of lenders who currently pay a procuration fee to intermediaries who recommend an existing client takes a new deal with them will see their ranks increased as more lenders realise that they need to work with intermediaries on a long term basis rather than just to acquire new customers. However, this will only work for lenders who offer new business rates, or similar, to existing customers as otherwise it is likely to be better advice for the borrower to remortgage.

One product which lenders don't yet appear to appreciate the retention potential of is the offset mortgage, particularly if linked to a current account or a savings account which accepts direct debits. In Australia current account and offset mortgages are far more common than in the UK, no doubt because they are priced in line with, or very close to, other mortgages. The premium on offsets in the UK is falling but is still too high. When lenders cease to insist on premium pricing for offset mortgages they will be the right choice for most borrowers and will give lenders a potentially powerful retention tool.

RICHARD BROWN

MANAGING DIRECTOR, BANK OF IRELAND PERSONAL LENDING (UK)

The big debate whenever talking to someone about the mortgage industry is house price movements because they affect us all. We are always in an over-heated market, a stagnant market or waiting for crash. We have now seen house price inflation fall from over 20 percent to low single digits in little over a year, so what will happen going forward? In my view the two key factors are what happens to interest rates which affects affordability and whether or not we have any recessionary trigger.

In terms of interest rates they drive affordability and the experience in the UK and Ireland shows that in a relatively short period house prices adjust in line with rates: ie if long term rates fall by half then prices double. In simple terms then if long-term rates continue to average in the 3.5% - 5.5% range then we should have a stable market. If rates fall to a lower long-term level in line with Europe then we will have significant further price inflation, but if long term rates were to move up by say 25% then we would see a significant period of stagnation.

The other key question is will we get a recessionary trigger or not? Relative to current rates prices are high but not excessively so. However, if we were to have a significant upturn in unemployment and corresponding change in sentiment then I think we would see real house price falls. Interestingly, in common with most mainstream lenders, I think Bank of Ireland and Bristol and West are more exposed to a downturn in housing transactions than house prices. We all have high quality secured books with a good deal of equity, but all need continued growth in earnings to hit our plans and this requires an active purchase as well as re-finance market.

If I were to stick my neck out, what else would I expect in the next few years?

- Buy-to-let arrears will continue to outperform the standard market but new business pricing will fall materially
- Self Certification arrears will move above the average even in the clean credit self-cert lenders
- We will all start to price up for first time buyer business due to the new capital regimes
- Churn will continue to grow, and average mortgage lives will continue to fall
- UK will still not enter the euro
- Stamp duty will not be reduced
- Single premium payment protection will cease to exist
- The UK element of the Spanish property market will hit problems
- A number of credit card and personal loan providers will show significant increases in bad debts and change their pricing

Given that I bought my first shares in July 1988, and my first property in March 1989, the best advice is not to follow mine!

ADRIAN COLES

DIRECTOR GENERAL, THE BUILDING SOCIETIES ASSOCIATION

Three key factors have shaped the mortgage market over the last five years, and these seem likely to have a strong influence over the next five. First, we have seen a sharp reduction in interest rates that, not surprisingly, has been reflected in a sharp increase in asset - ie house - prices. This one-off adjustment will not be repeated. As I write house price inflation has fallen to zero and seems likely to stay there. For new borrowers housing equity will not be created through house price inflation; 90% LTV loans will remain just that and borrowers will actually have to repay debt to create their own equity. This will have a powerful influence on how the market, and particularly trading up, will work in the future.

Secondly, margins will continue to narrow. The average building society margin has fallen from 1.42% in 2001 to 1.13% in 2004 - a 20% fall in just three years. Figures of other lenders reflect the same competitive pressures. The pressure will be on management to extract ever more cost efficiencies, while providing an ever-improved service to consumers. What some will see as unpalatable decisions or issues such as branch closures and offshoring will, in some cases, either be forced on, or embraced by, some institutions.

Third, regulation will continue to intrude on management and interfere with the management/consumer relationship. "Fairness" will become an overwhelming regulatory issue. There are currently seven regulatory regimes in the UK using the "F" word! The institution that works out best how to deal with customers fairly and efficiently, while coping with zero house price inflation will take the prizes in tomorrow's market.

MICHAEL COOGAN

DIRECTOR GENERAL, COUNCIL OF MORTGAGE LENDERS

Making accurate predictions in 1997 was a lot easier than it is now! Politically, we are better placed as an industry than for 20 years with a Government looking to increase home ownership levels towards 75%. This could mean a million extra borrowers by 2010. However, this political commitment will have to be backed by more action to reduce entry costs - a lower and fairer stamp duty - if first time buyers are to be encouraged to act in large numbers.

The introduction of home information packs is the Government's major reform agenda for the housing market. It will not be implemented on time at the beginning of 2007. Will it be introduced at all if the perceived long-term consumer benefits will be at the cost of significant market disruption in the house buying process?

Consumer confidence in home ownership will endure. Consumers will want to build an asset for the future. Conversely, attempts to increase saving in long-term investments will not succeed as trust in financial services companies remains low.

In the next five years, regulation will become more intrusive. The winners in the industry will be those who lead on the treating customers fairly agenda, seeing it as a commercial necessity rather than as a compliance issue. A review of the new mortgage rules will lead to few changes, as the FSA's moves to simplify their rulebooks stall due to lack of industry support. Consumers will become more used to key facts documents but shopping around will not increase.

We will face threats of new regulatory intervention from Europe as integration of mortgage markets is promoted for retail customers. These will not succeed as consumers are simply not interested in cross border borrowing.

The government and the FSA will extend their commitment to improve consumers' financial capability. Lenders will promote the new FSA developed debt test. Consumers' understanding of the potential risks of borrowing will improve. They will become more aware of their credit status, which they will seek to manage more pro-actively. This will be increasingly important as new capital rules drive forward risk based pricing in the mortgage market.

High levels of remortgaging will remain a permanent feature of the lending landscape. Despite industry and government efforts to encourage sustainability, the consumer preference will continue to be for higher-risk, variable-rate mortgage products, not 25 year fixed rate mortgages.

STEVEN CRAWSHAW

CHIEF EXECUTIVE, BRADFORD & BINGLEY

At Bradford and Bingley, we have been in the unique position of observing the mortgage market from two perspectives - as a lender and a broker. The market will continue to evolve - although things tend to change more slowly than many commentators predict. My predictions are as follows:

1. The UK consumer will continue to drive the mortgage market on in a period of measured house price inflation. A growing segment of long term "rent by lifestyle choice" consumers will represent a new social trend

2. The buy-to-let market will continue to grow at a more mature pace.

3. Lenders will continue to wrestle with the conundrum of how to retain customers. As "back book" and "front book" margins converge proactive retention lending will become increasingly standard.

4. But retention lending will not, as some have suggested, kill re-mortgaging or dis-intermediate brokers. Proc fees to brokers may evolve to reflect the longer game.

5. Lenders will continue to balance income between margin and fees, and intermediaries will play an ever more important role in helping consumers navigate through the various dimensions of pricing.

6. Some lenders will look to cement long-term relationships by offering ultra-low margin, long-term deals.

7. Lifetime mortgages will take off - the only question is when. There is already a huge need for equity release, but regulatory fear threatens to stifle distribution.

8. Customers will continue to benefit from an innovative market. Lenders will need to continue to examine the economics of all parts of the value chain.

CHRIS CUMMINGS

DIRECTOR GENERAL, AIFA & AMI

It is easy to reflect on the mortgage market and focus on an industry going through change. However, change is a part of our market, as the old adage goes: it really is the only constant. That means firms have choices: to wait till the impact is felt and then respond, endeavour to keep up with the curve, or to be bold and try to shape the market as they wish to see it.

Macro-economic and political influences are stronger in the market today than, perhaps, at any other time. The global nature of financial services is apparent as new players make their presence felt, and capital shifts around the world. Newer influences of statutory regulation and the increasing bite of European regulation are only just working through our system and the market requires a strong and robust defence against the excesses of regulations that would change the shape of the industry - often more by unfortunate error than deliberate design.

Closer to home, the relationship between intermediaries and lenders is moving through a cycle to develop into an increasingly mature relationship between strategic business partners. I fervently hope that the "bad old days" of intermediary distribution being seen as a necessary evil are long gone.

The last few years have been halcyon days for the mortgage market. Political, regulatory, media and consumerist scrutiny are coming more sharply into focus just at the time when the market feels less buoyant. Intermediaries will increasingly focus on a wider range of activities: protection, offshore, commercial mortgages and other types of lending in order to meet clients' wider needs. The move to holistic financial planning will see new business models emerge, many of which will be fee based.

Change may be constant but that does not mean to say its impact will be felt equally by all: those who seize the initiative will at least have the opportunity to see the market they want.

JOHN GOODFELLOW

CHIEF EXECUTIVE, SKIPTON BUILDING SOCIETY

When faced with the question, "What next for the mortgage market?" there is a part of me which is tempted to give some outlandish answer like, "By the end of the century, no-one will own their own home," or, "Houses will be bought and sold by bartering". And there's a part of me that wishes it were true, because the prospect of the real future seems full more of regulation and administration than anything revolutionary.

In 10 years' time, seeds that are already planted and being dealt with by the industry will bear fruit. The current issue of Basel II, dealing with lenders' risk with regard to loans, will drive individual mortgage pricing and lead to everyone knowing their own credit score. International Accounting Standards will also continue their metamorphosis of the balance sheet, making profitability more volatile. Carrying on from the changes mortgage regulation has already imposed, pressure will continue to be put on the intermediary market, meaning that in a decade, only the fit will have survived.

With regard to products, any innovation we see is likely to be minor, based on the principles already in place, because, let's be honest, price will always be king in this sector. However, I predict that in another 10 years, instead of the majority of mortgages being funded by retail savings, they will instead be funded wholesale, copying the existing US model. In addition, the popularity of short-term products will have waned slightly, with a greater acceptance of longer term products resulting in 80% of asset-rich pensioners having a lifetime mortgage.

ANNE GUNTHER

CHIEF EXECUTIVE, STANDARD LIFE BANK

Customers have changed the mortgage market in the UK substantially in the last five years or so. Before then, remortgaging hardly existed, professional landlords with commercial borrowings were the equivalent of today's much wider spread phenomenon of buy-to-let and mortgage business conducted purely by internet and phone was the exception rather than the rule. The changing returns on equities and savings have led to the widening buy-to-let market and the internet, particularly, has become an increasingly useful tool for customers beginning to create their own ideal mortgage, rather than accept a commodity product.

My hypothesis is that increasingly the home will be treated as a very real "piggy bank" with customers paying down their mortgage with bonuses and off-set savings and then drawing on the store to fund their lives, ranging from holidays and second homes to support for older relatives, school fees and university fees. There is a significant possibility that an increasing number of people will feel comfortable with debt secured on their home and will never totally repay, and possibly even convert the rump of the mortgage to a lifetime mortgage later in life to begin to spend the equity in their property. This leads naturally to a much greater flexibility and for lenders to be much more in tune with the overall commitments and aspirations of their customers. The mortgage will become a flexible asset management tool, rather than purely a means to fund house purchase, and customers will work with lenders, or more likely, the lenders' increasingly sophisticated websites, to develop their overall asset portfolio.

The combination of flexibility, service and expertise required by the customer will mean that lenders and brokers alike will have to up their game. Our own customer research already shows us just how adept our customers are at tailoring our flexible mortgage to deliver much of the above and in many cases customers will be well ahead of their lenders in their thinking, and attitudes to permanent debt are changing fast. As lenders, we need to catch up and learn from our customers.

MARK HARRIS

MANAGING DIRECTOR, SAVILLS PRIVATE FINANCE

The last 10 years have witnessed unprecedented success for brokers, packagers and lenders alike. For those that have failed to capitalise on a rising housing market, the buy-to-let boom and historically low interest rates, the future is undoubtedly bleak. The next 10 years will surely see consolidation in the mortgage sector as the strongest get stronger in their particular sectors and the mismanaged and those that have mistimed their entry to the market will be the victims.

The industry coped well with the introduction of regulation and it is only a matter of time before the FSA widens its authority to cover buy-to-let, second charge and unsecured lending. This can only be a good thing for the consumer as the quality of advice they receive from an ever more intermediary controlled market will improve further.

The Miles report published in March 2004 suggested the need for longer term fixed rates to create greater stability in the housing market. Almost 2 years on and the concept has been rejected by the ultimate decision maker, the consumer. Lenders continue to provide what the market requires, a plethora of short to medium term products with an ever increasing range of flexible features. I expect to see further advancements in product design with fully flexible fixed rates an obvious starting point.

Ultimately, I see an exciting future with greater sophistication, fully integrated trading platforms between the distributor and the lender and a more professional industry image.

HARRY HILL

CHIEF EXECUTIVE, COUNTRYWIDE PLC

Assuming the government implement their own proposals - and introduce Home Information Packs (HIPS) in early 2007 - there will be some fundamental changes to the way that homes are bought and sold in the UK, many aspects of which appear to have changed little since God was a boy!

One wonders, however, whether those changes - which will certainly have major impacts on surveying and conveyancing businesses in particular, will also impact traditional mortgage providers? In the new environment, would-be buyers will be, at the time when the buying decision is made, much better educated about the new home that they aspire to own. They will have had access to a Home Information Pack and will therefore have seen a very comprehensive condition report and a full legal title pack. Should they have also already received a mortgage offer "in principle" and had their personal status verified - there will be little or no reason for them to delay at all signing a binding contract to buy - particularly if they, themselves, have no home to sell first.

Sellers, however, will, before placing their home on the market, have had to fork out probably about £1,000 - much more for a large or expensive home - to have a HIP prepared- and with many ordinary folk probably a little challenged to do so unless they can put the price onto their credit card, the provision of the HIP funding creates some interesting questions.

Could, for example, a new entrant to the UK mortgage market consider that an interest free loan to home sellers to cover the cost of their HIP - on condition that the seller subsequently takes a mortgage from that company when buying their next home - be a viable strategy for a low-cost entry to the market? If so, would existing mortgage banks be prepared to risk losing market share - so simply match the offer?

Will internet "approvals in principle" to prospective buyers become much more the norm - particularly in brisk selling markets where access to the HIP for any would-be buyer will ensure that the buyer most ready and able to proceed will very quickly secure the home?

Will fees paid to introducers be under upwards pressure - particularly from those businesses that currently receive reciprocal survey work from mortgage providers as part "compensation" for large-scale mortgage distribution?

Will mortgage banks still need to retain anything other than a tiny in-house surveying capability?

Will England retain the Ashes in Australia in 2007?

I am not sure that I know the answer to any of the above questions either - but sincerely hope that I remain healthy and involved at some level to discover the answers in due course!

MARK LOFTHOUSE

CHIEF EXECUTIVE, MORTGAGE BRAIN AND MORTGAGE TRADING EXCHANGE

Over the course of the next few years there are two major technology related changes that I believe will take place, namely electronic trading through common trading platforms and the impact of compliance "reality".

Electronic trading is being embraced by mortgage introducers with many using the services provided by the lenders. The adoption of electronic trading platforms, like the Mortgage Trading Exchange, will continue to rise rapidly where an introducer can work with many lenders in a similar and easy to use manner from one place. With the ability to complete an application form and receive a Decision in Principle decision in under a minute, this fast and efficient "right first time" process is best for all concerned. Furthermore, I believe that lenders will substantially differentiate between the fees they pay introducers for electronic and paper-based applications, which will fast drive electronic as being the norm.

The introduction of compliance to the UK mortgage market on 31 October 2004 was a big day but I believe that its implications will not be realised for many years. Many lenders and introducers are only just starting to "realise the reality". Introducers have technology-based compliance point of sale systems but do not use them fully. This will have to change. The main change, however, is that lender produced Key Facts Illustrations (KFI) will be integrated with sourcing and point of sale systems through common trading platforms and this will be the main way to provide KFIs. This will be particularly true for larger lenders and those providing more complex products such as adverse and buy-to-let.

As can be seen, compliance and electronic trading are closely related and it is the closer coupling of technology based services used by intermediaries, integrated with those from lenders, that will produce service benefits and efficiency gains that all parties should ignore at their peril.

JOHN MALONE

MANAGING DIRECTOR, PREMIER MORTGAGE SERVICE

Since the publication of Stephen's book 7 years ago, the mortgage market has enjoyed spectacular growth in all product sectors.

The design and marketing of a variety of new products have created a mortgage for every individual's circumstance, coupled to the intermediary sector now controlling 60% - 65% of all mortgages placed in the market.

What can we expect in the next 5-10 years?

In the short-to-medium term the property market is not likely to grow in value or transactions. Despite very low interest rates, concerns over affordability, responsible lending, Home Information Packs and the lenders´ desire to treat customers fairly, business volumes are likely to reduce in all sectors of the market.

Lenders will also be introducing new accounting standards and the consequences of the Basel Accord may impact on lending.

Furthermore, with the first time buyer finding it increasingly more difficult to get onto the property ladder, the food chain in estate agency terms will impact across all buying sectors.

That said, it's not all "doom and gloom" in the short term - "boutique lenders" are likely to enter the market using packagers and mortgage clubs as their distribution, stimulating the specialist market.

The Self Invested Personal Pensions market may also create additional lending for those clients who already have an investment portfolio and are looking to include property to the mix.

Looking to the future I can see some major consolidation in the lending market, 80% of mortgages controlled by the intermediary sector, further sectors regulated, no paper- based mortgage applications and me enjoying my retirement!

JOHN MALTBY

CHIEF EXECUTIVE, KENSINGTON GROUP PLC

The UK mortgage market is the most innovative, competitive and vibrant in the world. We, in the mortgage industry, can build from this legacy but we face a material threat through standardisation, commoditisation and over-regulation.

Advances in risk appraisal, data mining and technology-enhanced distribution mean that we should be able to offer the right product at the right price at the right time to the right customer. Such mass customisation requires that market forces dictate the winners and losers, not regulators.

There is an alternative but less appealing future. A future of mass-standardisation where over-regulation (from the UK and Europe) discourages innovation in favour of safety in proven or accredited solutions. In this future Treating Customers Fairly would be interpreted as Treating Customers Equally. "CAT" standards and product-based regulation would encourage a "one size fits all" approach. Consumer choice would be seriously eroded with financial exclusion the inevitable result of lenders sticking to the "middle of the road" in product design.

Fear of retrospective interpretation of advice or retrospective changes to contract terms would undermine consumer confidence in lenders and advisers. All of this would blunt our invention, dull our ambition, and subdue our spirit. We would have a mortgage market, like so many in the world, where products are comparable certainly but only because they are all the same and chosen solely on price and not on whether they are the right solution for the customer.

The future of our market is in the balance. We must ensure that the power of competition and the power of market forces prevail to protect consumer choice. We must resist the power of intervention and the power of fear. In 10 years time I would like to still be part of the most innovative, competitive mortgage market in the world. I hope that I am.

DAVID MILES
MANAGING DIRECTOR, MORGAN STANLEY

There are three factors that will shape the environment for mortgage lending over the next few years.

First, houses are likely to remain more expensive relative to the incomes of potential new buyers than has been the case in the past. There are fundamental economic factors at play here. With inflation lower and more stable than in the past interest rates will likely stay lower and less volatile than in 1970s, 1980s and 1990s. The number of households continues to rise strongly and land available for development is - for good environmental reasons - stretched. Both factors mean the equilibrium house price to income ratio is probably higher than in the past, even if it might fall a bit in the very short term. This means that mortgage products that help potential home-owners borrow more, but in a manageable way, will be greatly valued. With real interest rates now low it may be that indexed mortgages - those where monthly payments are fixed in real terms and rise in nominal terms gradually with the general rate of inflation - might emerge as a popular form of lending.

Second, more households may look to tap the equity in their homes as a means to supplement pension income. Demographic change, pressure on the cost of state pensions and the shrinkage in company defined benefit coverage will generate rising interest in equity release products. Lenders who can offer equity release products that allow them to handle the risks of uncertainty over life expectancy, while letting home owners tap their housing wealth in a way that is easy to understand, will do well. But designing products and making them transparent is not easy.

Third, there may be initiatives from the European Commission to create a more "integrated" European mortgage market. There are real dangers here that there will be a Directives-led and highly prescriptive strategy from the Commission to create more uniform mortgage products. It would be highly undesirable to go down a road where integration was pursued though standardisation in mortgage products which is forced through detailed regulations on product features. Thankfully that is not the most likely way things will go, but the industry, the FSA and the government need to be aware of the risks.

GORDON PELL

EXECUTIVE CHAIRMAN - RETAIL MARKETS, ROYAL BANK OF SCOTLAND GROUP

Following a long period of heady growth and dynamic change, there now appears to be growing evidence that the UK mortgage market is entering a more mature phase.

Stability is the new by-word with house price inflation cooling off as anticipated, and the regional trends now converging, following the lead set by South East England. That said, with mortgage approvals bouncing back to levels in line with the ten year average it seems unlikely that a repetition of the early 1990s is on the cards with comfortable single digit growth for house prices for the immediate future.

Re-mortgaging has formed the mainstay of many lenders' activity, with the knock-on effect that SVR back books have dwindled and can no longer be relied upon to finance aggressive discounts to entice new business. Hence, it is our feeling that loyalty and customer retention will be key to future growth.

The decline in the First Time Buyer sector has also robbed the mortgage market of some much-needed liquidity, and with some evidence of affordability pressures easing, a wholesale uplift in FTB confidence could see the market receive a boost, though we would need to be cautious of the credit implications of large numbers of First Time Buyers entering the picture.

At the other end of the spectrum, the Equity Release market remains intriguingly under-serviced; with an ageing population, many of whom have made insufficient provision for their retirement yet have benefited from the housing boom. We feel that capacity exists to really transform this sector with the right offering.

Overall we see the UK mortgage market entering an era of reduced but sustainable growth, with some re-balancing towards giving good value products to existing customers rather than using them to offset aggressive acquisition, and exciting possibilities at the opposite ends of the property lifecycle.

ROBIN PHIPPS

GROUP DIRECTOR (UK OPERATIONS), LEGAL & GENERAL

Technology has always played an important role in the supply of mortgages to the consumer. It will be the key source of competitive advantage to all those financial services firms who work within the sector.

New systems will facilitate sales and ensure proper compliance enabling the winners to operate efficiently and successfully.

In a marketplace where scale will be critical to success, technology is the only solution for recovering productivity and providing a consistent sales process. In this environment, compliance will be an intrinsic but not obtrusive part of the sales process so that sales volumes can be maintained and grown.

This seamless push button approach will offer providers and sellers management systems which not only enable them to accommodate the complexities of compliance but also offers significant levels of management information to allow a much tighter control over their day-to-day operations.

Technology will also be central to the transition to new processes for house purchase, particularly the new Home Information Packs (HIPs). As technology costs accelerate, there will be a major consolidation of the existing distribution networks.

Delivery of HIPs will prove to be a high-risk venture as firms try to meet fluctuations in demand, tight timescales and the production of these complex documents.

As more innovative products develop, mortgage sourcing will have to fundamentally change, to some form of aggregated on line Acceptance in Principle, including credit scoring for effective risk assessment by lenders to meet their new Basel II requirements.

Apart from advances in technology, a further important feature of the market will be the ever-increasing importance for consumers of housing in asset accumulation. With 46% of an individual's wealth typically now held in property, the industry will have to find innovative new ways to release this locked up wealth to support consumers' lifestyle expectations, both before and into retirement - a challenge but also an opportunity for us all.

TREVOR POTHECARY

GROUP CHIEF EXECUTIVE, MORTGAGES PLC

At the time of writing, Moody's had just released its verdict on the state of the UK mortgage market which it says is heading for a slowdown but not a crash and, although arrears will rise, they will do so modestly.

Moody's does express concerns about smaller lenders, whose profitability will be squeezed in a slowing market, but it says most lenders are well placed to face more challenging circumstances and it remains "reasonably sanguine" about the overall health of the sector. "Fit for a tougher future" seems to be the experts´ prognosis!

I believe there will also be a number of specific changes which will have a profound impact on the mortgage market. For example, we have already seen technology start to change the way in which lenders do business, but the pace of change will almost certainly accelerate.

Many lenders are developing systems which will support the direct submission of applications and interface with trading exchanges and sourcing systems. Mortgages are perfectly suited to the world of electronic trading and lenders have not been slow to recognise the cost saving and benefits of increased efficiency which e-trading can deliver.

Wherever possible, lenders will also strive to forge direct relationships with brokers which, in the non-conforming sector, will make life more difficult for the packaging community. Large packagers who can benefit from the economies of scale will prosper and some may even consider becoming lenders in their own right, but small and mid-sized packagers may find life far tougher.

Product development will continue apace and we will see more prime lenders move down the credit curve into niche and non-conforming markets, whilst at the same time non-conforming lenders will move up the credit curve into prime lending! I never fail to be amazed at the sheer number and diversity of mortgage products which can be created from two simple ingredients: capital and interest!

The mortgage market has always been a fast paced and exciting place to work and it is my belief that the adrenalin rush is not going to abate in the years to come. If anything, life is going to become even more exciting.

NEVILLE RICHARDSON

GROUP CHIEF EXECUTIVE, BRITANNIA BUILDING SOCIETY

Growth in the mortgage market this year is lower than in the last few years. However, there are some good reasons for expecting reasonable levels of growth in the long term.

At a macro-economic level, the mortgage market is influenced by the availability of housing. As the Barker report from 2003 identified, the UK has a backlog of 950,000 households requiring new housing at the present time. In addition, the UK needs an extra 175,000 homes to be built each year to meet the increasing housing demand caused by the growing adult population, increased numbers of single households and immigration. In total, therefore, over the next fifteen years the UK needs an additional 4 million housing units. At today's (Barratt) prices this equates to £700 billion of housing stock.

This level of building will require funding. Whilst some of it will come from Government, at least for the initial build (e.g. through Housing Associations, and local authorities), a large proportion will be funded - at some time - by the mortgage industry. Potentially this could amount to an additional £500billion of mortgages (roughly 50% of the current mortgage stock).

The challenge - and opportunity - for the mortgage industry is to develop funding structures for both the initial developers and the future prospective owners of the housing such that the supply of housing to meet this demand is not constrained by the cost or availability of funds.

GRENVILLE TURNER

CHIEF EXECUTIVE - BUSINESS-TO-BUSINESS, HBOS

Over the last decade there can be few industries that have given so much value to its customers, injected so much into the UK economy and received so much press coverage as the mortgage sector. This is set to continue!

In my view, the economic fundamentals underpinning the UK housing market are sound. The UK economy continues to grow, average earnings growth is robust and employment is high.

Past major housing market downturns have all been caused by a combination of economic recession, steeply rising unemployment and significant rises in interest rates directed at controlling retail price inflation. There is very little likelihood of a similar combination occurring over either the short or medium term.

The easing in economic growth over the past year to a level that is currently below the UK's long-term average rate of growth, together with a ratio of house price to average earnings that remains historically high despite some decline in 2005, is expected to constrain housing demand and therefore prevent a renewed surge in house prices. Overall, we expect both house price growth and activity levels to be broadly stable over the near and medium terms.

Significantly, the shape of the mortgage market will change over the next few years. In particular, I expect the proportion of first-time buyers to increase steadily as affordability improves. Average earnings growth is now outstripping house price growth for only the second time in 10 years. This trend is expected to continue causing the ratio of house prices to earnings to fall, which will begin to make it easier for first-time buyers to get onto the housing ladder. Remortgage activity is also expected to decline over the medium term.

PHILIP WILLIAMSON

CHIEF EXECUTIVE, NATIONWIDE BUILDING SOCIETY

Will the mortgage of the future be seen as a millstone around the neck or as a flexible friend? The answer ultimately depends on whether the regulation of today creates too many obstacles on the road to genuine flexibility for the future.

Today's regulation is a millstone around the necks of consumers and of the industry. Not only does it make the mortgage process longer and less efficient but it is also hard to see how it actually helps the consumer over the long-term. Most importantly, for many people, the time required to obtain quotes and advice makes the process of choosing the right lender much harder than in the past.

In the future consumers will need to be able to differentiate between lenders, not just by the rate on offer, but also by the increasing range of fees and charges that are part and parcel of the mortgage deal. Fees and charges have already become a key source of income for mortgage providers and this trend is likely to continue if consumers, and brokers, focus only on headline rates.

As a result, the remortgage market is likely to hold up in the next year but will slow markedly over the long-term. It just won't be economical to switch lenders if exit fees, reservation fees and administration charges have continued to grow. The millstone of fees and charges will only be replaced by market flexibility if consumers become less preoccupied with rates and more focussed on the overall cost of a mortgage over the long-term.

Of course, mortgages can also be the consumers' friend and the market should always be listening to what consumers want. Product flexibility will be as key an issue as market flexibility as more people decide to use their mortgage in a way that meets their changing lifestyle needs.

MARK WOOD

(FORMERLY) CHIEF EXECUTIVE, PRUDENTIAL UK

Running out of money whilst staying surprisingly healthy into old age are the positive and negative of retirement in the 21st Century. Low investment returns and a stock market downturn of historic proportions have hit the value of savings so that, for many, savings are short of what they need to provide an adequate retirement income. The shortfall has been calculated at a staggering £65bn. Those starting their careers need to save and be certain that they will work longer than their parents and grandparents.

Today's fifty-somethings will also work longer than they had planned. Even then many don't have time to make up the savings shortfall and will need to look elsewhere for their pensions.

Increasingly, they will look to the family home. Massively generous defined benefit pension schemes can no longer be relied upon. Releasing equity from the family home will be the overwhelmingly important way of accessing wealth. Indeed, drawing on the equity in property can have the benign side effect of reducing a household's liability to inheritance tax.

So, releasing equity to purchase an annuity or progressively drawing down equity to fund or supplement a pension will move from being a slightly shady solution, a last resort of impoverished pensioners, often at too high an interest rate, to a mainstream, value for money, convenient way of drawing on value accumulated through home ownership.

Enabling people to draw on the equity they own in their home may well become the biggest thing in financial services.

JOHN WRIGLESWORTH

MANAGING DIRECTOR, THE WRIGLESWORTH CONSULTANCY

Sustained low levels of interest rates, sound consumer confidence and relatively stable house prices should see the mortgage industry remain robust. However, competitive pressures continue to be intense, with business volumes unlikely to repeat the record levels of 2004. As a result, lenders will look for margin in order to maintain revenues, focusing on higher yielding product areas such as non-status/sub prime, equity release, buy-to-let, etc.

A new opportunity for lenders will be to provide mortgages against residential properties invested in Self Invested Personal Pensions (SIPPs) - permitted from 6 April 2006. A maximum of 50% gearing will be allowed, so a member who has invested £100,000 in his SIPP can raise up to £50,000.

Some observers believe that this will over time lead to an explosion in second home purchase and that, as a knock-on effect, that lenders will enjoy a bonanza of new business.

The reality may be rather different. Notwithstanding the attractive tax breaks on offer, SIPPs are and are likely to remain a niche product that appeals mainly to the well-heeled. While the existing rather low contribution limits for SIPPs will be replaced by a new, 100% of annual earnings ceiling, how many people actually have sufficient spare cash to inject large amounts of money into a SIPP in one fell swoop? Not many.

Of course, individuals can progressively build up their SIPP over several years (investing the funds within the SIPP until used for property purchase), and supplement the fund with a mortgage, but will they bother with such a cumbersome procedure?

As we all know, the entry ticket for property purchase has become very high in most parts of the country: little can be found in the southern part of the country for less than £100,000.

On top of that, any good financial adviser will recommend that individuals spread their risk when deciding on the investment strategy for their SIPP. The alternative, of investing in a residential property fund, may prove a more attractive way of diversifying your pensions assets without putting all your eggs in one basket.

Add to this the spectre of mis-selling, and I would conclude that residential property investment within a SIPP and related mortgage lending will remain a limited, specialist activity rather than a mainstream one. It will add incremental niche business to specialist lenders rather than spurring a new boom in the housing and mortgage markets.

Food for thought, from our experts. Their words certainly made me think long and hard about what my predictions for the future might be.

How did I get on last time?

Before I get onto that, I made ten meaningful predictions in my part of the "What Next?" chapter of my last book. There has been much to-ing and fro-ing in my mind as to the merits of including in this book an analysis of how I got on last time. Nobody likes a smart arse, that is for sure.

I have decided to include it, however, because (a) I did get a few things wrong, and (b) it is a good illustration of the fact that the mortgage market is still wrestling with many of the same issues, some eight years later. Figure 8.1 sets out the previous predictions, plus comments, in tabular form:

STEPHEN'S PREDICTIONS IN 1997

Prediction	✓ or ✗	Comment
There will be statutory regulation of the UK mortgage market	✓	Not certain in '97 as the Mortgage Code was just being introduced
There will be a drift to European tax harmonisation on housing, with CGT a possibility for UK residential property	✗	This assumed greater European market integration, which has still not happened, although it is being talked about more
Lenders will introduce automated decisioning for the underwriting of mortgage applications	✓	We were one of them
The availability of regional house price indexing will permit automated valuation models to be developed	✓	The big impact of this on UK mortgage market delivery is yet to come
Title insurance will be accepted across the mortgage market and speed up completions	✗	Although more lenders are accepting title insurance, I cannot say that it has been accepted "across the market"
Interactive TV will become the norm for delivering financial services	✗	This could still be one for the future
One payment covering all mortgage-related insurances, and the monthly mortgage payment itself, will be introduced	✗	IT systems cannot cope in the face of regulatory requirements
Kensington has paved the way for the launch of more virtual lenders using warehouse lines	✓	There seems to be a new lender a month at the moment
Consumer banks will dominate influence and share, but the building society sector will survive	✓	Some bets were being placed at the time on the long term demise of the building society sector on the one hand, or a resurgence against plcs in favour of mutuality on the other
Flexible/lifestyle mortgages will remain as a niche product, but offset mortgages are an exciting new innovation for the future	✓	Many thought that flexible mortgages would take over. Some still do. Offset was still a theory in 1997

Figure 8.1

For my next batch of predictions, I am going to have a go at another ten. Some do not describe a precise outcome: rather, they are predictions of the choices that will need to be made by those who have the power to make them. Hopefully, in another eight years, I will be on the beach when you phone me to tell me I was wrong!

1. UK mortgage regulation

The Government, and the FSA, have a stark choice. Either they are going to continue down a highly prescriptive route, where regulation is of individual products; thematic reviews are undertaken to dig deeper into various aspects of individual products and IT-intensive requirements will continue to be specified on how products are illustrated, or there will be a move to a better methodology. One year on from the introduction of UK mortgage regulation it is too early to say what that outcome will be.

The FSA is doing a good job with a difficult brief. I have found the people I have met at the FSA to be responsive and willing to consult and debate. On the other hand, I feel that some of the requirements are based on logical purity rather than business pragmatism. As a result, the consumer may be inadvertently suffering.

Take statutory regulation as a whole. I report separately in this book that the IMLA chairman thinks that the cost to the mortgage industry has been £200m while the BSA chairman thinks that the cost has been £500m. Whichever it is, those costs will find themselves in borrowers' bills in due course. Has the "protection" offered therefore been proportionate? Or are all borrowers paying for something that only a few borrowers would ever have suffered from?

Having been an initial fan of the Mortgage Code, I have come round to thinking that statutory regulation was inevitable. There were too many organisations, in my view, bending self-regulatory definitions to allow previous business practices to continue. Nobody is doing that with the FSA, which must be right. My issue is that it may be possible to cover most of the perceived industry problems at a fraction of the current cost, instead of trying to cover all of the problem at ten times the cost.

A good example of this is the KFI. If lenders had been required to produce certain generic statements when presenting an illustration to a customer then, for sure, they would all have presented this information in a slightly different way. Customers would not have found comparison between products as easy as if all the information was consistently displayed in the same order. But they would still have received the information.

However, to present the same information in a consistent format has required systems investment amounting to hundreds of millions of pounds. Programming new information to be covered in a specific order in a specific way with no flexibility has sent IT costs soaring across the industry.

Putting the required information in front of the customer in generic form would have produced a fraction of the IT cost. Do those of us in the industry who deal with customers on a day-to-day basis really believe that they read the KFIs in such detail that the investment of hundreds of millions of pounds into technology could be justified on a proportionate basis?

Typically an intermediary might offer customers three product alternatives, which means three pre-sale KFIs (say 18 pages in total). Many customers will change their minds once about either the exact amount they wish to borrow, or the property they are going to buy. That will trigger another 18 pages.

When the offer is issued there is a further six pages by way of the offer KFI. Do we have any evidence to suggest that typical customers have the appetite to read 42 pages of KFI detail in a way that enables them to make an informed decision?

These are questions the answers to which can only be guessed. But there must come a time soon when proper research into borrower reaction to KFIs must be undertaken in an objective and thorough manner. Only then can we assess the full cost implications.

The impact of the highly specific KFI can be felt in relation to some of the Government's own initiatives, such as the Homebuy shared equity idea. The Government wishes to offer key workers the opportunity to borrow 75% of a property's value by way of a normal mortgage, with the remaining 25% underwritten on a shared equity basis. This is where borrowers give up a proportion of the equity growth in the property they are buying in return for a lower outlay on the 25% portion (say a "rent" of 3%). This structure, in turn, enables a higher income multiple to be granted overall - hence key workers might be able to afford to buy previously unaffordable property.

The initial problem with this product was that the rules-based regulatory regime did not foresee it. The current thinking is that the KFI for this product should use the existing lifetime mortgage rules. There must be a calculation showing the amount of the equity that the borrower will be giving up after 25 years at annual property price growth levels of 1%, 5% and 10%. This calculation must be applied to the specific value of the property being purchased.

To be so prescriptive in that requirement will involve another massive IT investment for the participating lenders for what will almost certainly be a small scheme. As a result, the Government has currently attracted only three lenders (as at the time this book goes to press) willing to participate in shared-equity Homebuy.

It may be helpful to advise a young nurse that, based on the modest property she is buying under this scheme, she may lose an enormous six figure sum in shared equity growth in the extremely unlikely event that she stays there for 25 years, and in the unlikely event that her property grows by 10% per annum compound every year for 25 years. But is the value of that information proportionate to the IT investment involved?

If lenders were permitted to hand over a generic statement with a 'normal' KFI showing house price growth for each of the 25 years on a range of property values, and at a range of house price growth assumptions, this might (a) be more helpful and (b) massively cut down on the IT costs. As all practitioners will know, as soon as you change one part of the engine you have to test everything else just to see that there is no inadvertent impact on the other moving parts. So introducing a new KFI just for the shared-equity product is a massive undertaking.

As I write, the FSA is also scrutinising self certification. Non-conforming is next. Our experience has therefore been that there has been a particular weighting towards discussing individual products with our regulator, and this has been unexpected from a "principles-based" regime.

Statutory regulation can either continue down this route, in which case it could end up with a bland, less innovative and more commoditised mortgage market where customers pay more than they would have done. Or, after an initial couple of years of getting used to what the market is doing, the FSA may feel comfortable enough to back off a little and talk instead about broad principles at proportionate cost.

I would obviously vote for the latter outcome and I am reasonably optimistic it is the one we could get. The FSA are approachable and open about these matters and it is for the industry to engage with the regulator on partnership terms as part of this important debate.

2. European Integration and Regulation

There are proposals currently under discussion which seek to achieve greater harmony of mortgage products and services across Europe. The only problem is, as the CML has pointed out, the UK will be a net loser from such harmonisation, whereas almost every other European country would be a net gainer.

As an organisation that operates lending arms in the UK, Germany, the Netherlands and Spain, we perhaps understand more than most the different cultures that exist in those countries and, in particular, their attitude to housing. The fluid, imaginative, innovative, dynamic, competitive, fast-moving UK mortgage market is nothing like any other market that operates in Europe.

We have over 5000 mortgage products available for the UK consumer to choose from. To try and bring such a market as the UK into "harmony" with the rest of Europe can only hold it back.

This seems like a solution searching for a problem. Where is the demand for cross-border borrowing or lending which more regulation would unleash?

Relatively recently, I was in discussion with a consumers' representative in Germany who was a great advocate for such harmonisation. He was arguing, for example, for the use of a standard APR across Europe. He had no understanding of the complexity of fixed, discounted, variable, capped and tracker options the UK borrower has, often mixing two or more of those options in the same mortgage. An APR in those circumstances is worse than useless: it is potentially misleading.

My co-debater also argued that European regulation should be prescriptive about how and when a valuation is commissioned across Europe, what fees should be charged and so on. The tools with which some in favour of European mortgage regulation wish to damage the UK mortgage market are sharp, and dangerous.

My understanding is that the UK Government sees the pitfalls that this attempt at European harmonisation might deliver. Some of the proposed regulations, currently being consulted upon, go much farther than our own statutory regulation.

Cross-border lending will certainly not be achieved by prescription and regulation. Lenders who are determined to succeed in Europe can do so by understanding and respecting how local markets operate, hiring senior management from those countries and trying to attract business towards a broader model, rather than trying to contract it by regulatory enforcement. The diversity of cultures and markets are there to be embraced and celebrated, and highly prescriptive regulation which seeks to standardise one approach to mortgage lending, is a step too far.

The UK Government therefore has a choice. It can either oppose this damaging attempt at over-regulation or it can accept it. Upon this choice rests significant costs, including opportunity costs, for the UK mortgage borrower.

A related point is the whole question of the common currency. It is difficult to see how currency harmonisation can occur without taxation harmonisation, particularly in the key area of housing. This is the point I was making in my previous book, which I have marked with an "X" because there have been no moves towards tax harmonisation.

There will be such steps, however, if sentiment towards the common currency were ever to be reversed, such that the UK embraced it. The current sentiment is against the single currency so I do not repeat the prediction of tax harmonisation, but things can change.

Basel II probably sits best under this sub-heading, since it is regulation coming from Europe, even though it is inspired by international treaties. I believe that this particular development will be broadly beneficial to the UK market. The sort of risk management techniques we have to employ, given our business model, go farther than any I have seen prescribed under the Basel II regulations, so I feel that we will be largely unaffected. The development of more sophisticated risk management techniques among Europe's lenders, and the allocation of capital according to precise asset class, are to be welcomed.

Any major piece of regulation of this kind is going to produce outcomes that are not easily predictable. If greater capital has to be allocated to non-conforming lending, for example, then this may arrest price reductions in that sector, or it might attract more mainstream lenders. It might even spawn more sophisticated balance sheet sharing between lenders. Freeing the capital currently backing mainstream, full status loans may trigger market-distorting acquisitions, or other investments in new products or services. The only safe prediction that can be made about Basel II is that, in the years that follow its introduction, there will be developments in the market that would not have taken place had this particular regulation not been introduced.

On a lighter note, a friend of mine, who worked in a senior position for a large international organisation, trialled a pan-European call centre a few years ago (this is a true story). The level of complaints about the service being provided by this call centre was worrying, so there was some follow up research. This revealed that the complaint subject matter differed country-by-country.

Callers from Germany were not worried about how friendly or polite the call centre staff were, so long as they were quick and efficient. Callers from France were less bothered about efficiency: they wanted the call centre staff to be warm and friendly. Callers from the Netherlands did not really mind whether the call centre staff were efficient or friendly, as long as they were not German!

My friend's company closed down the call centre.

3. Equilibrium Pricing

All those who can or will remortgage to new business offers, will eventually do so. That is the stage when there will be a form of equilibrium pricing operating in the market, with the result that new borrowers will be paying a similar rate to that being paid by existing borrowers. The issue is one of timing.

Heavily subsidised new business rates have been around for the last 15 years. They are not going to disappear overnight. But the trend has been inexorably towards equilibrium pricing, as evidenced by the gradual reduction in new business incentives over the last few years. I do not think that, in our very competitive UK mortgage market, we will ever eliminate new business incentives altogether. But the rates will inevitably come closer together, and we will end up with something approximating the pricing continuum that I mentioned in chapter 1 which was, in fact, a consideration in our original strategic plan. When that point is reached, lenders had better be sure that their cost:income ratio is as low as they can get it, because margins will be even tighter and the emphasis will be on delivery. More and more lenders in those market conditions will turn to the established niches to try and obtain a better margin - this is where offset could come into its own.

My experience of marketing mortgages in the equilibrium-pricing environment of the 1970s and 1980s suggests that there would be a return to greater emphasis on product innovation and presentation. We used to major on aspects of the mortgage delivery unconnected to price. The regulatory environment is different now, but competition will manifest itself in different ways if price becomes commoditised.

A particular area of focus will be remortgages. The smaller the gap between back and front book pricing, the less incentive there will be for borrowers to remortgage. Lenders are also actively discouraging their own borrowers from remortgaging, trying to find ways to incentivise intermediaries to encourage customers to stay where they are. Since remortgaging accounts for a significant percentage of gross lending in the UK, there are some interesting battles yet to be fought on the remortgage front.

In the US, I have seen sophisticated "fee free" products being launched that maybe only cut $10 per month off a borrower's mortgage payment. But the broker is incentivised by a 1% fee to arrange that transfer. The intermediary explains to the customer that there is no work to be done, because the intermediary will undertake it all online. Although $10 per month is not much, it is better in the borrower's pocket than in the lender's. It is possible, therefore, that borrower perceptions as to when a remortgage is "worth it" may be revised by intermediaries.

A possible outcome of a reduction in remortgage activity is for lenders seeking new business to increase the intermediary incentive to a level that will more than offset the incentive being offered to keep the mortgage where it is.

4. The role of the home in financial planning

Some of our experts believe that a borrower's principal private residence will become more closely integrated with their overall financial planning and management. This is not, of course, a new concept. But it has gained extra momentum because of the so-called pensions crisis in the UK.

A long period of low interest rates, combined with low investment returns and higher taxation, has certainly hit the value of pensions, at exactly the time that people are living longer. This mis-match therefore requires a solution, so it is argued, by tapping into housing equity. The value of residential property has risen significantly over the period when these other factors have been impacting, so the crystallisation of equity into cash appears to be an inevitable conclusion.

This is entirely logical. The key point, however, is: will regulation and consumerism allow these economic and social factors to play out in a way that permits borrowers to fully maximise the opportunity? I have already argued in chapter 2 that lending to elderly people, when they are on the cusp of vulnerability, contains high reputational risk. Indeed, the chief executive of the FSA is on record as saying that he will hold CEOs personally responsible for what the regulator decides is irresponsible lending in the lifetime mortgage arena.

Are we therefore going to see newspapers in ten years' time criticising lenders over terms which elderly borrowers do not today understand, but which they might have understood perfectly well a decade previously? This is where, I feel, the Government and the regulator need to step in in order to protect lenders. If the asset rich, cash poor elderly population are to be able to have choice and flexibility in topping up their pensions with cash generated from the equity in their homes, then lenders have to be better encouraged to participate in this market, in my view.

For lenders prepared to take this risk, I personally favour the reverse mortgage. I was a non-executive director of a company called Home Income Trust that launched such a mortgage into the UK in 1992. It was far too ahead of its time and did not, in the end, gain any momentum. But the product did not involve any investments, nor were there complicated caveats. According to the age of the applicants, and the value of the property, a monthly amount was available to be paid by the lender to the applicants.

This was a guaranteed payment for the rest of the borrower's natural life. The lender took the risk of the regular payments, plus accrued interest, moving past the property value which, in the case of the scheme in which I was involved, was covered by indemnity insurance. I know that similar products are starting to appear now, and it is the simplicity of these schemes that mitigates the subsequent reputational risk.

One of the problems with lifetime schemes, of course, is the balance sheet capacity they use up. If it were possible to securitise such loans then significantly more liquidity would be introduced to the market, thereby driving further choice, flexibility and product innovation. Perhaps the Government could have a role in stimulating a secondary market.

While we may, therefore, see significant progress in the area of equity release mortgages over the next few years, I am still not persuaded by the idea that younger borrowers will be prepared to use their homes as a core part of general financial planning. When flexible mortgages were first introduced, with their payment holidays and opportunities to increase or decrease monthly payments, it was stated by some that these mortgages would take over and become the norm.

The problem with these products, however, is that they are expensive to administer. If those costs are properly reflected in the pricing then the audience of borrowers prepared to pay more to receive such services diminishes.

The launch into the UK of flexible and offset mortgages was clouded by subsidised new business offers, and extra intermediary incentives. The extra flexibility offered therefore proved to be an incentive, *all other things being equal,* and the products took off.

However, as lenders started to price these products more appropriately, it was demonstrated that there is only a limited, and niche, demand from customers prepared to pay more in order to have the so-called flexibility. The vast majority preferred to separate their banking and savings from their mortgage and were not prepared to pay more in order to integrate them.

While flexible and offset mortgages will therefore continue to extend choice in a most welcome way, and be attractive to a substantial niche, I do not believe that they will ever become mainstream because of the way they have to be priced, and the way that most borrowers conduct their finances.

5. Point of sale offers

Here is a short topic, to reflect its subject matter. So long as it is not prevented for non-commercial reasons, I believe it will be possible for customers to walk into an intermediary's office, and walk out twenty minutes later with a formal mortgage offer.

I have already explained in chapter 4 how automated decision making can be more predictive, and "safer" for lender and borrower, than manual underwriting. I feel the same about automated valuations, which I touch on later in that same chapter.

Put the two together and you have a binding mortgage offer, subject only to the subsequent non-detection of fraud, and subject also to the provision of an application form that agrees with the inputted data. The use of electronic identification can be built into the process to verify the borrowers' identity.

I agree wholeheartedly that lenders and intermediaries should not rush applicants in relation to the decisions they need to make. Applicants must be given sufficient time to make comparisons with other products. But that is different to slowing down the pre-offer process for non-commercial reasons.

Of course, regulation did not foresee such a service. The MCOB rules currently provide for a KFI to be supplied at point of sale and at offer stage. If technology allows both stages to be merged, there will presumably either need to be a change of rules or we will have to print two identical KFIs for the customer, one pre dating the other by several seconds.

Nonetheless, what a revolutionary service for borrowers and the market generally point of sale offers would be! It will speed up chains, allow property purchasers to drive harder bargains, increase certainty, remove costs that can be reflected in mortgage rates, and give lenders a more objective valuation for their portfolios. I think it will happen.

6. Home Information Packs

An extra boost will be given to automated valuations if HIPs are introduced, since there will have been a physical inspection of the property prior to the submission of a mortgage application. I do not think that this is necessary for the success of automated offers, and I believe that the disadvantages which will accrue as a result of introducing HIPs will be greater than the advantage a prior physical inspection might deliver to lenders.

The problem with HIPs is: who is going to believe them? You are about to purchase your dream house, but you are being asked to rely on information about the property's condition, and its legal title, that has been commissioned by the vendor. OK, so there will be indemnity insurance if things go wrong. But you would prefer them not to go wrong in the first place.

Of course, 99.9% of surveyors and solicitors are honest, professional and trustworthy. But what if you encounter the 0.1%? They do exist - ask the managers of the Law Society Indemnity Fund. Would you be prepared to risk taking on a property in those circumstances? I genuinely do not know the answer that most people would give to those questions. But I know what my answer would be.

HIPs are not only, in my view, therefore in danger of amassing a pile of information that a significant number of purchasers might not be prepared to accept without double-checking with their own professionals, they are also introducing delay and substantial cost to the property-selling process. Herein potentially lies the most damaging aspect of HIPs.

The UK property market is different to most other European countries in its trade-up, trade-down cycle. Typically young first time buyers start with a small house or a flat. They then trade up several times until they find a property they live in for a while, before then trading down again in later life. This is in contrast to many European countries where people either buy later or stay pretty much in the same area without moving anything like so often as they do in the UK.

A property move in the UK is often triggered by vendors "testing the water". When they receive an offer they then understand what they can afford to buy. A chain is created. If HIPs are introduced, however, it will be a giant roadblock imposed on that first stage.

It will not be possible in the future to "test the water". You may still get a free indication of value from an estate agent, but you will not be able to market the property and test that valuation with a real offer without incurring the expense of producing a HIP.

Estimates vary as to how much a HIP will cost. I have heard £600 and I have also heard £1000. If it turns out to be anywhere near this range then all but the determined movers will be deterred. Far from speeding up the market, and making property purchase easier, HIPs could cause a chronic reduction in the supply of homes coming onto the market as the discretionary or "whim" movers, who only get going when they receive a real offer on their properties, will be deterred from entering the fray.

It would be nice to have some representative research on which to prove or disprove this theory. Unfortunately, the research that the Government has so far undertaken in support of HIPs relates to a handful of transactions in Bristol, so far as I can tell. With something as major as making every residential property vendor in the land pay out £600 - £1000 for a package of information that some purchasers will not trust, you would think that there would be, say, a year-long review of many different geographic regions involving thousands of borrowers before committing to legislation. But that has not been the background to the introduction of HIPs, and I think it could be such a disaster that might even need to be reversed.

It cannot be reversed until it is actually introduced. Therein lies another problem. It is estimated that approximately 2000 new quasi-surveyors will be needed just to cope with providing the property assessment that goes with HIPs.

I say "quasi-surveyors" because my understanding is that the individuals concerned do not need to be full chartered surveyors, but will instead be allowed to undertake these property assessments based on a lesser qualification. As far as I know, that qualification has not yet been defined and nobody has spelt out in any detail where these surveyors will be recruited from.

The sort of economically-viable price that the assessors will be able to charge in order to produce their report for HIPs does not suggest that the pursuit of a career as a quasi-surveyor will be high on the list of those graduates in search of fame and fortune. The Government wants to introduce HIPs in June 2007, but this is a big risk.

I know that many of the large estate agents welcome the introduction of HIPs. But secretly I think that some of them realise only too well the disruption HIPs will cause to the flow of properties coming onto the market for sale. They just hope that that particular disadvantage is more than outweighed by the extra income that compulsory property assessment will deliver. I think they may have got their sums wrong.

7. First time buyers

The main reason that the percentage of first time buyers has reduced as low as it has can be demonstrated at a glance by figure 8.2:

UK HOUSE PRICE TO EARNINGS RATIO (HPE)

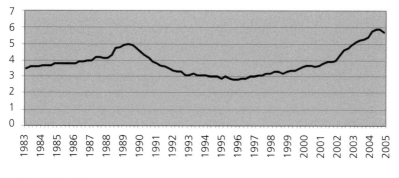

Source: Nationwide

Figure 8.2

At nearly six times average income, the HPE is too high for most first time buyers. This is why affordability was described by 50% of that group as being the main reason why they were not in a position to purchase a home in research we undertook for public policy reasons, as described in chapter 5. Now, only 50% quoted affordability. As that chapter discusses, the other 50% are deliberately putting off property purchase for a variety of other reasons. We concluded from that research that there is no initiative that the Government and the lending industry could undertake which would return first time buyers to their previous percentage levels. To address those who are precluded for affordability reasons, however, will require some product innovation where, currently, there are some non-commercial barriers.

Whilst the Government's Homebuy shared-equity scheme is a good one, we believe it is possible to introduce a broader-based product which would allow income multiples up to six times, involving monthly payments that are no different to a "standard" three and a half times income loan. I believe that somebody in the market will crack this issue and launch a shared equity product which will be extremely valuable in getting first time buyers back to the market, so long as the IT issues arising from the bespoke KFI can be viably overcome.

One lender tried to solve the problem in another way by introducing a loan which advanced up to 125% LTV. To recognise the fact that many borrowers topped up their mortgage borrowing with expensive credit cards and personal loans, this lender gave purchasers the opportunity to wrap all of those borrowings into one, at a much cheaper overall rate. The lender imposed strict credit scoring rules in order to weed out those who were statistically likely to get into trouble. But it is fair to say that this lender was nonetheless hammered by the press.

Without any regard for the fact that borrowers in general were free to take out personal loans and credit card debt, and often did, the lender was accused of irresponsible lending. To its credit, it stuck to its guns and maintained the product, but what is it that some of these critics want? Do they prefer multi-source borrowing at high rates, which is the practical alternative?

Non-conforming lending also gets a bad press sometimes, but do commentators really want us to return to the days when I first started out on my mortgage career, when borrowers who had incurred credit problems in the past were not given a chance to rehabilitate and were, instead, thrown to the mercy of the secondary market? Because there was precious little mercy shown.

We have a similar issue with buy-to-let among some analysts and market commentators. Based on what I call the "should-be" principle of analysis (this product "should be" performing badly, so I am going to assume it is without looking into it any deeper), we also have buy-to-let earmarked by many as being a risky product. The argument is that the loan is not on the security of the borrowers' principal place of residence, and is a commercial transaction, and will therefore perform worse than a mainstream loan. Whereas in practice, our experience is that buy-to-let loans perform better than mainstream loans.

Buy-to-let has a particular role to play in the first time buyer market because it is providing privately-rented property to pick up the demand from those who are choosing to rent rather than buy. But the point of mentioning it here is that it is another example of the barriers, unrelated to the real world, that stand in front of lenders wishing to innovate to help first time buyers.

I do not think that this problem is going to be solved by a crash in house prices making property more affordable. As I discuss in the next point, a house price crash is unlikely to happen. First time buyers are unlikely to therefore again comprise 50% of new gross advances, as they once did. But we can as an industry get more first time buyers back into the fold by innovative product design, particularly in the area of shared equity or 100% lending. I just wish that everybody else involved in the process was working with the lenders, instead of against us.

8. House prices

The following three diagrams are the most instructive to me on this subject. Figure 8.3 shows the steady decline in the number of people per household in England from 1971 through to 2003, which is projected to continue into 2011.

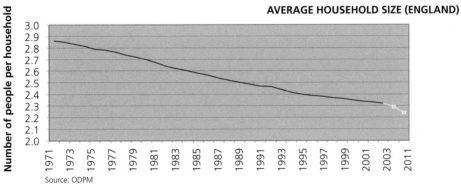

Figure 8.3

This is part of a trend by which divorce, in particular, is creating a larger number of smaller households which is, in turn, creating a demand which the current supply of property is unable to match. However, it is not just divorce which is creating new household demand, as figure 8.4 demonstrates.

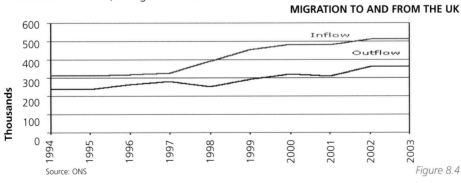

Figure 8.4

These figures show that there has been a steadily increasing net migration into the UK in the ten years between 1994 and 2003 inclusive. This is creating still-further pressure on housing supply. So what are we doing about meeting that demand? Figure 8.5 tells its own story.

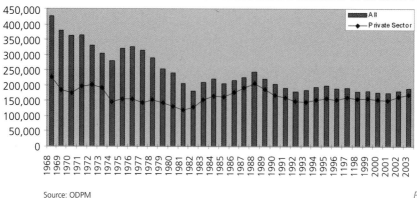

UK: PERMANENT DWELLINGS COMPLETED PER YEAR

Source: ODPM   Figure 8.5

As you can see, the private sector has been unable to bridge the gap created by the reduction in new build for social housing. Indeed, housing starts in 2003 in the private sector were less than they were in 1968. We are simply nowhere near to meeting the demand for new household formation.

The Government recognised this with the Barker Review, which agreed that there was a substantial shortfall in housing supply that could amount to several hundred thousand units. As a result, the Government announced some measures to increase new building.

But there is only so much that can be done on our limited-space island. Supply is unlikely to ever meet demand for housing in the UK in the foreseeable future. It therefore follows that any form of significant house price correction could only be triggered by severe economic conditions.

I am sometimes reminded that a shortfall of housing supply to household demand existed in the early 1990s when there was a significant house price correction. But this property price adjustment occurred because there were forced sellers.

Inflation was in double figures, interest rates were at 15%, unemployment was high, there were two consecutive calendar quarters of no growth and the economy was in trouble. People had no option but to crystallise the value in their homes, resulting in a house price fall notwithstanding the excess of demand. Purchasers were simply taking advantage of the fact that it was a buyers' market.

The same thing will happen again if all of those economic conditions occur at the same time. But even the most pessimistic of forecasters in the UK, and around the world, are not currently predicting recession for the UK economy. Inflation looks relatively benign. Unemployment is rising, but is still at quite low levels historically. Interest rates are also historically low, so there are no grounds for constructing a case for a large number of forced sellers coming onto the market at the same time.

I can subscribe to the view that we might be in for a relatively long period of flat or slightly increasing property prices. This is what happens in low interest rate, low inflation economies. I can also appreciate that there may be corrections in some regions where, for example, property prices may have accelerated due to a particular type of demand.

But my prediction is that it is very unlikely that there will be a crash or significant downturn without a major deterioration in economic prospects. We will instead enjoy a period of stability with flat or low house price inflation subject of course to the picture not materially being distorted by Government action, or world events, which cannot be foreseen today.

9. Lender consolidation

As this book goes to press, there are 147 members of the CML, with several new lenders planned for launch in 2006. My good friend, Michael Coogan, Director General of the CML, may be rubbing his hands with glee at the prospect of all this new membership income. But is it sustainable? Can all these lenders survive?

The laws of economics dictate that significant over-supply will lead to long-term consolidation. With the top ten lenders accounting for more than 80% of all mortgage lending, it could be argued that this is already taking place.

I think there are three groups to aim for, namely the big group, a significant, identifiable and sustainable niche or regional. I believe that all lenders need to be shooting for one of those groups.

In the big one there will be commoditisation. Technology, delivery, product innovation and cost:income ratio are all going to be factors that dominate the ability to compete.

There will be many aiming for that group who are, for one part of the year, on a trajectory to maintain a place and, in other parts of the year, not getting there. There will be other lenders who are on a long term trend to miss out, but who do not intend to go out without a fight.

This is therefore a great opportunity for those lenders with our business model, under which assets are created and traded, and we hope to satisfy that demand for many years to come. In the end, though, the big group could only realistically expand to a total of 15 at most, so there will have to be mergers.

There are, currently, clearly identifiable niches including buy-to-let and non-conforming. Some specialist lenders undertake substantial, and profitable, lending by specialising in those areas. This may continue. Moreover, other niches may develop that we cannot today foresee.

A big challenge with niches, of course, is their lack of scalability. In the end, if a niche becomes important enough to attract the attention of the big group then, as they start joining it, the niche becomes mainstream, and so does the pricing.

Buy-to-let lending to standard borrowers is almost there, and the big niche in that sector now is lending to partnerships and corporate landlords. Non-conforming is getting there, but I believe that a substantial niche may still remain in that sector involving the more toxic areas of lending. This will still be offering borrowers a better deal than throwing them to the loan sharks.

Offset is another identifiable niche. There are barriers for entry in terms of the investment necessary to maintain such a product. This investment, and the extra administration involved, needs to be priced into the products for profit sustainability. But it is a great customer retention product.

Strong regional support, particularly when enhanced by a local retail deposit-taking facility, has as good a chance of survival as any other. The theory is that customers will always want the cheapest mortgage rate, or the highest savings rate. But actually, real people make decisions beyond pricing considerations. Service, loyalty and familiarity are all reasons to buy, which could sustain a local or regional presence for many years to come.

The net position, however, is that, if I have enough brain cells left to repeat my cycle of a book every eight years, there will not be 147 lender members of the CML when I come to do the "What Next?" chapter. If I had to place a bet, it would be on the number 50.

10. Intermediaries

Most commentators feel that intermediaries now account for 50% - 60% of all mortgage demand. I think it is probably nearer the latter than the former. Reflect again on those 5000+ product choices that Moneyfacts revealed. Would you be comfortable making a selection from that lot based on one conversation with one lender?

I assume you are probably connected with the mortgage industry in some way (because, otherwise, why on earth would you be reading this book?). If you are uncomfortable with making that selection personally, it is easy to see why the majority of the public might be equally unhappy.

The power of intermediaries is set to grow, but not just because of choice. Getting applications in directly from the public is an extremely expensive and speculative business. By way of contrast, getting business in through intermediaries involves paying out only when the loan completes.

The market is going to have to focus on the fact that intermediaries are growing in importance. Which means that, while many are predicting a reduction in procuration fees, I actually think it will go the other way. Since we are heading for equilibrium pricing, I look to two markets close to home, that already have equilibrium pricing, to inform me as to what might happen here.

In Ireland and the US, intermediaries typically receive 1% of the loan. It is built into the product pricing. I think that is where we are heading. As soon as the subsidies mainly disappear from mainstream lending, the competition could well be around the services and payments made available by lenders to intermediaries.

At the moment, UK intermediaries probably receive a fee on average between 0.50% and 0.75% on their mortgage business when you take into account a weighted average mix of mainstream, niche and non-conforming. They top this up with fees charged to customers.

In a more commoditised equilibrium-pricing environment, fees to customers are going to have to come down. So this can only mean one thing. You guessed it - fees to intermediaries will have to go up.

So we at GMAC-RFC are certainly planning for intermediaries to be even more important to us in the future than they are today. I include packagers in this. I think there could be a healthy future for packagers who concentrate on value-added services to their customers, priced so that everybody can see what they are getting for the extra mortgage rate paid.

Estate agents will also continue to play a vital intermediary role. Although I suspect that more buyers are viewing properties on the web than via estate agency windows or mailings, there is still a deal to be negotiated and advice to be taken. Estate agents have an important opportunity to influence right at the start of a property purchase transaction, and this influence will grow if HIPs are ever introduced, as estate agents employing suitably-qualified assessors are guaranteed a role in pre-purchase. Maintaining good connections with estate agents will therefore be important for all lenders.

I therefore expect business introduced by intermediaries of all types will increase over the next few years, and that will not come cheap for the lending industry.

Wrap Up

So there you have the views of 22 leading industry figures on the subject of what is going to happen next in the UK mortgage market. You also have my views. Now is the time for you to reflect on how much of that you believe, and how much of it you do not.

I cannot foresee market conditions which would prevent the industry from making progress in terms of the breadth and diversity of products and opportunities. Regulation and media comment will sometimes hold these things back, but they do not have to. I am personally optimistic that regulation might be lighter touch in the years to come.

The UK has an opportunity to bring its rich diversity of products to more customers with point of sale offers and I hope this is allowed to happen. I particularly hope that the UK market is not held back by the unachievable dream of European harmonisation.

More than anything, I believe that the future is going to be better than today. Having that belief puts a spring in your step and helps you better address life's challenges. I said on page one that I was lucky, rather than clever. Luck visits more with you when you are smiling.

Now, where's that cat?

Index of Names

Page numbers for figures have suffix f

Index of Companies and Organisations
Page numbers for figures have suffix f